The Protestant
in the Great Plains
and Mountain West,
1865–1915

The Protestant Clergy in the Great Plains and Mountain West, 1865–1915

Ferenc Morton Szasz

With a preface by the author

University of Nebraska Press
Lincoln and London

Preface © 2004 by the Board of Regents of the University of Nebraska
© 1988 by the University of New Mexico Press
Manufactured in the United States of America

First Nebraska paperback printing: 2004

Library of Congress Cataloging-in-Publication Data
Szasz, Ferenc Morton, 1940–
The Protestant clergy in the Great Plains and the Mountain West, 1865–1915 / Ferenc
Morton Szasz; with a preface by the author.
p.   cm.
Originally published: 1st ed. Albuquerque: University of New Mexico Press, c1988.
With new pref.
Includes bibliographical references and index.
ISBN 0-8032-9311-9 (pbk.: alk. paper)
1. Protestant churches—Great Plains—Clergy—History.   2. Protestant churches—
Rocky Mountains Region—Clergy—History.   3. Great Plains—Church history.
4. Rocky Mountains Region—Church history.   I. Title.
BR545.S95   2004
280′.4′097809034—dc22
2004000605

Preface

As the morning paper and evening news regularly remind us, organized religion plays a prominent role in twenty-first-century American life. The theme runs like a red skein through both foreign policy and vital domestic concerns. It is not hard to imagine that the forces of organized religion were equally central to the American past, and I am delighted that the University of Nebraska Press has agreed to reissue *The Protestant Clergy in the Great Plains and Mountain West, 1865–1915*.

Except for quietly correcting a number of pesky errors, I made no major alterations in the text. But a large question sat on my shoulder and continued to whisper in my ear: how would the book have been different if you had written it—from the same research—in the early twenty-first century rather than the late 1980s? Were that the case, I concluded after some thought, the book would probably have stressed the following three themes.

To start with, I would have included far more discussion of the idea of sacred space. Both the rugged expanse of the Rocky Mountains and the vastness of the Great Plains abound with places made sacred by organized religious activities. Take the issue of names. When people designate a place as New Braunfels (Texas), New Waverly (Texas), or Prague (Oklahoma), they are harkening back to a European past. But to call a spot Hope (New Mexico), Mount Hope (Kansas), Fairplay (Colorado), Beulah (North Dakota), Love County (Oklahoma), Bon

Homme County (South Dakota), or Comfort (Texas) is to look in the other direction. There is even an Eden, Wyoming (presumably not named in January). To etch such names onto the soil is to place one's faith in both the future and in the land itself. "There is something in the western soil that tugs me," Wyoming writer and rancher Candy Moulton recently wrote. "There are times when the power of the land is so strong as it surges through me that I cannot keep the tears from rolling down my cheeks."[1]

The American West—especially Indian Country—abounds with such sacred places: Bears Lodge and Medicine Wheel (Wyoming), Bear Butte and the Black Hills (South Dakota), Treacherous Mountain on the Crow Reservation in Montana and Blue Lake on Taos land in New Mexico, and, of course, Montana's valley of the Little Bighorn. Equally sacred are the red rocks of Sedona, Arizona, the nearby Grand Canyon, Chaco Canyon (New Mexico), the valley of the Great Salt Lake, and many regions of the Rocky Mountains. The West does not lack for sacred places.

Many of these locations have earned their sacred status because they witnessed tragedy. As Professor W. Scott Olson has observed, trouble may be as essential to sacred places as the Fall is to Salvation. (Perhaps Eden, Wyoming, was named in January after all). Kiowa writer N. Scott Momaday defined such venues as follows: "Where words meet the land, that is what makes a location sacred."[2]

Second, I would have expanded on the conflict-cooperation link between the various organized religious bodies. The Great Plains and Rocky Mountains had their share of conflict, of that there is no doubt, but since religious faith calls forth the most intense of all human emotions, some degree of tension is inevitable. But usually this conflict revolved around a "standoffishness" or hard words rather than outright violence. Moreover, the hard words were usually restricted to denominational periodicals rather than loudly voiced in the public realm.

Very little anti-Semitism was found in the region. Indeed, Jewish settlers on the northern Great Plains were viewed as simply another ethnic colony. The rabbis (usually Reform) were highly respected in their communities. In the eyes of the majority the rabbi was simply "the Jewish minister." Although the longstanding cultural tension between Protestants and Catholics smoldered in the Southwest and at times in Lutheran-Catholic communities of the upper Midwest, for the most part it remained within acceptable bounds.

The folk poetry and song that emerged from this region reflected a broad western ecumenicism. A surprising number of cowboy poems dealt with religious themes. God was "Herd Boss," "Trail Boss," or "Sky Boss." A person was headed for the "Golden Stairs," "Last Round-up," or "Judgment Day." Damnation and salvation seemed equally open to all. Take the poem "The Hell Bound Train," written by Rev. J. W. Pruitte in 1909. One verse reads:

> The boiler was filled with lager beer,
> And the Devil himself was the engineer,
> The passengers were a most motley crew,
> Church member, atheist, Gentile, Jew.[3]

If Hell was ecumenical, so too were the rewards of living a just life. The lyrics of Charles Badger Clark Jr.'s now-classic poem "A Cowboy's Prayer," reflect this to perfection. A South Dakota Methodist minister's son, Clark wrote the poem in 1902 while ranching in Arizona. First published in 1906, it was so often reprinted that it was frequently attributed to Anonymous. As the "Battle Hymn of the Republic" is to patriotism and "Amazing Grace" to hymnody, "A Cowboy's Prayer" has evolved into an all-inclusive statement of western religious faith. Today it is often read at funerals, regardless of the affiliation of the deceased.

A Cowboy's Prayer

(Written for Mother)

Oh Lord, I've never lived where churches grow.
I love creation better as it stood
That day You finished it so long ago
And looked upon Your work and called it good.
I know that others find You in the light
That's sifted down through tinted windowpanes,
And yet I seem to feel You near tonight
In this dim, quiet starlight on the plains.

I thank You, Lord, that I am placed so well,

That You have made my freedom so complete;
That I'm no slave of whistle, clock or bell,
Nor weak-eyed prisoner of wall and street.
Just let me live my life as I've begun
And give me work that's open to the sky;
Make me a partner of the wind and sun,
And I won't ask a life that's soft or high.

Let me be easy on the man that's down;
Let me be square and generous with all.
I'm careless sometimes Lord, when I'm in town,
But never let 'em say I'm mean or small!
Make me as big and open as the plains,
As honest as the hawse between my knees,
Clean as the wind that blows behind the rains,
Free as the hawk that circles down the breeze!

Forgive me, Lord, if sometimes I forget.
You know about the reasons that are hid.
You understand the things that gall and fret;
You know me better than my mother did.
Just keep an eye on all that's done and said
And right, sometimes, when I turn aside,
And guide me on the long, dim trail ahead
That stretches upward toward the Great Divide.[4]

As I view the evidence, the central pivot of the story of religion in the Great Plains and Mountain West rests less with the clash of one faith against another than with the fact that each group faced the vastness of the region and found a way to create a niche for its particular point of view.

Finally, if I were writing the book today, I would have spent a little more time exploring the question of why historians have given the theme of religion in the West such a wide berth. Most of the books and articles on this subject—and there are not that many—tend to focus on a single denomination in a particular state. Rarely does one come upon a multi-denominational overview. For many observers, it's as if organized religion played little or no part in the western story.

Some critics trace this omission to the primarily secular nature of the Academy, but I think the cause extends further than that. Religious history—especially in the late nineteenth to early twentieth centuries—tended to be largely local in emphasis. With few exceptions, church efforts focused on regional concerns: establishing Sunday Schools, building and maintaining churches, holding regular services, setting up schools, erecting hospitals and orphanages, resolving quarrels, surviving scandals, and trying to "clean up" the seamy side of western life. Important though these items may have been on a local level, they lack the high drama that one finds in other realms of western history: the Texas Rangers, the bitter Cripple Creek and Ludlow mining strikes, the numerous battles between Indians and Whites, the building of the Union Pacific Railroad, and so on. For many budding historians, to write western religious history is to engage in, well, a "parochial" enterprise.

There is another reason too. History graduate school training urges young scholars to master archival research techniques but places no emphasis on mastering a perspective that allows them to comprehend faith, ritual, or the idea of the sacred. Thus, most historians lack a vocabulary for understanding the role of religion in the West. Related disciplines such as folklore, religious studies, and anthropology are much more comfortable with these concepts than are historians.

An Orthodox theologian once termed secularity "a lie about the world."[5] Similarly, I believe that a purely secular version of western history is "a lie about the West."[6] The paperback version of *The Protestant Clergy in the Great Plains and Mountain West, 1865–1915* is a modest attempt to fill in at least part of this gap.

NOTES

1. Max Evans and Candy Moulton, eds., *Hot Biscuits: Eighteen Stories By Women and Men of the Ranching West* (Albuquerque: University of New Mexico Press, 2002), 234–35.

2. N. Scott Momaday; from a speech at the Albuquerque Kimo Theatre, March 2003.

3. John A. Lomax and Alan Lomax, comps., *Cowboy Songs and Other Frontier Ballads*, 2nd ed. (New York: The Macmillan Company, 1964), 236–37.

4. Julie Saffel, ed., *Cowboy Poetry* (Edison NJ: Castle Books, 2001), 154.

5. John Garvey, ed., *Henri Nouwen* (Springfield IL: Templegate Publishers, 1988), 17.

6. See also Ferenc Morton Szasz, *Religion in the Modern American West* (Tucson: University of Arizona Press, 2000).

Dedicated to
Mary I. Szasz
and the memory of
Ferenc P. Szasz,
Margaret,
Eric, Chris, Scott, and Maria

Contents

*The Protestant Clergy
in the Great Plains
and Mountain West,
1865–1915*

Introduction

The literature on the post–Civil War American West is abundant. Except for the War Between the States, no other aspect of the nation's past has evoked such enthusiasm. Historians, filmmakers, and novelists have all combined to create a West with universal appeal. It has become a story of epic proportions. Given this popularity, it is astonishing that there have been so few accounts of the western clergymen. "Most of the books written about the early days on the frontier," complained Nebraska Episcopal Bishop George Allen Beecher, "have had little or nothing to do with the story of the church."[1]

Bishop Beecher has a point. The religious dimension of the American West has been slighted. In fact, it would be hard to find another aspect of western life that has been similarly ignored. For example, a recent compilation of primary sources on the American West "in history, myth, and literature" contained only a single, brief ministerial account. In their extensive bibliography *The Frontier and the American West,* Rodman W. Paul and Richard W. Etulain list only forty-four titles under the heading "Religion." (The Mormons rate a separate category.) This comes to about one percent of almost three thousand entries.[2] The Buffalo Bill Museum in Cody, Wyoming, which contains a vast array of western art, displays few paintings on religious themes. Moreover, it offers no exhibit commemorating the faith of the early settlers. The list could easily be extended.

If western historians, artists, and museum directors have had dif-

ficulty incorporating the saga of the clergy and churches, the denominational historians have failed to point the way. In *The Episcopal
Church in the United States, 1789–1931,* James T. Addison devoted
about ten pages to "Home Missions" in the post–Civil War period.
None of the other surveys of the American Episcopal church im-
proves on this coverage. There is no Presbyterian, Methodist, or
Baptist history of western church life during this era. The authors
of *The History of American Congregationalism* despaired at even
attempting it. "[A] detailed history of the Congregational expansion across the continent," they confessed, "is here impossible."[3]

Those historians who have studied the American churches after
the Civil War have invariably concentrated on the South or the
urban Northeast. Focusing on these regions, they have analyzed
church reaction to Darwinism, immigration, urbanization, higher
criticism, the rise of the social gospel, millennialism, and revival-
ism. Lest I appear too harsh, however, I confess that I, too, neglected
the West in my first book, *The Divided Mind of Protestant
America, 1880–1930.*[4]

Filmmakers and novelists have faced an even greater challenge
in dealing with the role of the western ministers and their churches.
Here, however, the problem is aesthetic rather than historical. In
all fairness, authors have always had difficulty in portraying a basically "moral" person. The dilemmas of rakes and rascals make far
more interesting reading than does a life of righteousness. To para-
phrase an old adage, "goodness has no story." Whenever a fictional
clergyman is portrayed, he is vaguely designated, "Padre," "Bishop,"
"Reverend," "Preacher," or "Father." This title is wide enough to
include anyone from Roman Catholic to Southern Baptist. Willa
Cather's *Death Comes for the Archbishop,* a fictionalized life of New
Mexico Archbishop Jean Baptiste Lamy, is the exception that proves
the rule. Why have the western clerics been ignored? Why has the
western church story not been told?

The answer, surely, lies in the nature of the American religious
experience: denominationalism. The religious pluralism that characterized American life from the earliest days moved toward the
Pacific Coast with the settlers who traveled west. There was no
standard "American religion" on the post–Civil War frontier. Instead, the pioneers arrived as adherents of a particular faith. They
came as Roman Catholics, Northern Presbyterians, Southern Presbyterians, Northern Methodists, Southern Methodists, Northern Bap-

tists, Southern Baptists, Disciples of Christ, Congregationalists, Quakers, Greek Orthodox, Norwegian Lutherans, German Lutherans, Unitarians, Jews, Latter-day Saints, Mennonites, Hutterites, and so forth. One cannot speak of a generic "bishop," "priest," or "minister." The bishop might be Roman Catholic, Greek Orthodox, Episcopal, Methodist, Moravian, or Mormon; the priest might be Catholic or Episcopal; the minister might be Southern Baptist, Congregational, Presbyterian, Methodist, Unitarian, and so on. Each denomination retained its own particularities.

In the saga of the mythological West, however, most of the other characters adapt easily to generalization. The cattleman, cowboy, outlaw, sheriff, and schoolmarm have all achieved a timeless universality. Only the western religious figures cling stubbornly to sectarian boundaries.

The existing historical literature on religion in the trans-Mississippi West clearly reflects this denominational bent. Most of the major church groups have encouraged local historians to write the history of their individual congregations, usually for a fiftieth- or a hundredth-year celebration. Although frequently written in a hagiographic style, these pamphlets provide an excellent body of primary source material. Hundreds of them lie scattered in archives throughout the region.[5]

Other church historians have analyzed the role of a single denomination in a particular state. Their accounts carry titles such as *The Episcopal Church in Colorado, History of Methodism in Utah, Congregational Nebraska,* or *A History of New Mexico Baptists.* A three-volume study treats the Roman Catholics in Nebraska and a seven-volume history deals with the Catholics of Texas. Recently Harriet and Fred Rochlin have published a praiseworthy account of the Jews in the Far West.[6]

These books are valuable, but they seldom reach beyond their own boundaries. *Congregational Nebraska,* for example, ignores the Episcopalians, Presbyterians, Baptists, and Methodists—all of whom were working side-by-side with the New Englanders. In addition, many of the accounts serve more as hymns of praise to the denominations involved than as analytical studies of their role in the development of western life.

A few pioneering historians, such as William Warren Sweet, Clifford M. Drury, and Colin B. Goodykoontz, recognized the importance of religion in a frontier setting. Some contemporary scholars, such as Robert W. Mondy, Ross Phares, Will Kramer, Gary Topping, Louisa W. Arps, and Norman Bender continued to move in that direction. Nonetheless, the story of the churches in the trans-Mississippi West is still largely *terra incognita.*[7]

This book is an attempt to write on this neglected theme. My subject is the mainline Protestant ministers and the role that they and their churches played in the trans-Mississippi West from about 1865 to about 1915. Since this is a rather tall order, a word of explanation may be necessary. By "mainline" I mean the following groups: Methodists (both northern and southern), Baptists (both northern and southern), Presbyterians (chiefly northern), Congregationalists, and Episcopalians. These groups form the core of my study, but I will also draw on Lutheran, Quaker, Unitarian, Disciples, Holiness, and Mennonite examples as the occasion warrants. With reluctance, I have slighted the contributions of the numerous Lutheran groups that were so prominent on the northern Great Plains. As Eugene L. Ferald has noted in *The Lutherans in North America,* the chief Lutheran approach to home missions was to search out "fellow Lutherans of the same national background as themselves."[8] This concern with language and ethnicity only dimly reflected the outlook of the other mainline Protestant churches.

Although the first special religious census (1906) discovered well over two hundred denominations, my five mainline groups formed the core of Protestant America. In the census of 1850, for example, they were ranked (in the order listed above) as second through sixth in total number of churches. (The Catholics were first, a position they had held since the 1840s; the Lutherans were a close seventh. All the other Protestant groups were considerably smaller.) These rankings would shift only slightly over the course of the century. Thus, it seems safe to say that in terms of numbers (and probably influence) these five denominations ranked among the most important of the American Protestant churches.

In spite of the denominational rivalry, the clergy of these churches, at least in their better moments, saw themselves as engaged in a common enterprise. The popular Congregational minister Henry Ward Beecher once proclaimed all the churches of Christ as "sisters." In 1877 home missionary Zachary Eddy drew on military metaphors to describe the "Army of Israel." The "Army" included the Presbyterian infantry, the Congregational engineers and artillery, the Methodist cavalry, the Baptist gun boats and submarine monitors, and the Episcopal army of reserve. All presumably were engaged in the same "war."

After the constitutional separation of church and state in 1787, no single denomination could ever become America's equivalent of "the church." Consequently, each group provided its own unique contribution to the national religious scene. For the Episcopalians, this meant the dignified ritual of the Prayer Book and the power of the episcopacy; for the Congregationalists and Presbyterians, a New England–Middle Atlantic States emphasis on education; for the Methodists and Baptists, an insistence on God's free grace and the virtues of popular democracy. Since no single denomination had the resources to "tame the land" by itself, each agreed that the others were necessary to the enterprise.

In general, I have limited my geographical focus to the "Home Mission" region that encompassed the Great Plains (from Dakota Territory to west Texas) and the Rocky Mountain–Great Basin region of the interior. The isolation and scattered population of this area meant that it developed quite differently from the more easily reached Mississippi Valley and Pacific Coast states. Although the "New West" varied considerably in topography and climate, the clergy had similar experiences wherever they went.

My chronological boundaries, 1865–1915, are similarly flexible. Settlement began well before 1865, of course, and I chose 1915 as a terminus largely to symbolize the rise of the automobile. While the clergy were not unaffected by the political and economic currents of the day, the religious history of the region invariably established its own boundaries. The years 1865–1915 approximate one such boundary. A Methodist minister who had participated in both the settlement of Virginia City, Montana (in the 1860s), and Superior, Montana (in 1908), found little difference between the two. A 1922 sociological study of the country church in four western states (South Dakota, Montana, Nebraska, and New Mexico) cited the most crucial factors of rural church life as the extremes of climate and distance, the sparseness of population, and the mobility of both clergy and parishioners. These complaints were identical to those of the 1870s and 1880s.[9] As Methodist Edward Laird Mills observed of early twentieth-century Montana, "The frontier lasted a long time."[10] The religious life of the region did not change significantly until the automobile became common property, and the

Fundamentalist–Modernist controversy of the 1920s introduced a theological reorientation that is still under way.

The clerics who pastored these isolated regions were often perceptive observers of the life around them. They left a significant legacy of memoirs, diaries, and autobiographies. Stephen R. Riggs, *Mary and I: Forty Years with the Sioux* (1880); John L. Dyer, *The Snow-Shoe Itinerant* (1890); Ethelbert Talbot, *My People of the Plains* (1906); and Daniel S. Tuttle, *Reminiscences of a Missionary Bishop* (1906) have become minor classics. The more narrowly focused studies by Samuel E. West, *Cross on the Range: Missionary in Wyoming* (1947); George Allen Beecher, *A Bishop of the Great Plains* (1950); Ralph Hall, *The Main Trail* (1971); and Claton Rice, *Ambassador to the Saints* (1965) deserve to be better known.[11]

By ignoring the role of the Protestant clergy, the standard accounts of western life have been genuinely remiss. They have neglected a pivotal figure of the trans-Mississippi West. The pioneer clergy devoted countless hours to the needs of their own congregations. Moreover, their concerns did not simply end at the church door. Instead, they performed a variety of far-reaching social roles. Not only did they deliver general public sermons, they also served as librarians, counselors, social workers, educators, book sellers, peacekeepers, reformers, and general purveyors of culture. They came west by the thousands. It was a rare settler who did not cross the path of a minister from one of the five mainline denominations.

As I will argue in the following chapters, the mainline Protestant clergy wore many hats during the two generations after the Civil War. In the immediate postwar years, they raced west to found new churches so that they might "capture" the settlers as soon as they arrived. Once established, they tried to "clean up" the more obvious vices of their fledgling communities, although they seldom achieved this goal. By the early 1880s, however, the major western towns had matured considerably. Generally speaking, the vice districts had been segregated and the clergy usually ignored them. People from the "proper" side of the tracks, however, almost always viewed the clergy as community leaders. The ministers emerged there as the prime conveyors of the best of Victorian life: education, refinement, decorum, and personal compassion. The women of each community utilized their churches as a major means of social expression. For many people, "social life" and "church" became almost synonymous.

On the sparsely settled Great Plains, the efforts of mainline Protestantism revolved around revivals, camp meetings, and creative attempts at colportage. In New Mexico, Utah, and elsewhere, the clergy confronted what the Presbyterian Board of Home Missions politely termed "the exceptional populations": the Hispanic Catholics, the Latter-day Saints, and the Native Americans—groups who were "with us—not of us."[12] Virtually all denominations relied on parochial schools and itinerant evangelists as the major means of outreach for these groups. Denominational schools also lay at the heart of the Protestant missionary efforts to the Indians. Although eastern theological concerns were usually muted west of the Mississippi, the western clerics did develop their own unique version of the social gospel. Finally, all through the period the ministers touched people's lives through countless sermons, marriage ceremonies, funerals, and acts of spiritual or personal guidance. In short, the Protestant clergy and their churches proved an integral part of everyday life in the Great Plains and Rocky Mountain West. Their story is worth telling.

This study could not have been completed without the aid of numerous people. Let me, then, thank the following: Charlie Biebel, David Dunaway, and Hana Samek for their gracious sharing of materials; Bonnie Sykes for translations from Spanish documents; Ellen Foppes for her aid in gathering statistics; and Howard Rabinowitz and Paul Hutton for their reading of several sections of the manuscript. Floyce Alexander and Dana Asbury did yeoman editorial work under unique circumstances. I would especially like to credit the numerous archivists who helped me along the way: Emmett Chisolm of the Western Heritage Center of the University of Wyoming; Steven R. Wood and Gary Topping of the Utah Historical Society; the staffs of the Colorado Heritage Center in Denver and the Western Room of the Denver Public Library; those of the North Dakota Historical Society, South Dakota Historical Society, the Western Collection at Texas Tech University, the Nebraska Historical Society, the Kansas Historical Society, the Montana Historical Society, the Stowe-Day Library in Hartford, Connecticut, and the Bienecke Library at Yale. Credit should also go to the (Episcopal) Church Historical Society in Austin; the Presbyterian Historical Society in Philadelphia; the Southern Baptist Historical Society in Nashville; the Disciples Historical Society in Nashville; and the Methodist Archives, formerly at Lake Junaluska, North Carolina. I would also like to thank

Carolyn Atkins and Dorothy Stevenson of the Menaul Historical Library of the Southwest in Albuquerque; Betty Danielson, premier historian of New Mexico Baptists; and the staff at the Archives of the Episcopal Archidiocese of the Rio Grande.

In retrospect, it is clear that I owe a considerable debt of thanks to William Hale, Mark Banker, Philip Jordan, Richard W. Etulain, and Sidney E. Mead for numerous discussions on a subject of mutual interest. Rev. Francis Rath, pastor of the First Congregational Church, regularly reminded me of the power of a good sermon. A special mark of commendation should also go to Vi Palfrey, Sandi DeSolla, and, especially, to Penelope P. Katson for deciphering my handwriting through several drafts. Thanks, too, to Dorothy Wonsmos, head of the Interlibrary Loan Department, Zimmerman Library, the University of New Mexico. Finally, Margaret and Maria heard about this book so often that it is almost as much theirs as it is mine. Even as we traveled through the English countryside on our Fulbright year abroad, they listened patiently to stories about the Protestant ministers in the trans-Mississippi West.

Chapter One

The Beginnings

After the Civil War, much of the nation turned its attention to the region of the Great Plains and the Rocky Mountains. Here newly emancipated slaves, ex-Confederate and ex-Union soldiers, Chinese laborers, European immigrants, New England Yankees, midwestern farmers, and gold seekers from every nation on the globe jostled each other for the riches of the land. The clergy from the mainline Protestant denominations joined this exodus. Often they arrived with the first wave.

There is an old adage that "the Baptists came on foot; the Methodists came in a Conestoga wagon; the Presbyterians rode the train; and the Episcopalians arrived in the Pullman car." But this observation reflects social class more accurately than it does historical fact. Actually, ministers from all the major Protestant groups arrived in some part of the region at approximately the same time. Each denomination enjoyed its share of "firsts" in delivering sermons, organizing congregations, and establishing churches, schools, and hospitals.

The clergy went west for numerous reasons. The majority were "called" to serve in a sense that modern readers may find difficult to comprehend. "I wanted to go where others had not gone," recalled Idaho Presbyterian Edward S. Murphy, "where I was needed, where the gospel was not preached."[1] As an integral part of their calling, the ministers tried to provide the ordinances of their denomination—baptism, confirmation, ceremonies of marriage, regular worship services, communion, counseling, and funerals. This always remained their main task. In addition, they offered their version of the Gospel to whoever would listen. For example, when a young missionary from the Chicago Theological Seminary arrived in southwestern Missouri immediately after the Civil War, he was told that the region contained no Congregationalists. "I was not hunting Congregational people at all," he replied. "I was just coming to save men in the name of the Lord Jesus Christ."[2] Finally, the Protestant clergy went west to rescue the land from a variety of real and imagined dangers.

It was this last aspect that provided the sense of urgency to their mission. As historian Sidney E. Mead has shown, the mainline Protestant clerics clearly viewed themselves as the bearers of the national cultural tradition.[3] Drawing upon familiar millennial themes, they reminded their listeners that America was God's "New Israel."[4] The emergence of the "New West" held the key to the future of the nation. If it were brought into the Protestant camp, all would be well; if not, American liberties would end. Congregationalist Joseph Ward went to Dakota Territory "to pre-empt the territory in the name of the Lord," while home missionary W. G. Puddefoot placed the fate of Christian missions abroad directly on the success of missions at home. A Lutheran pastor said he could serve God better on the plains of Kansas than any other place in the land. The West, everyone agreed, would soon become as great an influence in national life as New England had been in the past. "It is the West, not the North or South," observed the editor of the *North Dakota Evangel* in 1888, "which holds the key to the nation's future."[5]

The success of the American political system, the clerics argued, rested primarily on the moral health of its citizens. If moral decay were to increase, it would invariably produce political decay. As Congregationalist Joseph P. Thompson observed in 1868, "The alphabet, the ballot, the Constitution, so much vaunted as the A.B.C. of a sound political system, cannot restore to soundness a society whose morality has begun to degenerate."[6] Many of the clerics who went west were convinced that they held the fate of the republic in their hands.

Such strident appeals to "save the West" were hardly new in the post–Civil War era. In fact, similar rhetoric characterized the home mission literature for the entire antebellum period. Hundreds of pre–Civil War pamphlets, sermons, and magazine articles had voiced identical fears about the dangers inherent in the "first" American West—the territory west of the Allegheny Mountains. This included the Old Northwest of Ohio, Indiana, Illinois, Michigan, Wisconsin, Minnesota, and Iowa; and (sometimes) the Old Southwest of Mississippi, Arkansas, Alabama, Louisiana, Kentucky, and Tennessee. Since the earlier home mission literature had left such a strong legacy, it is necessary to examine it in some detail.

Clerical concern over the future of this first West had deep roots. In 1812–13, Presbyterians Samuel J. Mills and John D. Schermerhorn visited the region, and in 1814–15 Mills joined Rev. Daniel Smith to make an even more extensive tour. Armed with 600 Bibles, 1,400 religious tracts, plus numerous sermons and pamphlets, the two Presbyterian ministers crisscrossed the entire trans-Appalachian frontier. In general, they were not pleased with what they saw. "The whole country from Lake Erie to the Gulf of Mexico," they concluded, "is as the valley of the shadow of death. Darkness rests upon it. Only here and there, a few rays of gospel light pierce through the awful gloom."[7]

Mills and Smith's 1815 pamphlet marked the opening blast of the clerics' "literature of warning" about life in the early West. The initial forays into the fur trading region of the Rocky Mountains only extended their concern. One of the first clerics to enter this distant region, Rev. Samuel Parker, observed that the western trappers had sought out a place where, in their words, "human nature is not oppressed by the tyranny of religion, and pleasure is not awed by the frown of vice." The fur traders of the Rockies had many good qualities, another observer wryly noted, "but they were those of animals."[8] Such warnings became standard fare from all the denominational spokesmen.

Within a few years, however, two clergymen took up the cause with notable success. Cincinnati Presbyterian Lyman Beecher wrote "A Plea for the West" in 1835, and twelve years later, Connecticut Congregationalist Horace Bushnell followed with "Barbarism the First Danger." Both pamphlets received wide distribution. They have become representative classics of the era.[9]

If the Protestant churches did not succeed in "Christianizing" the West, Beecher warned, the new republic would surely fail. He was especially concerned about potential Roman Catholic domination, emanating from the city of St. Louis. (By 1845, St. Louis had about fifteen thousand Catholics, slightly under half of its population.) While Bushnell did not discount the Catholic issue, he was far more concerned with what he termed "the bowie-knife style of civilization." Bushnell feared the descent of anarchy upon the land. Without the ministrations of the Protestant clergy, he predicted, armed bands of ruffians would roam the West at will. As a spokesman for the American Home Missionary Society observed: "*Mesmerism* is there to delude them. *Popery* is there to ensnare them. *Infidelity* is there to corrupt and debase them. And atheism is there, to take away their God as they go on to the grave, and to blot out every ray of hope that may beam on them from beyond."[10]

As a consequence of these warnings, the antebellum Protestant churches launched a concerted effort to bring the frontier under control. This crusade, moreover, was never viewed as a mere act of guidance or supervision. Rather, it was seen as a genuine battle between good and evil, one whose outcome would determine the fate of the nation. Eventually, the cause involved settled pastors, itinerant evangelists, and far-seeing bishops. It also enrolled a corps of well-organized wealthy organizations, such as the American Bible Society and American Tract Society, dedicated to the distribution of Bibles, tracts, and other appropriate literature.[11]

The home mission crusade also enlisted the women. Following her father's lead, Catharine Beecher voiced great fear over the threat of Roman Catholic parochial education on the frontier. As a consequence, she helped to establish in Boston the Ladies' Society for the Promotion of Education in the West in 1846. The society hoped to send "competent female teachers of unquestioned piety"—all had to attest to an experience of grace—to the western states. The group sponsored over one hundred young women before it merged in 1854 with the National Popular Education Board. By the Civil War, this organization had sent perhaps a thousand teachers to serve in western schools.

These women who went west to teach shared the same sense of mission as their male counterparts. When men teachers deserted their jobs for the lure of California gold, the women were expected to replace them. Commentators often labeled the male missionaries as decidedly mediocre, but that criticism did not extend to their female counterparts. As one observer noted in 1856, "the young women of New England succeeded in the West better than the men." Sunday schools with women teachers—far more integrated with public education than today—also grew rapidly during this period.[12]

In addition to secondary schools, the Protestant churches founded numerous denominational colleges on the antebellum frontier. They deemed this effort necessary because the West seemed so different from New England (the home of the most articulate home missionaries). The Yankees there had formed a homogeneous community that had esteemed education as the great ideal and goal of life, they said. But the West contained so many immigrant groups that it lacked "a strong educational heart."[13] If the West were to enter the Union with its voters unable to handle democracy, it would be like placing "a drawn sword in the hands of a giant maniac."[14] Until the West could boast its own colleges and theological seminaries to provide its own religious, literary, and scientific leaders, it would be vulnerable to all the evils of the day.

Thus, the Middle West became home to scores of denominational liberal arts colleges—Oberlin (Congregational), Ohio Wesleyan (Methodist), Wooster (Presbyterian), Denison (Baptist), Beloit (Congregational), and Wabash (Congregational), just to name a few. Some schools, such as Oberlin, also helped found satellite colleges in nearby states. When a friend once asked William McKinley why Ohio had produced so many great statesmen, McKinley quipped that it was probably due to the large number of small colleges scattered throughout the state.[15]

When the onset of the Civil War began to divert the ministers' attention to the issues of slavery and secession, it was clear that most of their earlier fears had not been realized. Although the Middle West remained rough in spots, it had not lapsed into barbarism. Except for a few isolated individual spokesmen, organized rationalism had staked few roots. Although the Catholic church lay firmly entrenched in the "German triangle" of St. Louis, Milwaukee, and Cincinnati, as well as in other areas, it showed no sign of "taking over" the nation. The much-despised Mormons had been driven from Missouri and Illinois to the far reaches of Utah. By 1860, then, the trans-Appalachian West had been "saved."

This pattern of success with America's "first" West provided the Protestant clergy with a model for the "New West" of the Great Plains and Rocky Mountains. So many of the conditions appeared identical: the wide variety of peoples, the frenzied pursuit of riches, the creation of instant communities, and the general collapse of social restraints. Consequently, in the post–Civil War years the clergy drew on proven methods to begin their work: traveling evangelists, distribution of Bibles and appropriate literature, women teachers, and the creation of colleges. "We go there [the New West]," said Presbyterian Timothy Hill in 1868, "to make a broader New England; that we may transplant her energy and skill, her schools and her finest religious faith on a broad field; that we may retain what is excellent of our own and mingle it with what is most desirable in the other portions of our land."[16] The frequency with which the missionaries drew on antebellum examples demonstrated that many viewed the New West as simply the second round of an old crusade.[17] "Home missions saved this country once," declared Congregationalist Richard S. Storrs, "and will save it again if necessary."[18]

But the situation in the New West was to prove quite different from that of the old. For one thing, as Walter Prescott Webb has noted, the topography, uncertain rainfall, and vast distances of the Great Plains offered a land that proved far more challenging to tame.[19] The general collapse of restraints that flowed from the Civil War, plus the outbreak of subsequent Indian wars, meant that "barbarism" continued to present a genuine problem. Moreover, the *bêtes noires* of nineteenth-century Protestantism—Rationalism, the Roman Catholics, and the Mormons—all had a decided head start in the region.

"Rationalism" or "infidelity" originally referred to the eighteenth-century pattern of deist thought. Its most visible weapons lay in the form of deist books and tracts, or in short-lived free thinkers' societies. Over time, however, the term evolved into a blanket form of condemnation. One Southern Presbyterian listed "the varied aspects" of infidelity as "pantheism, naturalism, indifferentism, and formalism."[20] The Roman Catholics proved a much more tangible foe. Franciscan missionaries had first arrived in the Southwest in the 1540s—over three generations before the Pilgrims had landed in Plymouth. Virtually all Hispanics were members of the church. The Latter-day Saints proved equally formidable. By the end of the Civil War, the Mormons had been settled in Utah for almost a generation. They had developed a culture that boasted a distinct self-consciousness. Clearly, the Protestant churches had their work cut out for them.

When the Civil War ended, the Protestants resumed publication of the "literature of concern." It remained standard fare for countless pamphlets, speeches, and all the home mission periodicals. The clergy compiled a list of dangers to the reunited republic, which, with variations, almost always included the following: lawlessness, immigration, rationalism, Roman Catholicism (usually described as "the Jesuits"), and Mormonism. Sometimes the enemies could be combined, as when a Baptist missionary said of the Mormons: "Their whole attitude is Jesuitical."[21]

Two of these postwar authors, however, emerged as especially significant: Congregationalists Josiah Strong and E. P. Tenney. Strong's *Our Country* (1885) and Tenney's *The New West as Related to the Christian College* (1877) played the same role for the post–Civil War West that Beecher's and Bushnell's pamphlets had performed for the pre–Civil War frontier.

Fresh from divinity school, Josiah Strong cut his ministerial teeth in the town of Cheyenne during the early 1870s. From this experience, plus considerable reading, he produced one of the most popular books of the period: *Our Country.* First published in 1885, by 1916 *Out Country* had sold over 125,000 copies. Separate chapters were reprinted as magazine articles or pamphlets. It was also translated into at least one foreign language. A prominent librarian compared the book favorably with Harriet Beecher Stowe's *Uncle Tom's Cabin.*[22] Strong offered the familiar litany of Protestant foes: socialism, Mormonism, immigration, wealth, the city, Catholicism, tobacco, and alcohol, among others. Far more important, however, was his earnest call to the nation's Protestant churches to evangelize the West. Historians have been somewhat baffled by the success of this rather strange volume, but the secret of its appeal almost surely lay in his clarion call to service. Strong reminded his Protestant readers that their efforts alone could "save the nation." If they failed to respond, the American experiment might fail.

Strong argued that God had designated the Anglo-Saxon race for the moment at hand. The Lord's plans were such that the American churches could no longer delay. The fate of foreign missions depended on the successful evangelizing of the American West. Thus, he concluded: "And our plea is not America for America's sake; but America for the World's sake."[23] Anticipating historian Frederick Jackson Turner's famous 1893 essay on the closing of the frontier, Strong predicted that the nation's public lands would soon be exhausted. When this occurred, the character of the West would have achieved its permanent imprint. In 1884 Strong suggested that the fifteen years remaining in the nineteenth century would mold the West forever. Thus, he described these closing decades as a focal point in human history. The importance of these years, he claimed, were second only to the birth of Jesus Christ Himself.[24]

Exaggerated though these claims might sound, Josiah Strong was not alone in his sentiments. As the first Episcopal Bishop of Colorado declared in 1866, "The ground here is *new* in every sense of the word." Three years later the bishop observed that Colorado's society lay plastic and ready to be formed: "We live in an age marked by developments which have no precedent in history."[25] In 1886, his Episcopal successor John F. Spalding expanded on this theme. Spalding saw the East as an inflexible society. The West, however, presented an open arena where Christianity could confront (and best) intemperance, infidelity, socialism, and "anarchic tendencies." The churches could accomplish more in the next twenty years, Spalding forecast, than in the century that would follow.[26]

E. P. Tenney's book, *The New West as Related to the Christian College,* proved only slightly less influential than *Our Country.* First published in 1877, it went through five printings in two years. Tenney derived his knowledge of the West from his term as the second president of Colorado College in Colorado Springs. Like Strong, he also cataloged the traditional litany of dangers from an unchurched West. Unlike Strong's millennial suggestions, however, Tenney proposed a plan of direct, practical action. Tenney would save the West by planting denominational colleges throughout the area. These schools would shape their regions as Harvard and Yale had molded New England, and as Oberlin, Beloit, and Wabash had infuenced the Middle West.

Tenney predicted that a string of western church-related colleges could have untold influence. Not only would they elevate the tone of their respective towns, they would also guarantee a supply of ministers for the area in a way that no eastern schools could duplicate. In addition, they would serve as normal schools to ensure sufficient Christian teachers for the West. In so doing, they would fend off the "Jesuitical" influence emanating from New Mexico, the Mormon thrust from Utah, and any rationalist trends that might arise from the local state universities. "It will be impossible to plant a Christian college in Colorado," Tenney concluded, "without doing much thereby toward modifying the future of New Mexico, Arizona, Utah, Wyoming, and every nearby state in that region."[27] With this rhetoric to guide them, the mainline ministers ventured forth into the Great Plains and Rocky Mountains.

The first Protestant ministers to arrive on the scene came in the late 1850s. Part-time itinerants, their primary motives were economic rather than spiritual. Nonetheless, at least in the experience of the Colorado gold rush of 1859, the miners usually treated them as full-fledged ministers.[28] They left no permanent legacy.

The first body of full-time clergymen did not arrive until the end of the Civil War. Their first task was to find enough members to organize a church. The ministers all agreed that a thriving church would serve as a magnet to attract the next wave of incoming settlers. This produced a genuine race to secure a "first strike" and command the primary theological ground. "Other denominations had taken the lead," complained Baptist R. C. Brant from Lawrence, Kansas, in 1857, "and of course the crowd run after the popular religion."[29] "The Catholics will be here [Salt Lake City] during the Spring and Summer," warned Episcopal priest Warren Hussey in 1867, "and probably the Methodists; and the first here will get [the] most support." The Methodist Church Extension Board actually gave Rev. E. M. Boggess a Kentucky thoroughbred horse to enter Oklahoma in the first land rush to secure a lot for the church. They justified the expense on the grounds that "the King's business requires haste."[30] As late as 1908, home missionary Ward Platt advised that "an alert missionary pioneers along new railroads and picks up corner lots for churches, and trusts his board to make good on first payments."[31]

The railroads and the various town corporations aided this denominational rivalry by donating lots to virtually every church that asked for one. Sometimes they gave away an entire city block. The great game of the time, of course, was town building, and the railroad's purposes were more economic than religious. In their eyes, church buildings denoted permanence. Local newspaper editors agreed. They always listed the number of churches as a mark of the town's "stability."[32]

The primary goal for many of the early ministers, then, was to organize churches. For most of the late nineteenth century, this remained a steady theme. It characterized the railroad boom of the 1860s, the mining rush of the 1870s, the Dakota expansion of the early 1880s, and the opening of Oklahoma and southern Idaho during the *fin de siècle* era. When Gilded Age agnostic Robert G. Ingersoll predicted that American Christianity would soon collapse, Rev. Charles McCabe, secretary of the Methodist Church Extension Society, produced church statistics to the contrary. In a famous telegram to Ingersoll, McCabe replied: "Dear Robert: All hail the power of Jesus' name—we are building more than one Methodist Church for every day in the year, and prepare to make it two a day."[33] Many of these new churches were in the trans-Mississippi West.

Several frontier clerics were remarkably successful in organizing churches. During his five years in the San Luis Valley of Southern Colorado, Rev. Alexander Darley founded ten Presbyterian churches. During his twelve years in North Dakota, Episcopal Bishop William D. Walker built twenty-two, plus six rectories. In his forty years in New Mexico, Methodist Thomas Harwood helped establish sixty-six churches, chapels, and schools. Colorado Episcopal Bishop John F. Spalding founded over fifty churches while Methodist Tabor Moore established seventy in North Dakota. Nebraska Congregationalist J. D. Stewart claimed to have founded over one hundred, many of which eventually joined other denominations because of a lack of Congregational ministers.[34] In his forty-seven years in Montana, Methodist William Wesley Van Orsdel established one hundred churches, fifty parsonages, six hospitals, and two schools.[35]

Few western clerics, however, could duplicate the church-founding reputation of Presbyterian Sheldon Jackson. From 1869 to 1883, this self-appointed "Rocky Mountain Superintendent" crisscrossed the region preaching sermons, establishing schools, and organizing churches. Jackson gained notoriety, among his contemporaries as "the Kit Carson of the Presbyterian Church," the "pioneer of the cross," and "the Francis Xavier of Protestant America."[36]

In 1869, Jackson became the "Superintendent of Presbyterian Missions for Western Iowa, Nebraska, Dakota, Montana, Idaho, Wyoming, and Utah." As he entered the region, Jackson broke with the established Presbyterian tradition of waiting until an area was settled before trying to organize a church. Instead, he often arrived on the first train, sought out a few Presbyterian families, established a church, and then moved on. In a twelve-month period from 1869 to 1870, he traveled about twenty-nine thousand miles and organized twenty-three churches. Between 1873 to 1876, he founded sixteen more. In one stretch in early 1872 he organized seven churches in sixteen days. Rawlins, Cheyenne, Laramie, Helena, Fremont, Grand Island, and Bozeman were just a few of the towns where he planted permanent Presbyterian roots. The total number of Sheldon Jackson–organized churches can only be estimated.[35]

Utilizing free passes from the railroad lines, which were indispensable to his work, Jackson averaged about thirty thousand miles a year in his efforts. Such frantic activity, however, soon brought charges of recklessness from national church officials. In truth, many of Jackson's churches collapsed shortly after founding. In several towns he organized churches with only five or six members. In Missoula, in 1872, he organized one with only two members. The day after the founding, half the congregation left town. Of course, the church collapsed. As the 1876 Montana Presbytery observed: "Roll of churches called and all found dead except those at Deer Lodge, Helena, and Bozeman. The former District Superintendent's work [Jackson's] was strongly condemned."[38]

Nonetheless, for over fourteen years, Sheldon Jackson loomed as the major Protestant figure in the New West. In 1872 he established the *Rocky Mountain Presbyterian,* the denomination's only western paper. Published monthly from Denver, the paper was sent to all Presbyterians in the region, as well as to numerous national church officials. Through his editorials and endless correspondence— he sometimes wrote fifty letters in a single day—Jackson sketched the drama of frontier life for eastern readers. With strident prose, he warned them of "the Mormon assassin," the "Papal mob," and the thousand other western perils. He directed much of his appeal to women readers.

Jackson's tales of hardship and heroism must have struck a responsive chord, for he soon tapped the financial resources of numerous eastern churchgoers. He placed these gifts in his special Raven Fund (as Elijah was fed in the wilderness by ravens) and distributed the money with considerable skill. His Raven Fund gave him a degree of financial independence from national church officials. When railroad construction declined in the early 1880s, Jackson turned his attention to establishing Presbyterian Mission schools in New Mexico and Utah. He might have accomplished even more had he not chosen to go to Alaska in 1883 to start yet another career. For over a decade, however, Sheldon Jackson played a significant role in the development of western Protestantism.[39]

Many of the churches founded by Jackson and others existed on paper long before they had any permanent home. Initially, church services were held wherever people could find room—in tents, private homes, courthouses, and schools. Few people, however, considered this solution satisfactory. "We met wherever we could find a place," complained Presbyterian Timothy Hill from eastern Kansas in 1868, "and at one period there were five consecutive Sabbaths in which we not only met in a different place each Sabbath, but on one Sabbath at least—we met in two places the same day. Such a condition could not long remain and the church have any prospect of life, much less of growth and prosperity."[40]

Virtually every person connected with an early church hoped for a separate building. Consequently, the minister's next challenge was the building of a permanent church home (and, occasionally, the procuring of a lot for a cemetery). All the denominational home mission societies contributed financial aid to this process, as only a fraction of the cost could be borne in the field. Even so, several churches quickly assumed mortgages. As the Arizona *Citizen* observed in 1879, "the new [Tucson] Presbyterian church is nearly $6000 in debt, which is quite a monument in itself."[41]

The beginnings of prefabrication and the arrival of the railroad aided the church-building process considerably. Sheldon Jackson, for example, ordered several buildings from Chicago, and within a few months they had arrived, each broken into sections. Occasionally, the railroads hauled church lumber without charge. Cheyenne Episcopal priest Joseph W. Cook ordered his wood from Chicago, hiring local carpenters to construct the doors, windows, and trimming. In 1906, Disciples of Christ minister Liff Sanders had his lumber shipped to Lubbock where voluntary labor built the structure. When it was finished, it was the tallest building in Lubbock and seated three hundred people (three times the number in the congregation). Boulder's First Congregational Church was also built by volunteer labor.

A wave of church construction characterized the period under consideration. Interestingly enough, no distinctive style of western church architecture emerged from it. Instead, the western congregations drew exclusively on eastern prototypes. Clearly, the fledgling congregations sought to transplant the most tangible evidence of their former roots to the new environment. The first Congregational church of Yankton, Dakota Territory, for example, looked as if it belonged on a New Hampshire common. This New England frame structure, with clapboard sides, gabled roof, and modest steeple, typified the early wave of western church building. Later variations on this design were dubbed "prairie Gothic."

Of modest dimensions, the early Protestant churches reminded visitors of a frame house with an added steeple. They were approximately thirty feet wide and eighty feet long, with seating capacity that ranged between one and three hundred. The typical cost ran from one to four thousand dollars. Episcopal Bishop William D. Walker of North Dakota (1883–97) encouraged his parishioners to build their churches out of stone, for he felt that stone churches implied more stability than those of wood. But he was the exception. The Mennonite Brethren built their wooden churches to resemble large houses. Since church was an all-day affair, the presence of a good stable nearby also proved an essential part of church construction.

Most church interiors were plain, for lack of money meant little ornamentation. The focal point lay with the modest altar and pulpit. Wood or coal stoves heated the interior, while kerosene and coal oil lamps provided light. If a congregation wished to be extravagant, it usually spent its extra money on windows. The churches on the upper Great Plains emphasized their spires. By 1890, the two churches in Harrison, South Dakota, boasted spires that reached sixty-eight and ninety-two feet in the air. Except for the cross at the top of a steeple, however, few could distinguish a prairie Catholic church building from a Protestant one.[42]

The steeples served more than just an ornamental function, however, for they usually housed the pioneer church's most precious possession: a bell. Cast in eastern foundries, these were carried west at considerable expense. A six-hundred-pound bell arrived at St. Mark's Episcopal Church in Cheyenne in 1869—the first church bell in Wyoming—as a gift from wealthy St. Mark's in Philadelphia. A similar bell came to Santa Fe by wagon. The bell for the Lake City, Colorado, Presbyterian church had to be hauled by pack train over the Continental Divide and two additional high mountain passes. The first church bell in Yankton was borrowed from a Missouri River steamboat that had run aground and burned. In 1871, Episcopal priest Joseph W. Tays hired a Mexican bell maker to cast a copper bell for his El Paso church. He was quite proud that it was the only Protestant church bell for a thousand miles. The bell that hung from St. Mark's Episcopal Church in Salt Lake City was the first for all of Utah. When a group of Montana Methodists canvassed their community for a new church, so the story goes, a nonbeliever who lived nearby said that he would contribute one hundred dollars to the fund—but only if the church ceased ringing its old bell.

These bells served a multitude of purposes. In a world before inexpensive pocket watches, they often tolled the time of day. In addition, they signaled the hour of worship, as well as births and deaths of the members of the congregation (an old New England custom). In some areas, they warned of fires, hangings, or Indian raids. In Manti, Utah, the bell on the Presbyterian church tolled the city curfew and also served as the fire alarm. Gamblers chose the Methodist church in Durango to house the funeral of a crooked Silverton gambler in 1881 largely because it "had a bell which would toll." The sound of bells often reminded the settlers of their roots. In 1872, a Colorado editor termed the sound of church bells as the symbol of "the advancement of the humanizing influence of Christianity and healthy progress."[43] When the Congregational church in Boulder, Colorado, got a church bell in the middle 1860s, people came for miles around simply to hear it ring.[44]

The early western communities generally admired their new churches. "Everyone is quite proud of our [Episcopal] church already," wrote Joseph W. Cook from Cheyenne in 1868. "It's an ornament to the place."[45] The Dickinson, North Dakota, *Press* described the new Congregational church as "one of the finest and most ornamental buildings in town." A Boise editor termed the town's first Presbyterian church "one of the most attractive buildings in our city."[46] As the Albuquerque *Morning Democrat* observed in 1893: "When we stop to consider that a church does as much to build up a town as a school, a railroad, or a fair, we are sure our people will not be slow to respond to this [Northern Baptist] call to help build up our town."[47]

In cases where religious faith overlapped with ethnicity, the entire community usually became involved in church building. Historian Frederick Luebke has suggested that the church on the Great Plains often became the key social institution for maintaining ethnoreligious group loyalty. Through this means, it gained a new dimension in America that it had not known in Europe.[48] When members began construction of a German Lutheran church north of Bethune, Colorado, for example, each able-bodied man was expected to bring several loads of rock. In western Kansas, a small German Catholic community built a church from labor donated by every male over twelve years of age. The First Mennonite Brethren church of Henderson, Nebraska, was built in 1880 from donations of sun-dried bricks. The father of each household contributed either money or bricks, and each man then worked one day per three weeks until the building was completed.[49]

Occasionally, even the more ethnically diverse areas joined in communal church-building enterprises. A group of Methodists south of Sundance, Wyoming, for example, built a thirteen-hundred-dollar frame church in 1891. They did so by assessing every person in the region an amount proportionate to the worth of his house. In a spirit of coooperation, the fledgling Jewish communities frequently contributed to these church-building programs. Tucson musician M. Katz performed in an instrumental duet to help raise funds to build the local Methodist church. The lone Jewish merchant in Deming, New Mexico, always contributed his share of the Episcopal clergyman's salary. Merchant Louis Hershfield helped Baptist minister A. M. Hough build his Virginia City, Montana, church, while Rachael Strassburger gave the Virginia City Catholics a lot for their hospital. In nearby Helena, Henry Klein donated a site for the Protestant Intermountain Union College.[50] The Seligman family of Santa Fe were very helpful in building Archbishop Lamy's Catholic cathedral there. In 1892, the Phoenix firm of M. Goldwater and Brother gave one day's profit to each of the three churches in town: Catholic, Episcopal, and Methodist. Clearly, the early Christian churches had an impact that extended well beyond their denominational boundaries.[51]

The traveling ministers soon brought their various denominations to most of the important western communities. By the mid-1870s, Prescott, Arizona, claimed eight churches, with the YMCA on its way. El Paso in 1896 had sixteen churches for its fifteen thousand people, while Albuquerque in the year 1900 claimed eleven, plus one synagogue, for its population of seven thousand. By 1906, Arizona Methodists had founded a church in every town of any size in the territory.

As far as can be determined, however, actual church membership remained small. In the 1860s, the gentile town of Corinne, Utah, could discover only 12 Episcopalians, 26 Methodists, and 41 Sabbath schoolers. In 1882, the Cheyenne *Daily Leader* recorded the following statistics:

Presbyterians	81
Congregationalists	130
Methodists	75
Baptists	100
Catholics	300
Episcopalians	50
African Methodist–Episcopal	23

The total church members was 759, or only 15 percent of the population.[52] Records of the Laramie Presbyterian Church show that from 1869 to 1904, church membership rarely exceeded 100. The Socorro, New Mexico, Presbyterian church membership remained for years at about 20. In 1883, Montana claimed only 650 Methodists; in 1892, Wyoming had but 487 Baptists; in 1893, Arizona boasted only 272 Episcopalians. In 1890, the Baptists, Presbyterians, and Congregationalists together included only about 1 percent of all the people in South Dakota. Sabbath school membership (actually Bible study classes for all ages) usually exceeded church membership until around the turn of the century.[53]

One reason for the slow growth of the denominations lay with the unsettled nature of these early western "turnstile" communities. A woman known to history only as "Stella" observed in 1866 that the motto of Nebraska City, Nebraska, ought to be "everybody for himself." The people, she observed, "rush up and down the streets in utter forgetfulness apparently of everything but rushing—rushing right on—not much matter where."[54] An early settler in Laramie recalled that he knew of no person except himself who intended to remain in the town. A woman recalled that in frontier Cheyenne, "all seemed to be working under the same great impulse, to make a fortune and make it quickly."[55]

When pioneer Methodist minister Jacob Adriance arrived in Denver in 1859, he found a town of one thousand people "with very few, if any, expecting to settle down and stay."[56] Adriance found that the same restlessness pervaded the entire area. In nearby Central City, people came and left with every report of new mines. Adriance located several Methodists in the region, but their transience made it impossible for him to hold services on a regular basis. "At one appointment I would take names," he complained, "and at the next they would be gone."[57]

Such mobility characterized much of the western religious experience. In 1867, Congregationalist James Wilkinson of Minnesota, Kansas, wrote to a fellow clergyman in Topeka that he and his wife were the only remaining church members there.[58] El Paso Episcopal priest J. W. Tays saw his congregation go from from four to fifty and then back to three during the early 1870s. Joseph W. Cook watched helplessly as his most promising vestryman and two candidates for confirmation left Cheyenne for greener pastures. "So it goes in this restless mass of humanity," he observed in his diary.[59] In a single year, five consecutive families held the same pew in a Virginia City, Nevada church, while Episcopal priest Edward W. Burleson complained that the patron saint of North Dakota should be "St. Exodus."[60] "If you stay here long enough, remarked Congregationalist Rollin L. Hartt from Helena in 1897, "you see a very long procession passing under your teaching."[61]

The mobility of the clergy mirrored the mobility of the parishioners. In New England, by contrast, a man might spend his entire career serving a single church. But the New England custom of asking a minister to deliver a "fifty year retrospective sermon" was unheard of in the West. Brief pastorates became the norm. In the first seven and a half years of organized Presbyterianism in Denver, for example, the church had five ministers and was without a pastor 40 percent of the time. In Tucson, the First Methodist Church had twelve pastors in twenty-four years, while First Congregational had ten in the same period.[62] While both Northern and Southern Methodists had a policy of rotating their ministers, the records of Trinity Methodist (South) in El Paso show that only five out of the thirteen who served from 1881 to 1911 stayed even three years. The Laramie Presbyterian Church clearly reflected this clerical mobility:

Organized 1869: 4 months without a minister

Frank L. Arnold	1869–1874
William E. Hamilton	1874–1878
J. McGaughty	1879–1880
E. J. Boyd	1880–1881
E. S. Chapman	1881–1883
J. H. Burlison	1885–1886
J. H. Boyd	3 months
W. S. Rudolph	5 months

W. M. Hicks	1886–1888
George Barr	1888–1891
Jacob Norris	1891–1895

Six and one half years passed before they had another permanent minister.[63] "Ministers come and go," remarked Wyoming Congregationalist W. B. D. Gray in 1904, "the work remains."[64]

These floating congregations and brief pastorates characterized Protestantism in the New West from the end of the Civil War forward. Because membership changed so frequently, many churches found it difficult to exert a consistent influence on their local communities. Instead, they served as a locus of welcome and farewell for their parishioners. For years, the wife of the Episcopal Bishop of Colorado considered it her duty to hold an open house to welcome all of Denver's newcomers. "Visitors Always Welcome" characterized many a western church notice. Much of the church membership in the New West remained ever on the move.

This transience also undermined the impact of the western pastor. The constant mobility prevented the ministers from developing a close relationship with either their parishioners or with their local community. An Episcopal priest departed Roswell, New Mexico, feeling himself an utter failure. In 1875, when Nathan Thompson resigned after a decade of service to his Boulder Congregational church, he wrote an open letter to the town. In it, he regretted that his ten years in Boulder had produced so few "manifest fruits."[65] As will be shown in the next chapter, only those ministers who spent years in a single region were able to have much lasting influence.

Chapter Two

The Wild Ones,
c. 1865–1882

The early Protestant clergy had more duties than the organizing and building of churches. As historian Ann Douglas has suggested, they teamed with the women to serve as the prime purveyors of Victorian culture. They were the "civilizers" of life. As such, they represented stability, decorum, and morality in the context of a harsh and shifting world.[1] Given the turbulent nature of many early western communities, the clergy faced a difficult challenge.

The persistent legend of the "Wild West" rests largely on incidents drawn from the early cattle towns, railroad communities, and mining camps of the 1860s and 1870s. Several historians have argued recently that this theme of western violence has been considerably exaggerated.[2] Nevertheless, there can be little doubt that the early frontier clergymen *perceived* their towns as excessively violent. Numerous examples attest to this assessment. In 1859, for example, one observer noted that the only need for a minister in El Paso was to bury the dead.[3] Presbyterian Alexander T. Rankin described Denver in 1860 as a land of no law, jails, penitentiaries, or courts, and, consequently, "no restraint on human passion."[4] During his four years in Montana in the late 1860s, Methodist A. M. Hough witnessed twenty public executions.[5] Two decades later, Baptist James Spencer confessed that he could postmark his letters from Butte as sent "from Hell."[6]

While these clerical observations may safely be discounted, they probably should not be dismissed completely. Parts of the early

West *did* lack the trappings of civilized life. In 1868, eight thousand people gathered in Omaha to witness a public execution. Arundel C. Hull's photographs, taken in the same year, of recently lynched Laramie outlaws still make uncomfortable viewing.[7] Enlisted men at Fort Stanton during the early 1870s overheard an officer say that horses cost money but men came cheap. Colorado Methodist John L. Dyer discovered that cattle in eastern Colorado carried a higher value than human life. A captured rustler was almost certain to be executed, but a murderer was likely to escape punishment. When a minister complained to an Arizona mine manager that certain mine shafts needed stronger timber framing, he was told, "Dagos is cheaper." The first organized religious service in Durango, Colorado, occurred December 26, 1880; community leaders deemed it necessary because three men had been shot the previous Christmas Eve. Episcopal priest Joseph W. Cook, who lived through several "reigns of terror" in Cheyenne during the late 1860s, complained to his diary, "Of so little account is human life in this rough region."[8] As late as 1912, Montana Methodist William Wesley Van Orsdel recalled the story of a man who had been shot and killed in a saloon fight only ten minutes after he had left one of Van's sermons.[9]

If the myth of a lawless West has any basis in fact, many of these facts probably came from the clergymen. Journalists, writers, and photographers were quick to seize on the ministers' stories, and the saga of lawlessness rapidly became an integral part of western folklore. The effects of these combined publicists catapulted Deadwood, Tombstone, Virginia City, Tonopah, and Dodge City into national notoriety. El Paso, Cheyenne, Denver, Tucson, Wichita, Leadville, and several others, however, were not far behind. Cheyenne was nicknamed "Hell on Wheels," while Phoenix became "The Whiskey Town," and El Paso, "Murder Metropolis," or "the Monte Carlo of the United States." Even Salt Lake City had its problems. These reputations spread across the nation. When the Presbyterians of Wichita asked for eastern financial assistance in 1873, they were told that they first had to improve the sordid reputation of their town.[10]

While the eastern cities of the Gilded Age were hardly bastions of virtue, they differed from the western communities in several important aspects. First, the eastern urban areas were usually segregated along class or ethnic lines. Residents drew strict boundaries between the "proper," middle-class sections and the immigrant areas. Police often feared to patrol the slums at night and few respectable people ventured there at any hour.

Since the immigrant areas were chiefly non-Protestant, the mainline Protestant churches—largely middle-class institutions by this time—could safely ignore them. Until the late 1880s, eastern urban churchgoers might legitimately claim ignorance of conditions on the other side of the tracks. The first institutions to confront the problems of the immigrants directly were a late nineteenth-century phenomenon. The Salvation Army did not arrive in the United States until 1880; the Goodwill Industries gained its first support in the following decade. It took the depression of the 1890s to spur the mainline churches into action with their social gospel campaigns.

The western towns witnessed a totally different set of circumstances. Most western communities were so small that no parishioner could claim ignorance of social conditions. Moreover, no western clergyman viewed his ministry as limited to a single section of town. Unlike their eastern brethren, the western ministers saw their "parishes" as encompassing the entire community. Thus, they tried to assume responsibility for the general morality.

This proved to be a considerable task. Much to the clerics' dismay, many violations of convention occurred in broad daylight. In Canon City, Colorado, in 1872, for example, a prostitute tried to set up business in the building next door to the Baptist church. When a similar incident occurred in Virginia City, Nevada, the townspeople responded by moving the church. In Yuma, Arizona, a local theatre group lacked a sufficient number of women for a melodrama; so, the prostitutes played all the feminine roles. In the early 1880s, an Albuquerque editor denounced the flagrant nature of the city's netherworld. Virginia City, Nevada, proved so wide open during the mid-1870s that police compared it to San Francisco's notorious Barbary Coast or New York's equally infamous Five Points.[11] "In the east, as a general thing," observed Joseph W. Cook from Cheyenne, "vice is obliged in some measure to keep somewhat in the dark, and a cloak of refinement is thrown over it. But here all is open and above board, and the eyes and ears are assailed at every turn."

As Savanarola attacked fifteenth-century Florence in the name of God, so these frontier clergymen denounced western life in the name of morality. The targets varied in detail, but they usually included cardplaying, theatergoing, dancing, hate, gossip, swearing, hurdy-gurdy houses, and even "museums," such as the ones in Cheyenne, which boasted a stereoscope with risqué pictures. A group of West Texas Presbyterians declared their intention to "make war" on the "frontier devils of liquor, dancing, Sabbath breaking, and ignorance of the Holy Writ."[12]

The blatant disregard of Sabbath observance proved particularly irksome. In 1864, Congregationalist Jonathan Blanchard, president of Wheaton College in Illinois, was appalled to discover that every Sunday in Montana was a great gambling and market day. Any criticism was met by derision, however, for territorial Montanans claimed that their religion had "played out."[13] There was a common adage in Kansas during the 1870s that "there is no Sunday west of Junction City and no God west of Salina." Leavenworth, Kansas, actually held an election to consider the issue of Sabbath observance. The question—should the tradition be continued—split the community in two, with the narrow victory going to the pro-Sabbath forces. A Cheyenne billiard hall owner told Joseph W. Cook, "We came out here to make money and we are not governed by the old puritanical ideas prevalent in the states."[14]

In the mining regions, the clergy who pressed for Sabbath observance often enjoyed support from the miners. During the mid-1870s, southern Methodist Alexander Groves engaged in fierce arguments in eastern Arizona over mandatory Sunday mine work. More than once he held services in a completely empty church to protest the mine's Sunday work policy. The Sabbath issue might have provided common ground for clerics and miners to advance other such issues, but it seldom did. Sabbath observance was changing nationwide, of course, and complaints about western violation of the Sabbath largely disappeared by the 1880s.

Although the lack of Sabbath observance remained a source of irritation, the frontier ministers leveled their most vehement social critiques against the "evil trinity" of gambling, prostitution, and saloon-keeping. Traditionally, these three occupations have had minimal contact with organized religion. Hence, ministers in the East probably had few dealings with representatives from any of them. Yet in the jumbled society of the early western towns, contact was unavoidable.

Recent scholarship has shown that gambling proved a legitimate profession in the trans-Mississippi West. Like the clergyman, the professional gamblers wore distinctive clothing—long black coats and white shirts—that announced their occupation. Historian Robert K. De Arment's discussion of frontier gambling centers includes virtually every important western community.[15]

While the clergy and the gamblers never exactly became intimate, they shared more interaction than one would expect. Ministers occasionally preached from faro tables in saloons, and they often asked the gamblers for donations. In 1882, Episcopal rector Endicott Peabody was dumbfounded when the local sporting fraternity volunteered several hundred dollars for his Tombstone church. In turn, the gamblers liked to place their winnings in a clergyman's hat, for there was an old legend that this brought luck. Nebraska Congregationalist A. E. Ricker once shared a tent with an itinerant "pea and shell" expert, a notoriously crooked con game. The gambler agreed to let Ricker read him a passage from Scripture since he "aint got nothin' again' the Bible." Later, the gambler moved out to ply his trade while the minister fell asleep. Ricker later marveled at how the gambler had to be on his guard at all times. There is little doubt that the clergyman used this incident as the source for more than one sermon.[16] In San Juan County, Colorado, Presbyterian Alex Darley was asked to give "a good send off" to a recently deceased faro dealer. After coping with the distress of the gambler's "girl," a local prostitute who attempted suicide in remorse, Darley did as instructed.[17] The clergy were much in demand when members of the underworld died. Following common understanding, they asked no questions about the past life of the deceased. Ministerial attacks on gambling continued throughout this period, but they seldom developed into full-blown crusades. This may have been because the various church bazaars often included a bit of "gambling" themselves.

Recent scholarship has also begun to reassess the role of prostitution in the West. Several historians have argued that the "soiled doves" played a vital economic and social role for the mobile and largely male population.[18] While this may have been true initially, over the course of the century—when the balance between men and women evened out—the Gilded Age "palaces" lost much of their earlier luster. By the turn of the century, most of them had fallen into disrepair. In several cities they had been replaced by cheap cribs or itinerant streetwalkers. The Progressive Era witnessed the official closing of most of the western red-light districts. This "success," however, came after almost sixty years of clerical agitation. One wonders, therefore, how much impact the clergy had on this social issue.

In the early and more unsettled period, the ministers and the madams often found themselves thrown in contact with each other. In no instance was this strange relationship better illustrated than in Rev. Josiah Strong's attempt to solve the problem of prostitution in Cheyenne.

In 1871, the twenty-four-year-old Strong moved to Cheyenne to pastor the local Congregational church. No sooner had he arrived when he decided to curb prostitution in the city. Much to the astonishment of his eighteen-member congregation, Strong approached the prostitutes, "supplied them with religious readings," and "gave to everyone a cordial invitation to attend preaching, with the assurance of a welcome at all times." None responded. Then he boldly offered to take them into "respectable" homes, if they would change their ways. This, too, produced little effect. In 1873, Strong led the Cheyenne clergy and townsfolk in a community crusade against "the social evil." The brothelkeepers, however, threatened to burn the town if they were prosecuted. The Grand Jury rejected their threat, and that night Cheyenne burned. The next day, the outraged citizens ordered all vagabonds and prostitutes evicted from the town. It was not long before they returned, however, and Josiah Strong moved on to another pastorate.[19] His later best seller, *Our Country,* drew heavily from this frontier experience.

Another minister thrown into contact with the women of the netherworld was Colorado Methodist Thomas A. "Parson Tom" Uzzell. Uzzell spent the years 1878–1881 in Leadville, where he buried over three hundred people, almost none of whom died under natural circumstances. Once he was approached by Maggie Ways, a prominent Leadville madam, who asked him to perform a funeral for the daughter of one of her girls. Almost fifty women, all wearing black silk dresses, attended. Uzzell delivered a stirring sermon:

> I talked plain, too [he wrote later], telling them there was a heaven to gain and a hell to shun. I talked to them of their mothers in eastern homes, who possibly did not know the lives some of them were leading. I never saw a more thrilling scene in a church. There was not a dry eye in the house. I stood in

the pulpit crying like a child myself while talking to them and the undertaker cried a little too.[20]

After the various western towns segregated their vice districts, the resident clergy had much less contact with the sporting element. Virtually the only spiritual attention the women received came from traveling evangelists. One such itinerant Chicago evangelist, K. A. Burwell, conducted a series of street meetings for prostitutes in Albuquerque in 1883. Assisted by the church women of town, Burwell preached several times in front of the houses. His appeal had mixed reactions. One prostitute treated him with scorn, but another broke down and wept openly. She confessed that she would like to abandon the life but "there was nothing for her to do by which she could earn a living."[21]

The saloon—as home of both gambling and prostitution—always drew the most severe clerical attacks. Frontier ministers despaired at the large number of western saloons. Since many hamlets erected a saloon before they built a church, this proved a constant source of irritation. Indeed, this institution became the symbolic enemy of proper behavior, and in many cases the embodiment of all evil. From the 1860s until the Progressive reform movement of the early twentieth century, it was a rare clergyman (some Episcopalians excepted) who did not attack the liquor industry. As late as 1922, a study juxtaposed a picture of a church and a saloon in a western town with the caption, "where the one is planted, the other cannot stay."[22] Yet the clergy and the saloons also found themselves strangely intertwined. Each wanted its towns to prosper, but for different reasons. In 1873, for example, the Boise saloon and sporting element sent Rev. R. M. Gwinn a gift of sixty-five dollars for his newly founded Methodist church. When saloon keeper Soapy Smith invited Rev. Thomas Uzzell to Creede, Colorado, he hired a full brass band to meet him. When the first Baptist church of Hinton, Oklahoma, held its initial service in 1902, it was the local bartender who walked up the aisle and set a pitcher of ice water on the pulpit.[23] In Tucson, the wives of several saloonkeepers were active in city church affairs. Many an early sermon was delivered in a saloon simply because the town had no other appropriate building.

An incident involving Methodist Andrew Potter, the "fighting parson" of El Paso, illustrates this unique relationship. Potter once entered an El Paso bar and asked for five dollars to aid his revival

meeting. The saloon owner refused on the grounds that he never
attended revivals. "That's your own fault," Potter told him. "The
services are there for you to attend." Nonplussed, the owner gave
Potter five dollars. A few days later, Potter received a bill for five
dollars' worth of whiskey. When he returned to the saloon to protest, the owner replied, "The whiskey was here for you." In the
spirit of the moment, Potter paid him back the five dollars.[24]

Modern historians Elliott West, Richard Erdoes, and Thomas J.
Noel have all argued for the central position of the early western
saloon. Since the tavern often appeared before the other institutions of society, it took on a many-faceted role. Saloons served as
political and economic headquarters, as well as providing needed
social companionship. Few Victorian clerics, however, could have
been persuaded to agree.[25] They denounced the saloon with vigor
for over fifty years.

The clerical attacks on gambling, prostitution, and saloon keep-
ing usually had minimal effect. Their denunciations never confronted the economic aspect of the "vice" industry. Consequently, the
criticisms remained limited to their congregations and an occasional reforming editor. Instead of abolishing their vice districts, most
western towns simply "regulated" them. By the early 1880s, the
community leaders had confined such activity to carefully deline-
ated sections of the city—Third Avenue in Albuquerque, Market
Street in Denver, Tenth Street in Omaha, and so on. Law officers
preferred this arrangement, for they soon got to know the "sporting
element" on a personal level. As such, they could control the vice
district more easily than they could manage the itinerant sharpers
and con men who drifted through on a regular basis. Periodic fines
and token arrests simply added moneys to support other, more
respectable civic ventures. As El Paso's premier historian has observed, sin on the border had become a business "like shoes and
real estate."[26]

If the ministers wielded only modest influence over the general
mores of the community, they had a little more success with the
behavior of their own members. As with so many other issues, here
they borrowed a leaf from the antebellum West.

On the pre–Civil War frontier, the churches frequently served as
"moral courts" to regulate behavior. Through the practice of "disfellowshipping," they punished both men and women for a wide
range of offenses. Some of these were covered by the legal system,

but many were not. Crimes for which antebellum churchgoers might be chastised included adultery, betting, sharp business practices, slander, dancing and frolicking, gambling, quarreling, abusing a slave, misusing a wife, thievery, intoxication, stealing, swearing, selling an unsound mare, running an incorrect line, refusing to obey the call of the church, and so on.[27] The frontier churches had no legal power, of course, so they relied exclusively on the force of moral suasion.

This antebellum tradition of community disapproval continued into the New West. In 1883, for example, the First Presbyterian church of Boulder suspended a member for public intemperance, but reinstated him upon the promise of reform. The next year, another man was dismissed from the Eldership (but not from the church itself) for the same offense. A few years later, "Miss A." wrote a letter of confession and penitence in an adultery case, and the charges against her were dropped.[28] In El Paso, August Furman, the "first man to be baptized in this place," was dismissed from the Baptist church on charges of drunkenness and attempted murder.[29] In Rawlins, Wyoming, a Mrs. Cockcroft applied for membership in the Presbyterian church but was refused because of unresolved business dealings. Similarly, a Valmont, Colorado, Presbyterian church expelled a member for nonpayment of debts. Congregational church records in Cheyenne show several people "dropped for unchristian conduct" or "dropped for cause." The Presbyterian church in Emporia, Kansas, suspended a member in 1879 for "contumacy" and "arresting proceedings." Evangelist W. Hamilton Wright recalled that a West Texas Methodist church trial resembled a civil court case. The minister and the "jury" heard the testimony from both sides and then reached a decision.[30]

Such disciplinary activity, however, seems to have been the exception rather than the rule. These incidents do not play a major role in the local church histories. (But, admittedly, church historians may have been reluctant to recall them.) Moreover, nationwide, church disciplinary procedures began to disappear by the 1890s.

The western clergy's efforts to regulate morality were further complicated by an atmosphere of general hostility. For example, when Jane T. Poore arrived in Boulder, Montana, with her Baptist minister husband, she expressed dismay that the area had no churches. "We can get along very well without them," a local resident replied.[31] In Middleton, Idaho, the citizens boasted that they had no need of organized religion. A crowd of rowdies in Sheridan, Wyoming, annoyed churchgoers by parodying "Nearer My God to Thee" as "Nero, my dog, has fleas." When Presbyterian George Smith first arrived in Bannock, Montana, in 1864, he was greeted with jeers. Because he carried an umbrella, they called him "pilgrim" and "tenderfoot." A Missoula sheriff actually had to protect one clergyman from the harassments of a mob. Methodist Jacob Adriance once asked a Colorado miner if he could pray for him, but the reply was, "No, I don't want any praying in my house." "I don't believe in ministers," a Nebraska settler told Congregationalist J. D. Stewart, "or in God or the devil." When Methodist John L. Dyer crossed the Great Plains to Colorado, his team boss threatened "that he did not care for my profession and would thrash me." Home missionary W. S. Rawlins once was introduced as a minister to a cowhand. The cowhand looked him over and remarked, "Well, he looks big enough to work for a living." Perhaps the most direct response was experienced by an Episcopal priest traveling on an early steamboat to Kansas. An inebriated man who recognized his clothing approached him and said, "We don't like you." West Texas–New Mexico Presbyterian Ralph Hall considered it unique that he had never been treated rudely because of his profession. As the Episcopal Bishop of Utah, Frank Spalding, once confessed, "Truly we are in the west because they need us, not because they want us."[32]

If the ministers were able to avoid expressions of outright hostility, they nevertheless often met an atmosphere of great indifference to organized faith. Captain Guy Henry complained in 1876 that of the four hundred soldiers stationed at Fort Russell, Wyoming, he never saw over ten at services on Sunday. A traveling Methodist minister once remarked that he found a larger percentage of backsliders in Montana than anywhere else in the nation. When Episcopal priest Cyrus Barry rode by a Nebraska sod hut and asked if he could be of any aid, the man at the door replied, "No, God's forgot us. Drive on."[33] Playwright Maxwell Anderson recalled his youth in Jamestown, North Dakota, as a time when religion was considered as a distant appendage to the dominant worlds of farming, banking, and trade.[34] Many western clerics confessed that the faith of their people had not survived the journey across the Mississippi River. "Goodbye God," a Connecticut girl once remarked, "we're going to Wyoming."

The social status of the western clergy suffered from this hostility and indifference. In the eastern cities, Protestant ministers often enjoyed positions of great prestige. Presbyterian T. DeWitt Talmage, Congregationalists Lyman Abbott, Henry Ward Beecher, and Washington Gladden, Episcopal Bishop Phillips Brooks, and Baptist George H. Lorimer all moved in the highest social circles. Each achieved a national reputation. When T. DeWitt Talmage died in 1901, his funeral in Washington, D.C., was virtually an affair of state.

This prestige failed to transfer when the clergy moved west of the Mississippi. Society on the turbulent frontier could not be forced into the established categories of the East. Here the world was turned upside down. In the East, the minister could expect a certain amount of social deference towards his profession. In the West, his status remained undetermined.

The popular terms used to describe the western ministers clearly revealed their ambiguous position. They were called "devil skinners," "Gospel sharks," "sin busters," "Gospel sharps," "soul doctors," or "sky pilots." New Mexico Episcopal priest Hunter Lewis was always "Preacher Lewis." West Texas Presbyterian Ralph Hall was simply "Preach." The term "Father" was used indiscriminately. In 1903, Episcopal rector Putman B. Peabody was nonplussed when a Wyoming rancher slapped him on the back and called him "Peabody." Utah's Episcopal Bishop once sat by a traveling drummer who asked him how long he had been "peddling salvation."[35] "The minister was a 'sis' to the average cowman," observed Colorado Congregationalist James F. Walker. That reputation, he confessed, "had to be lived down."[36]

The new social situation probably affected the Episcopal clergy as much as any. Accustomed to serving the more wealthy segments of society in the East, they met a very different situation west of the Mississippi. Missionary Bishop for New Mexico and Arizona, J. Mills Kendrick, spent much of his time trying to round up coreligionists. "I am the Bishop of the Episcopal Church for New Mexico," reads a typical letter. "Perhaps you have forgotten me. I have not forgotten you. Any other communicants in your town? I am hunting up the scattered sheep."[37] The Episcopal missionary Bishop of West Texas, James S. Johnson, was appalled at the indifference to religion in his region. In 1891, he concluded that the average southwesterner had little use for ministers, or " 'preachers,' as he calls them, excepting at weddings and funerals, and then merely for the sake of respectability." Johnson was especially dismayed when

the managers of a local townsite company offered him a free lot for
a church, but only if he would erect a tall steeple there to denote
social stability.[38]

Some of this lack of respect for the frontier clergymen, however,
may have been justified. Many young seminarians often considered
the foreign mission field or a prestigious urban pulpit to be far more
glamorous than an isolated home missionary assignment. In certain denominations, accepting a western mission post was tanta-
mount to admitting failure.

Consequently, a number of home mission clergymen proved
decidedly second rate. The preaching of the Methodist chaplain at
Fort Huachuca, Arizona, for example, was so poor that the prison-
ers preferred to cut wood rather than listen to his sermons. One
Coloradoan complained that his city got all the clerical "freaks,"
none of whom lasted long. Several ministers were called "petticoat
parsons," because they spent all their time visiting the women in
their parishes. One Presbyterian in Longmont, Colorado, wrote sil-
ly notes to the women in his congregation and walked about in
wet weather with newspapers tied around his feet. The Episcopal
rector in Grand Forks, North Dakota, so angered his parishioners
that they secretly changed the locks on the church door so as to
drive him away. A Presbyterian minister in Rawlins, Wyoming, was
dismissed when his sermons approached two hours in length. Another in Logan, Utah, was banished when he ran the church into
debt and refused to pay it off. Charles H. Book (Congregationalist,
then Episcopalian, later a Spiritualist) visited all the women of his
Colorado parish so often that they all hoped he would stay away.
One Episcopal rector was described as "effeminate" and another
as "an egotistical maniac." "I can send you a dozen men at short
notice," the Episcopal Bishop of Pennsylvania wrote to his New
Mexico counterpart, J. Mills Kendrick, "but I fear none of them
would wear well."[39]

The unique conditions of the western ministry meant that the
clergymen there could no longer rely on the status of their profession. Often they had to "prove" themselves in a manner that
would have been unthinkable back East. "Personality," as Ralph
Waldo Emerson once remarked, "never goes out of style." The
ministers who succeeded best in the West did so largely through
the force of personality. Some of the more representative of these
men include:

William Wesley Van Orsdel	Methodist in Montana
John L. "Father" Dyer	Methodist in Colorado
Daniel S. Tuttle	Episcopalian in Montana, Utah, and Idaho
Franklin S. Spalding	Episcopalian in Utah
Romulus A. Windes	Baptist in Arizona
"Bishop'" Hirum Read	Baptist in El Paso
Sheldon Jackson	Presbyterian in the Rocky Mountain area
James F. Walker	Congregationalist in Colorado and New Mexico
Ralph Hall	Presbyterian in West Texas
L. L. Millican	Baptist in West Texas
Thomas and Emily Harwood	Methodists in New Mexico
"Parson Tom" Uzzell	Methodist in Colorado
William Hobart Hare	Episcopalian in South Dakota
Ethelbert Talbot	Episcopalian in Utah and Wyoming
The Kansas Band and Dakota Band	Teams of young Congregationalists

These successful ministers proved themselves in a myriad or ways. Episcopal Bishop Cyrus Brady recalled that he had once lost face with his Great Plains parishioners when word spread that he had never plowed a field or seen a hog killed. In response, he quickly mastered that art of plowing a straight furrow.[40] His counterpart, Ethelbert Talbot, had never heard the term "good mixer" before he visited the Idaho mining camps in the late 1860s. But he soon learned that an honest, open interest in the lives of the men there spelled the difference between success and failure.[41] The Dakota Band of Congregationalists earned respect by traveling across the prairie in the harshest winter weather. Methodist Thomas Uzzell used a more direct method. When several Leadville squatters tried to jump the lot he had preempted for his Methodist church, he simply beat them up.[42]

Once they had established themselves, these innovative clergymen often found themselves in a position to exert considerable influence on the world around them. William Wesley Van Orsdel (Brother Van) was one of these. In 1872, he decided to do evangelical work in Montana Territory. During his forty-seven years there he became one of the most widely respected men of the area. For years he traversed the country, becoming known as the state's most recognized circuit rider. Toward the end of his career he served as a Methodist administrator, supervising the construction of churches, schools, and hospitals.

While Van had few educational advantages (he even refused to call his talks "sermons") he demonstrated a natural ability to get along with people. He conversed easily with miners, ranchers, and homesteaders. When he died in 1919, the Great Falls *Tribune* termed him "the best known and one of the most popular representatives of the church who ever labored in the Northwest."[43] For years afterwards, visitors could ask "Did you know Brother Van?" and receive a variety of replies.

Episcopal priest Joseph Wilkin Tays arrived in El Paso as a widower with two small sons. During his years there (1870–75; 1881–84) "Parson" or "Padre" Tays wielded considerable influence on the city. He served as an active member of the City Council, as a director of the First National Bank of El Paso, and as part owner of the El Paso *Times*. In addition, he helped build St. Clement's church and rectory, and founded a missionary day school, which launched the Protestant parochial school sytem on the Mexican border. He was also active in local charities and public works and personally helped several Jewish merchants establish themselves in business. He died in 1884 from smallpox, which he caught because only he was willing to officiate at the funeral of a Mexican who had contracted the disease. One observer called him "El Paso's first citizen."[44]

Congregationalist Richard Condley arrived in Lawrence, Kansas, in 1857 at age twenty-eight. He spent the rest of his life—forty-five years—as pastor of Plymouth Church there. During his career he served as director of the organization created to found a college at Lawrence (later the state university). In addition, he was also active in founding Washburn College in Topeka (which began as a Congregational school) and served for years as a trustee. He was also a regent of Kansas State University. For twenty years Condley served as a member of the Lawrence School Board, and from 1885 to 1891 he was its president. In 1879, he introduced the idea of planting shade trees on the plains, boldly declaring it a Christian duty to do so. This idea later developed into Arbor Day.[45] As a Methodist minister observed of his Congregational colleague, "We have always looked upon Plymouth Church as a leader of *everything* that pertains to the good of Lawrence."[46]

English-born Henry Martin Hart spent over twenty-five years in

Denver. He arrived there as a forty-year-old Episcopal priest and remained until his death in 1903. The driving force behind the first Episcopal cathedral (1881), Hart also played a considerable role in the city's development. Witty, argumentative, and urbane, Hart teamed with Catholic priest William O'Ryan and Rabbi William S. Friedman to become a major figure in the religious life of the city.

A fine speaker and a good administrator, Hart utilized his public position to air his views on a wide variety of subjects. He wrote scientific articles on chemistry, geology, and mineralogy, and helped bring the first smelter to Colorado. He promoted numerous social reform measures and for several years directed the city's charity organization. In addition, he spoke out vigorously against Christian Science and Sunday theatrical performances. Once he was hissed in church for his remarks about a recent society "masked ball." Despite his eccentric traits, however, Dean Hart exerted considerable influence on the life of Denver as "the conscience of the community."[47]

Romulus A. Windes graduated from the University of Chicago and moved to Arizona in 1879 to seek a cure for his wife's lung problems. After arriving in Prescott, he began teaching school and organizing Baptist churches throughout the region. One saloon-keeper complained that there were "too d——d many churches in Prescott already"; but the Prescott community, both Baptist and non-Baptist alike, helped contribute to his program. For years Prescott maintained a more sophisticated atmosphere than many of its neighboring towns; the large number of Prescott churches took the credit for this. Windes traveled all through central Arizona to establish Baptist churches. He introduced a Methodist-style camp meeting to the Globe area and also led numerous revivals. He ended his missionary days by traveling through the mining camps in a Gospel Wagon. Without his efforts, the Baptist influence in Arizona would have been considerably weakened.[48]

Probably no group of western ministers maintained as strong a record as the Missionary Bishops of the Protestant Episcopal Church. The most prominent figures here were:

Daniel Tuttle (1867–1886) in Montana, Utah, and Idaho;
Ethelbert Talbot (1887–1889) Wyoming and Idaho;
William D. Walker (1883–1897) in North Dakota;
John G. Spalding (1874–1902) in Colorado, and his son
Franklin S. Spalding (1903–1914) in Utah;

Ozi William Whitaker (1861–1886) in Nevada;
William Hobart Hare (1871–1909) in South Dakota;
J. M. Kendrick (1889–1911) in New Mexico and Arizona; and
Leigh Richmond Brewer (1881–1926) in Montana.

These Episcopal Bishops served as the ecclesiastical robber barons of their era. Relying heavily on wealthy eastern connections, they maintained the prestige of the bishopric west of the Mississippi. Their eastern contacts provided them the wherewithal to fund numerous projects. Through these "specials," they financed not only day-to-day diocesan affairs but long-term building projects as well. When each bishop arrived in the West, he faced sparse conditions. Nonetheless, each of them left a sizable legacy in the form of church buildings, rectories, schools, hospitals, and church members.[49] Ethelbert Talbot achieved yet another type of reputation. He became the model for "The Bishop" in Owen Wister's novel, *The Virginian.*

Perhaps the most fascinating Episcopal Bishop was Daniel S. Tuttle. Tuttle arrived in Salt Lake City in 1867 and spent the next nineteen years in the West. He established his reputation during the great Helena, Montana, fire of April 25, 1869. Although all able-bodied men in town joined to fight the fire, the most difficult task fell to those who sat on the various roofs. Their job was to keep the houses wet and prevent the fire from spreading. When the morning of April 26 arrived, only three men remained on the roofs, battling the fire: Bitterroot Bill, a desperado; Gentleman Joe, a Virginia-born gambler; and Bishop Tuttle. After that test, Tuttle's reputation was secure. As one Helena miner put it:

He's full jeweled and eighteen karats fine. He's a better
gentleman than Joe Floweree [a local gambler]; he's the biggest
and best bishop that ever wore a black gown, and he's the
whitest man in these mountains. He's a fire fighter from way
back, and whenever he chooses to go on a brimstone raid
among the sinners in this gulch, he can do it and I'll back him
with my pile.[50]

Tuttle crisscrossed the territory so often that he claimed to know all the stage drivers by their first names. By the time he accepted a call to become Bishop of Missouri in 1886, he had baptised over 3,000 people, confirmed over 1,000, married 146, buried 117, and held almost four thousand services. His *Reminiscences of a Missionary Bishop* (1906) provides an excellent firsthand account of life in the Gilded Age West.

Once missionaries like Tuttle had "proven" themselves with their community, they proceeded to adopt a variety of social roles. They gave sermons, counseled troubled parishioners, distributed social welfare, performed acts of personal charity, served as librarians, and tried to "elevate" life as best they could. In doing so, moreover, they often stepped outside the limitations of their particular denominations.

As in the East, preparing and delivering sermons consumed a good bit of time. The West, however, offered unique conditions for preaching. Western clergy spoke in saloons, dance halls, courthouses, schools, tents, shops, individual cabins, brush arbors, and under the open sky. When Methodist Father Dyer first landed in Denver in 1859, he spotted a large tent, which, he assumed, held a revival. Discovering, instead, a poker game, Dyer observed the play for two days and then stood on a table to announce: "Boys, I have looked at your game now for the past eight and forty hours. Now I ask you to give some attention to mine. Let us pray."[51] He then offered what was probably the first public prayer in Denver. Afterwards, the game continued.

During one Bishop Tuttle sermon in Virginia City, Nevada, the message was almost drowned out by the "orchestra" that was playing for a prize fight a few yards away.[52] During Endicott Peabody's 1882 Easter service in Tombstone, Arizona, a man crawled through the door on all fours. Peabody momentarily halted the service while he sat the culprit in his chair.[53] Episcopal priest Cyrus Brady held services at one location in eastern Kansas where the only woman able to read the responses was a prostitute.[54]

The western ministers were as much an everyday occurrence in western life as the miners, cowboys, and saloons. In 1867, a Reverend Bross (denomination unknown) delivered the first sermon ever heard in Lusk, Wyoming. Stopping his team in the midst of downtown, Bross turned his wagon around and used his seat for a pulpit. Without an audience, he read his text and proceeded to deliver his message. Word soon spread, and before long the street and saloons emptied; some even closed. Eventually an audience of about 120 cowboys, saloonkeepers, and shopkeepers heard him through. In 1869, a Methodist minister visited all the saloons in Laramie to invite everyone to the depot grounds for a service.[55] Whenever Ethelbert Talbot visited the Idaho mining camps, the miners always turned out in large numbers. Brother Van once preached in Butte to an audience that lacked only 10 of matching the entire population of the city.[56] No person visited the isolated Colorado mining camps more often than Father Dyer. One itinerant Colorado parson joked that every time he rode past a schoolhouse, his horse would automatically stop.

In general, these isolated and chiefly male audiences provided generous support for the services of visiting ministers. In 1885, Methodist John Hoskins preached to a group of placer miners in Diamond City, Montana. The bars closed for both his 11:00 sermon as well as his 3:00 follow-up. The miners then took a collection, with each man measuring a spoonful of gold dust into a chamois sack. As they said farewell, one miner told him to "be sure and tell the man at the assay office in Helena where you got this for he's apt to arrest you for robbing sluice boxes."[57]

Delivering sermons, however, proved but one of many duties. The clerics also spent considerable time in visiting the homes of their parishioners. Jacob Adriance, for example, utilized many hours in going from cabin to cabin in the Colorado mountains. Bishop Tuttle also felt that pastoral visitation was "a strong[er] force to win souls for Christ than is even the most eloquent preaching."[58]

An integral part of this visitation involved what we would now call counseling. Frontier families experienced all the strains of daily existence in a hostile environment and their problems ranged widely. Dakota evangelist C. S. Coddington found that the settlers approached him for advice on numerous subjects, ranging from spiritual questions to the best way to break sod. When Norwegian Lutheran minister John Blegen entered the sod home of a North Dakota immigrant, the man broke into tears. Amidst much weeping, he cursed the day he left Norway. "I reminded him that the faithful and merciful God was also to be found in this place," Blegen wrote, "and that He does not desert those who hold themselves near to Him."[59]

According to the clerics' accounts, one of the most serious problems they met among their parishioners was that of alcohol. Drunkenness seemed endemic to the frontier situation, and numerous ministers were forced to confront this condition. With counseling techniques in their infancy, they relied on common sense: they listened, they offered advice, and sometimes they scolded. When Bishop Tuttle was in Virginia City, Montana, he wrestled with the dilemma of a suicidal, alcoholic vestryman. In despair, he confessed that all he could do was pray for the man. Baptist R. A. Windes also observed that only God's grace could cure a drunkard.[60]

The paradox of how to advise this wide assortment of people proved a persistent problem for the western clergyman. Rev. Claton Rice depicted this dilemma with great sensitivity. After spending the summer of 1913 in tent evangelism in the barren region of northeastern Utah, Rice wrote:

> Just how to be helpful to such a heterogenous group, struggling hard to live in an unfavorable environment was always on my heart. What do they need most, I kept asking myself. A challenge to stop sinning and to straighten up? Praise for pioneers such as they? Comfort in their moments of disappointment and despair? A call to join the Presbyterian church? Perhaps all of these and more, I thought.[61]

In addition to individual counseling, the early clergymen also often played an important role in the social welfare of their towns. After a visit to the Cheyenne hospital, Joseph W. Cook became so appalled at conditions that he organized a "mite society" to get the "better class of people together, so as to shape society."[62] To his dismay, he discovered he had direct competition from the local Roman Catholic priest, who had organized a similar group. Cheyenne citizens were willing to donate to one charitable fund, but not both, and it was largely a question of who asked first. In 1868, Virginia City, Nevada, put on a comic benefit performance. The $106.20 raised was given to Bishop Tuttle to distribute as he saw fit.[63]

When disaster struck an area, the clergymen became, in effect, relief workers. Both Episcopal and Catholic priests joined hands to aid the victims of the 1864 Cherry Creek, Colorado, flood. During the hard times of the 1870s, many South Dakota ministers devoted considerable time to social work. The eastern funds sent to alleviate the grasshopper-devastated areas of the Plains in the 1870s were usually funneled through local clergymen for distribution. During the "grasshopper winter" of 1874, Nebraska Congregationalist Simon Barrows single-handedly organized the distribution of relief for all of his Polk county. During the harsh years of 1891–92 in Indian

Territory, several local clergy made trips to Dallas, Fort Worth, and Waco to procure carloads of food for hungry pioneers.[64]

In addition to organized charity, the ministers often contributed numerous acts of personal kindness. Bishop Tuttle found a paralyzed man in a cabin without food or fuel, and made arrangements for him to be cared for. Jacob Adriance brought home and fed a miner who had not eaten for a day and half.[65] When Sunday School missionary Albert Stewart found a tuberculosis victim waiting for the inevitable in the Arizona desert in 1919, he gave him appropriate religious materials and alerted the men in the nearest mining camp as to his condition.[66] In Virginia City in 1882, a battered wife sought refuge in the Methodist parsonage. The drunken husband fled only when the minister's wife raised her rifle at him. A Nebraska Congregationalist hid gifts of food during his visits so that his impoverished neighbors might find them later without embarrassment. When Tucson began to be overrun by indigent tuberculosis patients in the first years of the new century, the local clergy distributed free food to inhabitants of their "tent city."

The clerics performed other social functions as well. They were usually the first librarians. Presbyterian George Darley founded a Lake City, Colorado, Free Library Association and strove unsuccessfully to establish a public reading room with free letter paper for writing home. Ten years before Grand Forks, North Dakota, organized its public library, Episcopal rector William T. Currie established a parish library that he opened to the entire town. Almost all of the approximately thirty-five U.S. Army chaplains in the West during this period also operated the post libraries.[67] The wife of Jacob Adriance, Fanny Adriance, recalled that their few books and newspapers were much in demand by the early Colorado miners. "Our room became a sort of free reading room to all who wished to avail themselves of its reading matter," she wrote. "For several weeks we had no chairs, but our trunks, placed around the room, served as seats."[68] The 1876 Cheyenne *Daily Leader* urged the town's clergy to devote their pulpits to the issue of a public library so as to provide the children with a place to go during the winter.[69] In 1880, the Episcopal rector of Leadville, Colorado, convinced his eastern friends to send him back issues of such magazines as *Atlantic, Scribner's,* and *Harper's* so he could distribute them to the miners.[70] Even as late as the 1920s, circuit-riding Methodists in the Arkansas—

Oklahoma border carried the local county newspapers to distribute on their rounds.[71]

The better educated among the frontier clergymen—especially the Episcopalians, Congregationalists, and Presbyterians—took on yet another social task. They considered it part of their duty to give public lectures on religious and secular topics of popular interest. By serving as a virtual traveling college, they anticipated the famous Chautauqua of the early twentieth century.

The lectures varied with the lecturer. In February 1867, Bishop Tuttle gave a talk on "King Charles I and English Constitutional History" to a Helena audience. The next year he gave a series of lectures on the New Testament prophets. At one of these he attracted over 250 people.[72] Irish-born Episcopal priest John McNamara lectured in the Nebraska City region on "Paris, Geneva, and the Alps," and "Romantic Historic Places in England, Ireland, and Scotland." Joseph W. Cook gave a March 1868 lecture on natural history, "The Honey Bee," to the astonished soldiers at nearby Fort Russell.[73] Congregationalist Rollin L. Hartt lectured in 1897 in Helena on higher criticism and the new currents in theology. He was pleased to discover that the "best people" from all of the major denominations came to hear him.[74]

The Sunday evening service became a special forum for the dissemination of such information. By the 1890s, it was proving more and more difficult to gather a crowd on Sunday evenings. Gradually, these evening services became less "religious," and began to include discussions of current issues. Prescott Methodist H. W. Peck used his 1899 Sunday evening services to explain higher criticism to his audience. In 1914, Grace Episcopal Church in Tucson transformed their Sunday evening services into a popular lecture series. Drawing on the resources of nearby University of Arizona, the Desert Laboratory of Botanical Research, and state government officials, the church sponsored talks on numerous subjects. These ranged from "Life in Egypt and Algeria" to "Prison Reform" and "The Abolition of Capital Punishment." The governor of the state joined scholars and administrators as one of the lecturers. Hundreds of people who had never entered an Episcopal church in their lives attended regularly.[75]

During the early days of western development, then, the Protestant ministers served as a general public utility. Organized social services were almost nonexistent in the West during this period. Hence, the ministers filled the gap, just as they had on earlier fron- in American history. They assumed numerous social roles: distrib- utor of relief, social worker, librarian, counselor, good samaritan, and public lecturer. Thus, they moved well beyond the confines of their particular denomination and addressed their communities at large.

Chapter Three

The Settled Communities, c. 1880–c. 1915

"The 'hurrah' years of Dodge City are over," observed the editor of the local *Times* in 1882. "[T]he revolver is hushed and thieving and robbery [are] no more."[1] Although the dates might have varied with the region, virtually every western editor could have made a similar boast some time during the 1880s. In reporter Richard Harding Davis's phrase, the "mild West" had arrived. Naturally, the ministers were pleased with this development. In 1891, the secretary of the American Home Missionary Society noted that the days had passed when home missionaries frantically followed the track of settlers opening up new territory. Future mission work, he suggested, would lie in the areas of church development and consolidation. "The wild and woolley West," boasted missionary William N. Sloan in 1913, "has been transformed into a civilized, intelligent and progressive West."[2]

The ministers had played a major role in this transformation. They built impressive downtown churches, and inaugurated scores of public schools, private academies, and denominational colleges. In many locations they were also instrumental in creating the state universities. The churches often formed the heart of urban and rural social life. Throughout the region the churchwomen utilized the sociable and the bazaar to raise money for worthy causes, to provide entertainment, and to foster culture. Since local congregations remained small, the women always directed their sociables to include the entire community.

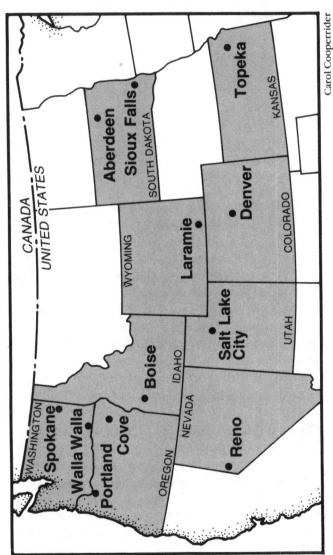

Protestant Episcopal Church academies in the New West. These schools catered largely to the sons and daughters of the elite and prided themselves on high standards of scholarship.

Carol Cooperrider

The rise of large, downtown church buildings was perhaps the most tangible manifestation of the church role in the maturation of the western cities. As the towns expanded, numerous congregations outgrew their early structures. Since these were all located in the heart of the central business area, the pastors were able to sell the land at considerable profit. With these expanded funds, the congregation then built a more impressive church in another part of town. Sometimes the process was even repeated. This pattern occurred in every major city.

By 1890, the first Methodist church in Cheyenne had replaced its 1870 white frame structure with a large stone church. The new building cost 30,000 dollars. When First Methodist in Tucson erected its 1906 building for 23,000 dollars, it was the largest church in the city, except for the Roman Catholic cathedral. First Presbyterian church in El Paso replaced its 1882 building with a new one in 1907 that cost 40,000 dollars. The next year St. Clement's Episcopal in El Paso erected a 60,000-dollar building. By 1913, the First Presbyterian churches of Helena and Bozeman each boasted structures costing over 50,000 dollars apiece. They rivaled each other in being the most elegant Protestant church in the state. Boise Episcopalians constructed their cathedral in 1899. Located within the shadow of the Idaho state capital, it gave the church access to elected officials. Laramie's St. Matthew's Episcopal cathedral, an English Gothic structure built in 1896, is still the most impressive building in town.

No city reflected this church building process as strongly as *fin de siècle* Denver. The Trinity Methodist church was built in 1886 at a cost of 173,000 dollars, while First Presbyterian followed in 1892 at 165,000 dollars. The first Episcopal cathedral (1881) cost 120,000 dollars while the second, built thirty years later, cost 400,000 dollars. These sprawling, materialistic structures reflected both denominational rivalry and the opulence of the era. Historian Lyle Dorsett has compared Denver's preoccupation with its large downtown churches with the cathedral construction of the Middle Ages.[3]

No distinctive pattern of church architecture emerged with this new wave of building. Instead, the western urban churches drew from the contemporary Romanesque styles popularized by architect H. H. Richardson or borrowed from the ever-popular Gothic. Dark and light sandstone; red and brown brick with terra cotta or light stone; or granite and boulder-like fieldstone proved the most popular building materials. These churches conveyed a massive, horizontal feeling that was broken only by an occasional pointed tower.

The horizontal shapes also reflected new church functions. By the 1890s the churches often needed space for numerous meeting rooms. These housed the library, youth groups, women's clubs, Sunday Schools, or men's organizations. Drawing on an awakened social concern, some congregations added a playroom or even a gymnasium. Thus, the church plant expanded to reflect these new interests.

These downtown churches dominated the urban skylines of the New West. Denver's Trinity Methodist Church still anchors the city center, while Holy Trinity Episcopal in Lincoln, Nebraska, is a textbook model of Victorian Gothic.[4] The Gothic Catholic church in Leadville, which had a seating capacity of 1,200, became the town's chief landmark. Located ten thousand feet above sea level, it was touted as "the highest steeple in the world." St. Clement's Episcopal church in El Paso, constructed in the old English style, was widely admired for its design, as was First Methodist in Albuquerque. For years, the Denver Methodist Church at Fourteenth and Lawrence (built in 1865, but no longer extant) was termed the most beautiful architectural structure between St. Louis and the Pacific Coast. The only exception might have been the Mormon Temple in Salt Lake City.[5] While the other large buildings of the era have often gone the way of the wrecker's ball, many of these church buildings still survive. Unlike the razed hotels, office buildings, and private homes, these downtown churches serve the same function today as they did in the past.

The rural and small town churches of the West were less affected by population increase. If a congregation moved on, the buildings were dismantled or hauled to a new location. Some were sold to another denomination. Others were remodeled, becoming schools or private residences. A few were even turned into scrap. A significant number, however, are still in use today. St. Paul's Episcopal Church in Tombstone, Arizona, the Presbyterian church at Lake City, Colorado ("the oldest church on the western slope"), and the Force Methodist Church in Kensal, North Dakota, have been serving their respective congregations for over a century.

The rise of public and private school systems also proved essential to the maturation process of the New West. In the field of education, the clergy became paramount. Here, their influence was unquestioned. All through the region they played vital roles in establishing the pattern of education for the territories. They contributed at all levels—primary schools, academies, colleges, and universities.

Regardless of denomination, ministers in a new community were virtually expected to introduce some variety of school. Although army regulations did not mention this duty, the chaplains were also expected to accomplish this task. Lutheran ministers blunted criticism from German and Scandinavian rationalists because they invariably performed an educational as well as a spiritual function. As will be noted later, the Congregationalists, Methodists, and Presbyterians were especially active in establishing parochial schools in New Mexico and Utah.

The Missionary Bishops of the Episcopal Church took an early lead in this field. They founded private primary and secondary schools—academies—all through the New West. By 1900 virtually all of the important western dioceses boasted an Episcopal academy. A partial list might include the female seminary in Topeka (1866); St. Helen's Hall in Portland (1869); Annie Wright School in Tacoma; St. Matthews Hall in Laramie (1895); St. Margaret's School in Boise (1892); St. Matthews (1886) and Jarvis Hall in Golden, and later in Denver; Wolfe Hall (1899–90) in Denver; and the West Texas Military Academy (1893). In addition, the church established St. Mark's Day School in Salt Lake City, with satellites in Ogden, Logan, and Plain City; All Saints in Aberdeen; St. Mary's Hall in Spokane; Platte Collegiate Institute (Kearney Hall) for western Kansas and Wyoming; Bishop Whitaker's school for girls in Reno; and the All Saints School for Girls in Sioux Falls. When Bishop Samuel French bequeathed a considerable amount of property for an Episcopal Girls' school to be located in Cove, Oregon, he remarked, "We are building the Church, but only as the heart of a religious education center."[6]

Officially, these Episcopal schools were designed to work in harmony with other fledgling public and parochial school systems. Actually, however, the Bishops introduced them "as a matter of self defense." As Joseph W. Cook wrote to his Bishop from Cheyenne, if they didn't begin a school, the "Romanites will come along and settle the matter."[7] In addition to their rivalry with other denominational schools, the Bishops also remained dubious about the emerging public school system. They feared that public classrooms would be unable to teach the tenets of Christianity that they deemed necessary for proper morality. Character formation always remained a central focus of their private school enterprise.

It was not long before these Episcopal academies began to serve college-bound students from the New West. In spite of the availability of scholarships for less privileged children, the academies largely educated the children of the elite. This focus led the schools to achieve high standards. For example, the prestigious eastern women's colleges were pleased to accept the graduates of St. Margaret in Boise. These young Idaho women were admitted into advanced standing without further examinations. The Episcopal academies, therefore, performed an important educational function in many western areas.

Where the ministers did not actually establish parochial schools, they invariably served on local school boards, and occasionally, as superintendents of public education. Richard Cordley did so for Lawrence, Joseph W. Cook for Cheyenne, Nathan Thompson for Boulder, and R. E. Hamilton for Laramie. Baptist George W. Baines (Lyndon Johnson's grandfather) sat on the school board that introduced the free public school system in El Paso in 1872. Lutheran Thomas Van Ness set up the first free kindergarten in Denver in 1887. Presbyterian Howard Billman, who had moved to Tucson for his health, soon found himself in charge of the Tucson Indian School. In 1895 he became president of the University of Arizona. Congregationalist Joseph Ward not only served as head of Yankton's Board of Education, he also framed the law that established the public school system for the entire state of South Dakota. The motto of the Congregational church in Dakota Territory reflected this emphasis. It read: "evangelism and education."[8]

Since the Protestant clergy established and/or supervised many of the public school systems, one may assume that a good bit of Christian doctrine found its way into the curriculum. Western church–state boundaries, however, generally remained flexible on this issue. While Nevada's 1865 school law specifically prohibited the use of sectarian books or doctrine, the first three territorial superintendents of public instruction were all Protestant clergymen. Oregon free thinkers encouraged Cumberland Presbyterian Will V. McGee to establish a school.[9] When faced with the choice of a church-influenced school or no school at all, the decision seemed obvious.

One finds only a few, scattered complaints about this church–state situation. All the Protestant clergymen, of course, denounced the Catholic influence on the public school systems. The editor of the *Arizona Miner* also complained that the 1875 Territorial Legislature's contribution of three thousand dollars to the Tucson Catholic school was wrong in principle. Three years later, Nevada elected its first nonministerial superintendent of territorial schools, largely because of prior disagreement about sectarian teaching. In 1907, Rabbi William S. Friedman publicly criticized the Denver public school system for assigning essays on the life of Jesus and for singing Christmas hymns in school.[10] Considering the prominent clergy and public school overlap, however, one might have expected a more vigorous critique.

In no area of education were the churches more visible than in the race to establish western denominational colleges. Many a western community fought to secure a college. Having a school marked a town as both mature and likely to prosper. The Congregationalists and the Presbyterians led in this crusade, but the Methodists and the Baptists were not far behind. Only the Episcopalians restricted their educational focus to the academy level. The theme of E. P. Tenney's *The New West as Related to the Christian College* obviously had considerable appeal to all the mainline denominations.

The campaign to establish western denominational colleges carried with it a familiar sense of urgency. "The whole valley is filling up with immigrants," Joseph Ward wrote from Yankton in 1871. "They are laying the foundations for a commonwealth larger than England, Scotland and Wales, and leaving out God. Dare we let them go on without the Bible and the spelling book?" Rev. M. M. G. Dana predicted in 1880 that the success of Christianity in America depended largely on the success of these denominational colleges.[11] When the Methodists planned a college in Denver, they stressed the urgency and need to cultivate the moral nature of their students. The clear implication was that the state schools could not do this. "Education only means 'clever devils,' " warned a Northern Baptist spokesman in 1883, "unless the education be permeated by the power of Christianity."[12]

Within a short time the ministers planted denominational colleges in every section of the New West. The list of those that survived is a lengthy one. The Congregationalists led the way with Doane College in Crete, Nebraska; Washburn in Topeka, Kansas;

Colorado College in Colorado Springs; Yankton College in Yankton, South Dakota; and Whitman College in Walla Walla, Washington. The Presbyterians, in addition to two unsuccessful attempts in Colorado, put their faith in Hastings College in Hastings, Nebraska; Huron College in Huron, South Dakota; the College of Idaho in Caldwell; the College of Emporia, Kansas; and Westminster College, Salt Lake City, Utah. The American Lutherans founded Bethany in Lindsborg, Kansas; Dana in Blair, Nebraska; Midland in Fremont, Nebraska; Concordia Teachers in Seward, Nebraska; and St. John's in Winfield, Kansas.

After many years of internal bickering, the Methodists consolidated their numerous Nebraska efforts into Nebraska Wesleyan at Lincoln. In Kansas, their main school was Baker University at Baldwin. The Methodists also helped to establish Rocky Mountain College in Billings, which was formed from an amalgam of Montana Wesleyan, the Presbyterian College of Montana, and the Congregational Billings Polytechnic Institute. Their Colorado Seminary (1863) eventually became Denver University. Their Denver-based Iliff Theological Seminary (1892) served as the major Protestant seminary for the entire West. The distant Presbyterian San Francisco Theological Seminary proved its only real rival. Although the Baptists entered the college race somewhat later than the other denominations, they tried to make up for it during the last years of the century. This era emerged as the great period of Baptist college-founding, and they established fifteen institutions in Texas alone. But the Baptists also founded Sioux Falls College, South Dakota; Colorado Women's College in Denver; Ottawa in Ottawa, Kansas; Baylor in Waco, Texas; and Oklahoma Baptist College, in Shawnee.

A significant number of western state universities are also indebted to the frontier clergymen. These state institutions grew from seeds that were planted by denominational representatives. Early Presbyterian activity in Kansas eventually evolved into the University of Kansas. The church's Henry Kendall College, established in 1894 in Muskogee, Oklahoma, moved to become the University of Tulsa. The Baptist academy in Yankton, founded by the remarkable Dr. Ephraim M. Epstein, laid the basis for the University of South Dakota. Episcopal St. Margaret's became Boise Junior College and eventually Boise State University. The Episcopal School in Golden evolved into the Colorado School of Mines. Congregational Dakota College in Spearfish, South Dakota, became Black Hills Teacher's College, and the Methodist Bluemont College grew into Kansas State in Manhattan. There is also a tenuous relationship between the Laramie Baptist academy and the University of Wyoming. Colorado Congregationalist Norman McLeod not only badgered the state legislature to charter a university, he also helped secure a large land donation for the proposed institution in Boulder. The Congregational Kingfisher College in Oklahoma survives today as the "Kingfisher College Chair of the Philosophy of Religion and Ethics" at the University of Oklahoma.

The race to establish denominational colleges provided the West with numerous opportunities for education that could have occurred in no other way. Since the main burden of educating western youth is now carried by the large state universities, one may overlook the significance of their denominational counterparts. Until the 1930s, however, these church-related schools carried more than their share of student load. They, too, proved vital components of higher education in the New West.

Having said this, however, it is also necessary to point out that few of the institutions ever achieved the stature envisioned by their founders. The denominational colleges failed to dominate the thought of the West as their predecessors, Harvard and Yale, had molded New England; nor did they sway the sentiments of a generation as Oberlin, Wooster, and Ohio Wesleyan had done for the Middle West. To the chagrin of the denominations, the New West continued to elude their grasp. It was simply too large, too sparsely populated, and too variegated in religious faiths to be so influenced.

The vastness of the West also led to other problems. The crusade to establish denominational schools often taxed church resources beyond endurance. A large number of schools that began boldly soon ran into financial problems. Within a few years they had collapsed. By the end of the era, the region was littered with extinct colleges. In Nebraska's thirteen years as a territory, for example, the legislature granted twenty-three charters for denominational colleges. Only five of them opened, and only Peru State (originally founded by the Methodists in 1866) survived. Montana witnessed numerous Presbyterian failures to establish colleges or academies; only one of six major Presbyterian attempts in Kansas survived. Arizona Methodists established a short-lived college in Phoenix in 1866. The annual report for the following year sadly noted: "Arizona is not ready for a Methodist University. Our members are too few and our resources too limited."[13] Thus, it too collapsed. In 1886, South Dakota housed seven faltering denominational colleges or academies scattered across the plains. Kansas established about twenty such schools, most of which had died by 1880. Too many western towns wanted a "college," complained one writer in 1891, but it was "immaterial with them whether the institution be a college proper, or a normal school, or a business college, or a school for the feeble minded."[14]

Consequently, many denominational schools soon turned into ghost colleges. Like their counterparts, the ghost towns, these extinct schools dotted the New West. Who has heard of the former institutions on the southern Great Plains: Della Plain Male and Female Institute, Lockney Christian College, Gunther College, Littlefield College, Monte Vista College, Central Plains College, Seth Ward College, or Floydada Presbyterian Academy (a West Texas school that boasted, in 1913, "We have almost the entire prairie for an athletic field.")? Who recalls Mallalico University (Nebraska), Nebraska University (Fontenelle), the College of the Sisters of Bethany (Kansas), Sedalia University (Kansas), New Mexico College in Artesia, Gooding College (Idaho), Redfield College (South Dakota), Presbyterian College of the Southwest (Del Norte, Colorado), Kingfisher College ("The Oberlin of Oklahoma"), Westminster College (Denver), or Montezuma Baptist College (Las Vegas, New Mexico)? Nonetheless, as Rev. Gabino Rendon once remarked about his alma mater: "a college isn't dead as long as its influence is still felt, is it? That's why it's wrong to say the Presbyterian College of Del Norte is a ghost college, even though it's been closed almost fifty years. There are still a few of us alive who went there and we've taught the Gospel and their letters to hundreds of others—so the influence is still felt."[15]

With a few exceptions, the race to found colleges died out with the great depression of the 1890s. Financial reasons precluded its renewal with the turn of the new century. The churches, however, developed an alternative plan, a pragmatic solution first devised by Texas Episcopal Bishop Herbert Kinsolving. Rather than a full college, Kinsolving established an institution known as "Grace Hall" and located it at the edge of the University of Texas in Austin. Grace Hall served both as dormitory and classroom for Episcopalians who attended the university. This idea proved eminently practical. A church-related building could offer classes in religion unavailable at the state school itself. Often the clergyman could also teach at the university. Moreover, it was very efficient to operate. Within a few years most of the Protestant denominations had established similar "halls" adjacent to the state universities.[16] This move eventually created a new variety of clergyman: the campus minister. Thus, while the college founding era drew to a close, the denominations did not relinquish their concern for higher education. They simply adjusted their desires to the realities of the day.

If the churches proved paramount in the field of education, they also dominated the social life of the New West. Here, however, the ministers usually took a back seat to their wives and to the other church women in their congregations.

In the New West, everyone agreed that the minister's wife was as important to the church as the minister himself. The most successful clerics almost always had crucial assistance from their spouses. In a western parish, a minister's wife assumed many roles. She was automatically expected to direct the Sunday School. In addition, she usually supervised many of the other numerous church organizations—Ladies' Aid, Foreign Missions, Young People's Groups, and so on. If she were musical, and many were, she either played the organ or directed the church choir. "A man without a wife's help," observed Idaho Presbyterian Edward Murphy, "fails to get with his people at many points."[17]

The ubiquitous women's organizations also proved essential to the day-to-day running of the church. A minister who arrived in a western parish to discover no "Ladies' Aid Society" knew he was in for a difficult pastorate. Sometimes, as in Silverton, Colorado, in the late 1890s, the Congregational Ladies' Aid Society reached into the community for a membership that extended well beyond the church proper. Their local charity work also encompassed the entire community. Most individual church histories stress the "great and indispensable work" of their various women's groups. In 1890, the Episcopal Bishop of North Dakota called the Women's Guilds the "lifeblood of the churches."[18] Given the prevailing mores of the day, church life provided a prominent arena for women's energies.

The women's groups seized on the institution of the bazaar as their chief arena of activity. In talented hands, these "sociables" proved capable of infinite variations. The major holidays—New Year's, Easter, Thanksgiving, and Christmas—all called for appropriate celebration. So too did Robert Burns's birthday, George Washington's birthday, St. Patrick's Day, and the Fourth of July. The Black churches usually staged an "Emancipation Day" celebration.

Western church women proved ingenious in devising ways to entertain or to raise money. In Colorado, a church sewing circle offered mending and button repair to single men. Others staged pronouncing contests, chicken pie sales, shadow picture contests, and box suppers. One society even put on a smiling contest. For the price of a nickel, a person had to smile on demand; if he failed, he forfeited his money. For years Phoenix Methodists supplemented their oyster suppers and sewing bees by conducting a regular public market every Saturday. Other churches raced dogs, ducks, cats, and roosters for various prizes. Methodists in Cheyenne held a "wittiest woman in Cheyenne" contest and also staged a "Martha Washington Tea Party" for the 1876 centennial celebration.[19] Fargo, North Dakota, Congregationalists held an Easter Social which featured a tree ringed with Easter eggs, each one accompanied by a written quotation from a famous author. The finder had to identify his quotation. An 1892 Episcopal fair in Laramie featured all members in the costume of a Mother Goose character. The puzzle was to identify the characters correctly.

Sociables provided ideal ground for flirtation and courting. In 1885, the Cheyenne Congregationalists held a "rosette sociable" where each man bought a rosette. When he found a woman with the same pattern in her apron, she was his partner for the evening. The year before, the Cheyenne Baptists had held an orange festival. When a man bought an orange at the door, he also purchased the companionship of the woman whose name was attached to it. At the end of the evening, the couple made orange juice. The Boulder First Presbyterian church women staged a "necktie party" during the Christmas season. The women provided the ties, and the men purchased both tie and partner for the festivities. If a partner became dissatisfied, he or she could be "divorced" for seventy-five cents.[20]

An example of the ingenuity that characterized these affairs may be seen in the 1892 Prescott Methodist "conundrum supper." Menus were printed with the following information.

The Cup That Cheers
Women of Grit
Boston Overthrow
Old Humpty Dumpty

Spring Offering
Food of the Spinning Wheel
New England Brains
A Palatable Mixture
What Every One Needs
Unruly Members
Logan's Stronghold
Fruit of the Vine
Tabby's Party
What a Boy Calls His Sweetheart
What Mankind Has Been
Doing Ever Since Eve Ate The Apple
Chips
Tramp Cake   Cake Hard to Beat
The Same to all men.

Some of these puzzles are obvious, and the next day's paper identified the best conundrum as: "What mankind has been doing ever since Eve ate the apple?" Answer: "stuffing." But the rest will have to be left to the reader's imagination.

Food usually formed the focus for these social events. The Congregational women of Albuquerque revealed their geographical roots when they staged a New England boiled dinner for the town. The women of the Cheyenne African Methodist Episcopal Church put on an 1876 Harvest Home Supper, complete with sweet potato pie, oysters, ice cream, pound cake, and grapes. The city's editors supported it to the fullest. Cheyenne Methodists also staged a more traditional strawberry and cream festival. Chicken pie, oysters, and fresh bread sales were also common.

With the food came entertainment. A Prescott reporter, whose wife dragged him to an 1878 Methodist benefit, has left a good account of such festivities. Numerous raffles dominated the affair. There was a doll lottery, which was won by a soldier at nearby Fort Whipple ("What will he do with it?"). Next came a contest for a gold ring hidden in a cake, and an "election" (twenty-five cents a vote) to determine the most attractive lady's hat. Plug hats, silver pieces, and miscellaneous dolls were all raffled off, interspersed with music from the Eighth Infantry band, vocal solos, trios, and guitar songs. The next evening, the church gave a free lunch to the town in order to get rid of the remaining food, and auctioned off all left-over articles. The 118-dollar profit was split between the Northern and Southern Methodist churches.[21]

Fund-raising efforts through the sale of ring cakes, grab bags, lotteries, and raffles became so common that certain ministers denounced them as gambling. One visiting cleric extended his disapproval to all church fund-raising. When he helped lay the cornerstone of El Paso's Second Trinity Methodist church building in 1895, Kentucky Methodist editor H. C. Morrison warned:

> Never turn this church edifice into an amusement hall or a restaurant. Let it be a place for the teaching of the gospel. Keep the ice cream sellers out of it, stop every strawberry at the door, and never let a boiled chicken go inside. Don't raise a dollar by entertainment and parties. Let the building you are putting up show you are for Jesus and make sinners acknowledge this church was built by a devoted and faithful people.[22]

The Roman Catholic church bazaars were identical to the Protestant celebrations with one exception: the Catholics always featured dancing. At one 1882 Catholic Fair in Cheyenne, the dancing continued for six days. Most of the mainline Protestant denominations eschewed dancing but the Laramie, Cheyenne, and El Paso Episcopalians all staged formal dances on occasion. At times the Episcopalians even sponsored a "masqued ball," but that event was considered very daring.

The church women aimed their sociables toward the entire community. Since the gatherings were primarily fund-raisers, they naturally needed as large an audience as possible. The First Presbyterian church in Tucson counted about sixteen people for worship during the late 1870s, but it staged a monthly social event for the entire town. Churches in the western Kansas town of Kinsley held socials every two weeks, as they formed the chief means of entertainment. The Central City, Colorado, newspaper urged all townspeople, whatever their faith, to attend a Baptist social. "We cannot have too many such influences in our midst," it observed, "for they regulate the moral tone of society, by elevating, purifying, and refining it."[23]

The church women saw the responsibility of "elevating" the moral tone of society as a serious commitment. Often they felt genuinely called to stage events to elevate the cultural level of their communities. The Ladies Social Circle of Plymouth Congregational Church in Lawrence considered it their duty "to amuse or instruct the public."[24] As such, they sponsored numerous lectures, concerts, spelling matches, and other occasions for uplift. In 1882, the Tombstone, Arizona, women put on a production of *Pinafore*—complete with elaborate costumes imported from San Francisco. The Parish Ladies' Aid Society of St. Marks in Cheyenne gave social entertainments at the rectory every two weeks during the winter of 1876–77. Their first performance of music, dancing, and food was praised by the paper as "the opening of the fall and winter season of gaiety."[25]

With outside entertainment at a minimum, the church became the pivotal focus for all age groups. This was especially true for western youth. The late nineteenth century saw the emergence of numerous young people's organizations. Baptist Young People's Union, Methodist Epworth League, and the Presbyterian Youth Fellowship all jostled with the interdenominational Christian Endeavour for the support of teenagers. Indeed, in the small towns and rural areas virtually all the young people's social life revolved around the church. The young played biblical games like "Ruth and Jacob" and "Going to Jerusalem," along with such standards as "Fox and Goose." At a Congregational supper in Fargo, each young person responded to roll call by reciting a verse of Scripture. If the schedule of the Congregational Church at Silverton, Colorado, is representative, church functions filled an enormous amount of time: Sunday services were held at 11:00, with Sunday School at 2:15, Choir at 3:15, Christian Endeavor at 6:00, and the evening service at 7:30. In addition there was probably a Wednesday prayer meeting.[26] With the opening of the new century, the churches reached out even further. They housed nurseries, employment agencies, gymnasiums, and the Boy Scouts. Some even served as polling places. Regardless of denomination, the mainline churches were often very much a part of general western life.

Black churches played the same central role for their constituents. Nationwide, the Black minister was always viewed as a leader and their church as "a nation within a nation." By 1909, African Methodist Episcopal, African Methodist Episcopal, Zion, or Black Baptist groups could be found in any community with a significant number of Black residents.[27]

From the start, these Black ministers and churches assumed a multitude of functions. Denver's Shorter Chapel (founded in the early 1880s) remained active as both a social and religious center, as did Omaha's St. Johns African Methodist Episcopal Church. Rev. Daniel Hickman served as an aggressive promoter of North Central Kansas' all-Black Nickodemus Colony. Yet, like the white churches, they too suffered from the constant turnover of population and pastors.

Supporting such a wide range of ecclesiastical activities demanded considerable financial outlay. Consequently, the western clergy faced a constant worry about money matters. The national Home Mission Boards all realized that they had to provide some aid to western parishes, but they invariably hoped that each congregation would soon become self-sufficient. For many western outposts, however—mining camps, railroad towns, and sparsely settled regions—that proved impossible. As an extreme example, in 1888, sixty-seven out of sixty-nine South Dakota Presbyterian ministers still received some support from the National Board of Home Missions.[28] Historian Colin B. Goodykoontz has estimated that the Protestant churches may have poured 76 million dollars into their western parishes.[29] While the major western urban churches all became self-supporting—largely through rental of pews—those in more rural areas required help far beyond the anticipated time.

The denominations handled the financial issue in a variety of ways. In the category of salary, the Home Mission Boards tried to provide a modest stipend that, with supplements, usually allowed a single man to scrape by. It was totally inadequate for a family, however. As one Episcopal priest wrote to his bishop in 1899, "a wife and baby cannot live on wind and sawdust pudding."[30]

When the local congregation could not supply its share of the cleric's salary—as was often the case—the ministers had to find additional employment. This was true for all denominations. Methodist Jacob Adriance worked both as a carpenter and handyman, while Presbyterian Lewis Hamilton mined gold and sold groceries. Father John Dyer carried the mail over the Rockies on snowshoes. Episcopal priest J. W. Tays worked as county surveyor. Southern Methodist R. W. Fields dabbled in real estate to make ends meet. Many Baptists and Methodists farmed on the side. When Methodist Protestant minister William Vance Shook pastored his Oklahoma community during the first years of the century, he worked primarily as a farmer. During that time he expected no remuneration for his sermons, since his people had nothing to give.[31] South Dakota Congregationalist B. B. Nichols served as postmaster and Disciples Liff Sanders clerked in a Lubbock store. Presbyterian Ralph Hall worked as a ranch hand by day and did his preaching around West Texas campfires at night. A large number supported their families by teaching school.[32]

Salaries varied considerably. In the 1880s, the average salary of a Methodist minister approached 663 dollars a year. During the first decade of the twentieth century, however, the Disciples were still paying their men only about 220 dollars annually. The more affluent Episcopal church tried to provide its western rectors with 600 dollars a month. But even its annual reports urged only single men to apply. The most successful Episcopal Bishops were those with wealthy eastern friends. Missionary Bishops complained that they were forced to spend much of their time in the East "begging" for their diocese. Many denominations had to rely on men who were willing to work long hours for very low pay. Consequently, several churches encouraged their theological students to spend summers on a brief home mission assignment. In the 1880s, the Congregationalists paid these men about 50 dollars a month, plus traveling expenses. Through such means, scores of young ministers received their first taste of western life.

Concerns about money form a large part of western clerical correspondence. One Phoenix Methodist noted in 1881 that he had been paid only 50 dollars of his promised salary and had already donated more from his own pocket than he had received. Many a farewell social was held primarily to pay the delinquent salary of the minister. An Episcopal rector refused to come to New Mexico unless he was assured that he would be regularly paid. A Congregationalist from Provo threatened to take his woes to the local press if his fledgling congregation did not pay the 65 dollars they owed him. If the letters to the Congregational American Home Missionary Society are representative, the denominational boards were frequently tardy with their payments. "I don't know now how, with a wife and five children, we lived," recalled Nebraska Congregationalist, M. F. Platt, "but we did."[33]

When the economy turned sour, the ministers suffered accordingly. Frequently, they were thrown back on community largesse. Methodist William Perryman Garven of Throckmorton, Texas, found that without the gratis support of his community, he would have starved. Often he would return to his home to discover a box of

canned goods on his doorstep. A rancher who had gone to town
for supplies had stopped to share his larder. The local butcher supplied Garvin with this staple, remarking "You're the only preacher
in town. I reckon we can keep you in meat."[34]

Sometimes congregations would surprise the minister and his family with a "pounding," where every family donated a pound of food
to the clergyman. Anne Moore Simpson, wife of Boise Methodist
William G. Simpson, recalled her 1877 pounding. When the family
returned home from a prayer meeting, she was astonished to find
the kitchen table and chairs piled high with vegetables, fruit, and
groceries. Easter Reaves, wife of an early twentieth-century Oklahoma Baptist preacher, found herself speechless at her first pounding. Her dining room table lay buried under sacks of flour, sugar,
lard, potatoes, bacon, ham, coffee, canned goods, and scores of home-
made pickles, jellies, and preserves. Since any item of value was
considered acceptable, however, many of the "pounding" contributions must have been of minimal use. One Methodist pastor in
Gooding, Idaho, for example, was given a wagon load of turnips.
Consequently, the family ate turnips all winter. Not surprisingly,
the children developed a lifelong aversion to them.[35]

The mainline denominations also supplemented the salaries of
their western missionaries by sending out missionary barrels. Western clerics described their needs in detail to the various Home Mission Boards, and those lists were distributed to more wealthy eastern
congregations. Much of eastern women's and children's church activities involved the preparation of these parcels.

The arrival of the missionary barrels proved a time of great excite-
ment in a western cleric's household. In Nebraska, Congregationalist Reuben Gaylor recalled the occasion when he and his family
received their box in 1861. Even before they opened it, they knelt
and offered prayer for the senders. Every fall, Colorado Presbyterian
Frank L. Moore took the measurements of his seven children and
sent them off to an eastern church. For years he and his family wore
primarily secondhand clothes. "None of us hardly realized what new
clothes were," Moore recalled in his autobiography. "During all of
my ministry, I did not buy a new overcoat."[36]

Many of the missionary packets, however, contained cast-off clothing or wildly inappropriate items. Seldom was anything new sent
in a missionary barrel. As one minister's wife remarked, the missionary barrels contained "things that aren't good enough for city

folks to wear any more, so they send them to missionaries' families and get themselves new."[37] Reminiscences by missionary children reflect the anguish of continually having to wear hand-me-down clothing and shoes to school. There is an old story that a deacon once commented at the installation of a young minister, "Oh, Lord, if Thou wilt only keep him humble, we will keep him poor."[38] That statement surely applied to the Home Mission frontier of the post–Civil War era.

In spite of the poverty, hardship, and shifting populations, the frontier ministers performed many tasks as their communities matured around them. They helped found academies and colleges, often the pride of the region, and assisted in the formation of the public school system. In addition, they served as lecturer, social leader, and general purveyors of culture.

The churches ever remained at the center of the "proper" social whirl. Women's groups used them to sponsor a variety of community-wide social events. Moreover, the buildings housed countless lectures, debates, and young people's gatherings. Like their arch-rival, the saloon, the early churches assumed a multifunctional social role in western life, one that reached well beyond denominational lines.

As the next chapter will show, the ministers also devised several unique means of spreading their Gospel message.

Chapter Four

The Vastness of the Great Plains

The New West encompassed an enormous variety of terrain. Virtually all the home mission literature marveled at the distances involved. New Mexico territory, one pamphlet claimed, could hold two New Englands, England, Ireland, Scotland, and Wales, with still room to spare.[1] The state of Colorado equaled Switzerland, New England, New Jersey, Delaware, and Maryland.[2] Wyoming could encompass New Hampshire, Massachusetts, Connecticut, Rhode Island, New Jersey, Michigan, Vermont, Delaware, and Maryland, plus two-fifths of Pennsylvania and three-fifths of New York.[3] Not only was Texas 210 times as large as Rhode Island, the entire population of the world could be placed within it; even so, the density would still be under ten people an acre.[4] Routt County, Colorado, was almost as large as Massachusetts. Montana was "an empire in itself." "Think of it," Episcopal Bishop Daniel S. Tuttle wrote to his wife from Virginia City, Montana, in 1867, "only one Protestant minister now in all this territory."[5]

In spite of this geographical diversity, however, the various churches usually viewed the region as a whole. One observer referred to the New West as a "physical unit" and a "moral unit."[6]

The confrontation with this vast expanse of land challenged all the major Protestant denominations. Basically, however, they all relied on one institution to meet the challenge: the tested methods of the Methodist circuit rider. As Congregationalist William Kincaid noted,

> If there cannot be a preacher for every village or hamlet, let preachers go from point to point. Especially let men of evangelistic fervor visit the weak and discouraged churches to promote revivals and encourage the hearts of the brethren and strengthen the things that remain.[7]

Historian Hunter Farish has written a study of the southern Methodist church after the Civil War, entitled *The Circuit Rider Dismounts*.[8] That may have been true for the South and East, but west of the Mississippi the Methodist ministers mounted up again.

So, too, did ministers from the other denominations. Along the lower Rio Grande Valley, for example, Roman Catholic priests developed portable "Mass kits," which they carried on horseback as they rode from ranch to ranch. Along the Idaho–Washington border, a Lutheran minister devised a portable communion kit that he carried in a similar fashion. Other Lutheran ministers also worked as "Reisepredigers," or circuit riders. The majority of small-town ministers had outlying "mission stations" that they were expected to visit on a regular basis. Pioneer rabbis also "rode circuit" as they performed their various duties.

Ministers in the New West spent an enormous amount of time on the road. Episcopalian Hunter Lewis, Baptist L. R. Millican, and Presbyterian Ralph Hall all spent their careers itinerating across the vast region of eastern New Mexico and western Texas. The other churches utilized the Methodist circuit-rider technique to perfection. As a Texas Methodist Bishop once observed, the other denominations had "out-itinerated the itinerancy itself."[9]

In no region of the West was the factor of distance more evident than on the Great Plains. The Plains, of course, proved to be both the first and last of the New West to be homesteaded. After the passage of the Kansas–Nebraska Act of 1854, settlers began to stream into the eastern sections of both territories. Yet the high, dry regions that marked the western stretches of the states were not completely settled until the twentieth century. One missionary dubbed the twentieth-century opening of the High Plains to irrigation as "a new Frontier."[10] "The U.S. Census Bureau, which said the frontier had gone in 1890," observed a Montana minister, "missed it by thirty years."[11]

From the earliest residents until the present day, the controlling factors of life on the Great Plains have been weather, distance, and the scattered nature of the settlements. One woman recalled her North Dakota homestead as a spot where nothing existed to make a shadow. Another described her Dakota prairie life as having "no wood, fuel, shade, or shelter, few streams and too little rain." In the 1870s, the Northern Pacific decided to run winter passenger trains on its northern division only after the trains agreed to carry blankets and ten days' provisions.[12]

Prior to the automobile, of course, travel outside the railroad relied entirely on horse and wagon. Charley O'Kieffe, who was born on a Sheridan County, Nebraska, farm in 1879, recalled that "seeing a neighbor—or seeing anybody, as far as that goes—while not unusual as to be a real novelty, was certainly not something that happened every day."[13] Mae Embrey remarked from her girlhood in eastern New Mexico that a visitor was "the most precious thing in the world."[14]

Almost all accounts of Plains life accord the church a prominent role. Even those who had been indifferent churchgoers in the East became strong church supporters on the Plains. In a world without telephones, magazines, motion pictures, regular mail delivery, or newspapers, the churches provided the main social focus. Sunday was a special day. If a congregation lacked a minister, someone usually read from Scripture or from a printed sermon. A prayer closed the meeting. In addition to Sunday services, many churches held evening gatherings to discuss questions of religion, politics, and ethics. Literary societies, tableaux, and even plays were also held there. The churches always served as the center of Christmas celebrations, and if a community erected a Christmas tree, they usually placed it in the church building. Wilfred T. Knight summed up his youth in frontier Oklahoma succinctly: "For our social life, we went to church." "Grandma" Rogers of Wichita Falls, Texas, illustrated this to the extreme; during the year 1889, she attended 115 sermons.[15]

Since the Plains churches were so scattered, the ministers had to travel great distances. During the early years of the century, Disciples of Christ pastor Liff Sanders visited all Disciples families in the Lubbock area. As there were no restaurants or hotels, he observed, "you just stayed with the Brethren." Baptist evangelist S. Y. Jackson was frequently on the road in eastern New Mexico, for he realized how helpless people felt when real tragedy struck.[16] The wife of Baptist L. R. Millican estimated that during her sixty years of married life she spent thirty years alone while her husband was on the circuit.

Episcopal ranchers in Colorado hoarded their hard theological questions for the periodic visits of the Missionary Bishop. In his travels across west Texas in the early twentieth century, Ralph Hall would occasionally find a home where the people had saved up an entire year's questions to ask him. "They don't have the opportunity to visit very often," he noted, "and will keep you up until the wee hours of the morning talking and visiting."[17]

The role of distance loomed large in the lives of these missionaries. While he was rector at Valentine, Nebraska from 1888 to 1903, Rev. John Mallory Bates had charge of twenty Episcopal mission stations. When he moved to Red Cloud, Nebraska, where he worked from 1903 to 1920, he still had ten mission stations to serve. In 1920, the South Dakota Episcopalians officially recognized this situation when they created "The Church League of the Isolated." As Nebraska Bishop George Allen Beecher admitted in 1934, "all our missionary fields cover so much territory, and our people are so widely scattered that a real representation of our church life is out of the question."[18]

The 1891–94 journal of Bishop Beecher at the Nebraska Historical Society illustrates how one Plains cleric spent his days. Stationed in North Platte, Beecher often called on his parishioners throughout the state. When he visited nearby Lexington, he also negotiated with town businessmen on the prospects of a new church building. In between, he attended to numerous baptisms, funeral services, and visitations to the sick. Occasionally, he gave communion in a private home. During one visit with a dying woman, he held a lengthy discussion with her about heaven and the future life. A cultured gentleman, Beecher was ever in demand to speak to local groups, ranging from King's Daughters to high school graduating classes. Interspersed with these tasks were numerous religious services, where his congregation might range from six to two hundred. Only rarely does his diary record: "Spent day in my study at North Platte."[19]

Since itinerancy formed a central part of the lives of most Plains clerics, they naturally sought out the best means of travel. They used horses, buggies, wagons, stages, and free railroad passes. One clergyman in Idaho relied on dog team and sled. A surprising number experimented with bicycles.

The most ingenious means of clerical travel, however, came with the advent of the railroad Chapel Car. In the early 1890s, William D. Walker, Episcopal Missionary Bishop of North Dakota, conceived of the idea of turning an ordinary coach car into a Cathedral Car. Eastern financiers, such as Cornelius Vanderbilt, responded generously, as did numerous Sunday Schools and churches. Eventually the Pullman Corporation built a car at a cost of three thousand dollars. The coach was remodeled into a small "church," with several chairs, a lamp, and a bed which converted into a desk. The words "The Church of the Advent" were printed above the windows and "The Cathedral Car of North Dakota," below. Eighty people could be seated within it on folding chairs.

The car was dubbed the "Episcopal Palace," and Walker first took it on a three-month trip through his diocese in 1891–92. He visited fifty-three small towns along the way and held services on an almost daily basis. The turnout was enthusiastic. Often he drew crowds well beyond the population of the town. In one hamlet, Walker preached to thirty people. "The same service in a cheerless schoolhouse, if there had been one," he noted, "would probably not have called out one-quarter of the number of people. . . . The compactness, the dignity, the simple church beauty of the car wins the people."[20]

Walker found that the car proved useful in reaching many diverse individuals: railroad workers, "men in shirt sleeves," barefoot boys, Negroes, "tramps," unbelievers, and agnostics. After one Chapel Car service, Walker sensed that the congregation seemed reluctant to disperse. So he led them in an extra hour of singing hymns. "Thus," he noted, "a bit of social joy was flung into the loneliness of their prairie life."[21]

The Chapel Car idea quickly spread. Several Baptist leaders approached John D. Rockefeller who helped to finance "Evangel," the first Baptist church on wheels. It, too, was equipped as an office, living quarters, and a tiny chapel. In its first year "Evangel" visited 88 railroad towns and held 424 services. Other cars, with names like "Glad Tidings," "Good Will," "Messenger of Peace," "Herald of Hope," and "Grace" followed. "Glad Tidings" had John 3:16 printed on its side in large, bold letters. By 1900 the Baptists boasted five Chapel Cars and eleven Chapel Wagons. "Glad Tidings" served Wyoming from 1915 forward, and "Evangel" became a permanent part of the Rawlins church in 1930. "Emmanuel," which boasted an organ and seats for 100, also toured Arizona and Kansas with great success. A retired "Grace" may still be seen at the American Baptist Assembly in Green Lake, Wisconsin.[22]

The Chapel Car idea soon was adopted internationally. Clerics in North Africa, South Africa, and England borrowed the concept and developed similar vehicles. In Russia, the Russian Orthodox Church utilized the idea on the Siberian Railroad. Here was an idea from the American West that spread around the world.

The first Episcopal Chapel Car, however, had a relatively short life. Its success depended on the Northern Pacific Railroad's willingness to haul it without charge, and by 1899 the railroad had begun to demonstrate some reluctance. In 1900, therefore, Bishop Samuel C. Esall sent the car to Carrington, North Dakota, to be used as a stationary chapel, and a year later it was sold.

It was not long, however, before Auto Chapel Cars emerged to replace the railroad version. These vehicles, really the first campers, proved to be marvels of engineering. The Baptists developed one that contained a washroom, complete with toilet facilities, a stove, table, fifty-gallon fresh water tanks, wardrobe closet, and bookcase—all built into the frame. The rear platform of the vehicle converted from a daytime reception room to sleeping room. In addition, the car carried numerous collapsible chairs, lanterns, and even a small pulpit organ. Part of the equipment was a 30' × 60' tent, built to accommodate about one hundred people. The tent was so constructed that the chapel auto could be backed into it to become a pulpit platform. Dakota Episcopalians devised a mobile bus chapel for the hinterlands. On the west coast, the ministers even developed Gospel Boats.

As they made their rounds from home to home, these itinerant ministers frequently distributed literature. In this, they were often aided by a group of similar itinerants called "colporters." The term, derived from the French *colporteur* ("neck peddler"), originated during Reformation times when traveling evangelists carried baskets of tracts balanced on a neck yoke. Sometimes the colporters were ordained, but more often than not they were laymen. These men were termed "supplementary missionaries," and the churches designed them to reach "a class that is not and cannot be reached by ordinary means of grace."[23] In part, these colporters served as traveling book agents for denominational publishing houses, but they also gave away much of their material. The American Baptist Publication

Society proved especially active in this regard. Their colporter ministry proved very economical, for the men received no salaries or traveling expenses but worked solely on commission.[24] In 1860, for example, the Baptists had 202 colporter agents; in 1890 they had 1,640 in all states of the union. By 1912, the Baptists boasted 50 colportage wagons, with colportage automobiles soon to come.

Baptist minister Thornton Kelly Tyson spent his career on the Nebraska and Oklahoma frontiers. While serving as State Evangelist and Missionary for Western Nebraska from 1894 to 1898, he averaged ten thousand miles a year. One of the main goals of his itinerancy was the free distribution of Bibles, testaments, tracts, and temperance papers. Many of these he received through an organization called "The Paper Mission."

His material covered a wide range. It included boxes of Sunday School cards, religious and temperance tracts, and the major evangelical newspapers: *The Standard, Examiner, Watchman, Western Recorder, Christian Herald,* and *Youth's Companion.* Occasionally, Tyson also received copies of national newsmagazines, such as *World's Work* and *Review of Reviews,* to distribute.

Tyson dubbed his literature "seed corn," and he distributed it as Johnny Appleseed did his apples. If no one was home at a dugout or shanty, he left the material by the front door. Whenever he stopped at a livery stable to feed and water his horses, he quietly put some literature in the back of every wagon he could find. When he traveled by train, he preferred to sit by an open window where he could throw out literature to the section gangs. Tyson's standard greeting was, "Well, boys, what do you have to read these long evenings?" He estimated that during his career he might have given away over a million pieces of literature.[25]

Baptist L. R. Millican used to stuff his saddle bags full of tracts, twenty-four pounds per side, before he went on a long journey. On one occasion, his horse bolted, and the materials were scattered across the West Texas countryside. From 1884 to 1913, Presbyterian Edwin M. Eller ("Montana's Bicycling Minister") pedalled over 36,000 miles across Montana to distribute his literature. He adopted modified saddle bags and wire racks to carry it all.

How much effect these reading materials had, of course, is impossible to say. But in many cases the literature had few rivals. In some places, newspapers, magazines, and books were exchanged on a regular basis. In 1869, a Congregational woman estimated that there

were not one hundred useful books in all of Montana Territory.
Charley O'Kieffe recalled that his Sheridan County sod house held
no book, magazine, or paper (excluding the family Bible) until he
was about ten years old.[26] When one missionary asked a small boy
if he had a Bible, the lad replied, yes, two, and then pointed to the
Sears and Montgomery Ward catalogs. One retired Baptist minister
in southern New Mexico was so appalled at the lack of available
reading material that he opened his sermon barrel for the free use
of the neighborhood.[27]

Overlapping with the colporters were the various Sunday School
missionaries who also emerged during the latter decades of the nineteenth century. Baptists, Congregationalists, and Presbyterians all
utilized them considerably. They hoped that the Sunday School
would fill the gap between regular church organization on one hand
and no services at all on the other.

The denominations discovered that the Sunday Schools offered
many advantages in the New West. Essentially nondenominational,
they were far more likely to succeed amidst a variety of nationalities and church preferences. Their flexibility also allowed them to
serve the temporary railroad construction camps, logging camps,
or early homesteaded areas. In addition, Sunday Schools did not
require the services of an ordained minister. Any person with an
interest could be appointed a Sunday School superintendent. Soon
each denomination prepared a course of lessons to assist whoever
took the job. If the region began to develop permanency, the Sunday School could easily form the nucleus of either a church or a
public school.[28] In 1914, the Presbyterians estimated that 80 percent of their new churches formed in missionary synods had grown
from these Sunday schools. In 1931, Colorado missionary W. H.
Schureman noted that of the 215 Sunday Schools he had planted,
35 had become permanent Presbyterian churches.[29]

The Sunday Schools provided yet another opportunity for frontier women to participate in church affairs. Even more than the
men, the women lamented the absence of regular religious services.[30] Few denominations allowed women to become ordained
ministers, but all were delighted to have them head the Sunday
Schools. When a Mrs. Blake sought to recreate the amenities of the
East in Deming, New Mexico, in 1882, the first thing she did was
to establish a Sunday School. The pioneers who settled Sulphur
Spring Valley of Arizona in the 1880s came from so many denomi-

nations that only a Sunday School met their needs. The first religious organization in Tulsa in 1882 was not a church but a Sunday School. One 1904 Nebraska report observed that the Sunday Schools were an agency for good, which could be done in no other way in "the neglected places of our country."[31]

The Sunday Schools also proved to be very democratic organizations. They were conducted by the people themselves. Charley O'Kieffe recalled his childhood Sunday school as a time when from six to sixty people would sit around a room. A self-selected teacher would read a verse or two from the Bible and then ask the various people how they might interpret it.[32] J. D. Stewart prided himself on being able to give "a single commonsense interpretation of the teaching of the Word of God."[33] Baptist Eugene Parsons later observed that the schools' greatest contribution was their insistence on the memorization of Scripture.[34] This rote method of learning tended to produce a conservative biblicism. Higher criticism of the Scriptures, an issue prominent elsewhere, seldom reached the rural and small-town Sunday Schools.

Hundreds of western ministers devoted much effort to these Sunday Schools. Presbyterian Sabbath School missionary W. H. Schureman was based in Cheyenne, but his "parish" included the 97,500-square-mile territory of Wyoming and eastern Colorado. Providing his own traveling equipment—in his case, a horse and open buggy that averaged four miles per hour—Schureman traveled over 300,000 miles in his twenty-five years of Sunday School service. During this time, he made fourteen thousand visits and conducted thirteen thousand meetings. In like manner, Congregationalist Jeremiah Everts Platt established numerous Sunday schools in southwestern Kansas, an area that he continually boosted for settlement.[35] Ralph Hall averaged 2,000 miles a month for the Presbyterian Sunday Schools in New Mexico and west Texas. J. D. Stewart, who farmed in Nebraska for thirty years, also served as State Superintendent of the Congregational Sunday Schools. He estimated that he organized perhaps eight hundred of these schools. When the Kincaid Act of 1907 opened 20,000 square miles of the western Nebraska sandhills region for settlement, the Sunday School played a major role. As one observer noted, "As the new settlements push out in the sand hills under the Kincaid Act giving section entry to homesteads, the missionaries also push out and plant the Bible school [Sunday School] as soon as it is possible to find a place of meeting."[36]

The Sunday School proved equally viable in Arizona well into the early twentieth century. As late as 1918, Sunday School missionary Albert Stewart found numerous communities without any public Christian gatherings and thus organized schools for them.[37] He concentrated on the railroad construction towns, expressing special concern for the crews who lived in the railway cars moving from site to site. He met one woman who had lived thirteen years under such mobile circumstances. Sunday Schools also proved their merit in serving isolated lumber camps, where settled church life proved impossible.

The early Sunday Schools involved all ages, ranging from Bible classes for adults to religious entertainment for children. Teaching of the children, however, was seen as crucial. W. H. Schureman realized that if he could win the hearts of the children, he could more easily convince their parents to participate in church life. Accordingly, whenever he stopped at a wayside home, he left cards and pamphlets for the children. Sometimes he even carried small presents—dolls, picture books, balls, and pocket knives.[38]

Although most of these introductory gifts have disappeared, the Colorado Heritage Center has been fortunate in obtaining a valuable set of Sunday School cards. They range in size from 1" × 3" to 4" × 6", and closely resemble modern bubble gum cards. They portray attractive pictures of birds, flowers, or other scenes from nature, and usually include Bible verses. In 1902, the Congregational Sunday School printed a series of cards that resembled playing cards. These 250 cards narrated the major Old and New Testament stories in picture form. Each reproduced a "golden text" for daily memorization. The reverse side contained biblical questions and answers. These cards offered the first "comic book" format for biblical tales. In 1916, the Congregationalists also created a religious card game entitled "Biblico."

The American Bible Society and the American Tract Society did yeoman work in this regard. Over the course of the century, the Bible Society either sold or gave away almost a million copies of Scripture. They approached their goal of placing a Bible in every home in the nation. Similarly, the tract society distributed countless pamphlets and books that stressed the importance of virtue and faith and warned of the dangers of vice.

In addition to distributing Sunday School literature, the Plains clerics also assumed a variety of social roles. An Oklahoma Baptist minister was asked to resolve family quarrels, both within and outside his congregation. A Nebraska Baptist helped build barns, houses, and windmills, and occasionally served as a physician. W. H. Schureman was able to match a childless Colorado Plains couple with orphaned "little Marjorie," to the mutual satisfaction of both. In the depressed years of 1911–1912, he established a Brotherhood Relief Committee that distributed over five thousand garments, fifteen hundred dollars worth of groceries, and three carloads of coal to over one thousand families. Episcopal rector J. M. Bates became fascinated with the bird and plant life of western Nebraska. In the course of his travels he began collecting specimens, which he later classified. In 1899, the federal government licensed him to report on the migratory pattern of birds in the region. In addition, he became an authority on the native grasses of the area. His private herbarium eventually included about twelve thousand specimens. Bates donated his collections to the University of Nebraska, and later several varieties of plants were named for him.[39] The traveling clerics on the Great Plains wore a variety of hats.

The southern region of the Great Plains developed a distinct religious milieu. Among the last areas to be settled, it was dominated by the conservative evangelical churches—Baptists, Methodists, and Disciples of Christ. Their influence helped the region achieve a religious temper all its own.

As late as 1890, Lubbock still remained largely a tent city. The Santa Fe Railroad did not arrive there until 1909. Thus, Lubbock and other west Texas and eastern New Mexico towns (El Paso excepted) did not undergo the "wild period" associated with the cattle or mining towns of the 1860s and 1870s.

The exaggerated film and television version of western life is totally out of character for the southern Plains. The towns there featured few saloons, gambling halls, or fancy women. Temperance sentiment discouraged the sale of alcohol. Liquor proved hard to get and few people could afford it anyway. In 1909, Alamogordo, New Mexico, boasted that it had four thousand people and only one saloon.[40] "Alcohol didn't play a part in these early settlers' lives," recalled Mae Embery, "but religion did."[41]

From the beginning, the southern Plains ministers also played a prominent role in this society. Settlers were eager to share in singing, preaching, and camp meetings. They welcomed visits by itinerant "ministering brethren." The "evangelical" mentality that emerged at the turn of the century continues to dominate the region. Even today, Lubbock is locally known as "the city of churches."[42]

One of the most famous of the *fin de siècle* ministers on the southern Plains was Baptist Leander Randon Millican. Born in Brazos County, Texas, Millican moved to El Paso in 1893 to pastor the First Baptist Church. He immediately found himself in trouble when he led an 1894 crusade to ban the Maher-Fitzsimmons prize fight scheduled to appear there. The El Paso *Times* attacked Millican as one of those "puffed toads, asses, putty-headed sky pilots and pulpit pounders who tire of minding their own business and court notoriety by dabbling in government affairs."[43] Suddenly he became so unpopular that his friends feared he might be shot on the street. A year later, when he discovered his congregation would not obey his strictures against dancing and card playing, he resigned.[44]

After his resignation, Millican found a field more to his liking. For the rest of his life, he served as a traveling Baptist evangelist for the southern New Mexico and west Texas region—an area larger than the state of South Carolina. During his sixty-one-year career, he became known as "Brother Millican," "The Cowboy Preacher," and the "Minister of the Mountains." He was to achieve the distinction of baptizing, marrying, and burying more people than any other man west of the Mississippi. Millican established so many small Baptist churches that his biographer could not name all of them. Once, when his horse was stolen, he waded across the Rio Grande into Old Mexico to ask for its return.[45] During his lengthy ministry, Millican discovered a continuity in the types of problems faced by his parishioners. "I do most of my work among the ranchers and farmers," he wrote in 1933. "There hasn't been much change among them."[46] As the El Paso *Herald-Post* observed on his death, "the man of God of the type of Brother Millican was as much a part of the West as the greasewood, the rancher, and the steer. His was the leavening influence that was always present and always working for better things and better days."[47]

Revivals and camp meetings extended their influence over the Great Plains. Although no regional evangelist such as Dwight L. Moody, Sam Jones, or Billy Sunday emerged to forge a national reputation, anonymous itinerant revivalists retained their popularity. Virtually all of the Protestant denominations—the Episcopalians excepted— utilized the revival technique. The crowds for these gatherings numbered in the hundreds. One 1872 Nebraska revival drew four thousand worshipers. Colorado Baptist Joshua Gravert organized over one hundred revival meetings in his adopted state. Nebraska Congregationalist C. S. Harrison listed his participation in over forty revivals as one of the great accomplishments of his life. Colorado Presbyterian Franklin Moore always maintained that the revivals were essential to church growth. Lauretta I. Randall, wife of a North Dakota Methodist minister, confessed that she disliked the coarseness of their yearly revival services. Yet she admitted that afterwards numerous people confessed their sins and that neighbors forgave their enemies. Oregon Circuit Rider John F. Nessley, however, staunchly defended the revival technique. The heart influenced the entire person, he maintained, and if an evangelist could move the heart, he could change the individual.[48]

Revivals also offered the mainline churches an avenue into the many ethnic communities on the Plains. While most of the immigrants remained members of their birthright denominations, many families chose to join new churches. Icelanders often became Congregationalists, and Reformed Hungarians and Bohemians frequently joined the Presbyterians. The Baptists and Methodists each had significant German- and Swedish-speaking congregations. Nebraska's Doane College established a short-lived German theological "proseminary," and many Protestant theological schools introduced foreign-language study for their students. While many of the graduates ministered to eastern urban immigrants, a significant number engaged in "foreign work" in America's heartland.

The southern Plains clergymen virtually institutionalized the revival technique. It reached its greatest level of popularity there in the organization of numerous camp meetings. Born of the religious enthusiasm of the antebellum frontier, the camp meeting also played a significant role in the post–Civil War years.[49]

In the decades after the Civil War, the camp meetings began to flourish in several areas along the East Coast as permanent and rather fashionable family "resorts."[50] In the New West, however, they retained their earlier, more rough-hewn flavor. In middle or late summer, after planting and before harvest, local committees selected a special site for a week-long religious gathering. The men in charge located a grove of trees with an abundant water supply. The next step was to create a "brush arbor." This was done by topping the trees and, if necessary, driving posts among them. These were then covered by a roof of leaves and branches. Logs or rough hewn planks formed the benches. Often a visiting clergyman carried a portable organ, for music formed an integral part of the services. The services were usually ecumenical, and often boasted a wide variety of social and religious gatherings, including formal sermons, prayer meetings, holiness meetings, love-feasts, evangelistic services, and the celebration of communion. The popularity of these meetings was unequaled. Every age group looked forward to them. "We pitched our tabernacle out on the praire," wrote Baptist evangelist James H. Davis in 1886, "[and] people came for 20 miles."[51]

As with the revivals of the antebellum era, the ministers measured success in terms of the quantity of converts. But the participants might well have measured their version of success in the hours of gossip and conversation. "[H]owever great may have been the need for salvation," Mrs. Sam Maddox recalled, "the need for recreation was given preference."[52]

· Great Plains ministers also directed their camp meeting and revival programs to the cowboys and ranch hands of the area. While the cowboys frequently lived by a distinct code of ethics, usually based on earlier teaching, they scorned formal churchgoing as unnecessary and unmasculine. This position may be seen in the following cowboy ballad (supposedly based on a real incident) where "Silver Jack," who had not always "used the Lord exactly right," attacked a rationalist coworker for maligning the faith of his mother. The last four verses read:

> But at last Jack got him under
>   And slugged him once or twice
> And Bob straightway acknowledged
>   The Divinity of Christ
>
> But Jack kept reasoning with him
>   Till the poor cuss gave a yell
> And allowed he'd been mistaken
>   In his views concerning hell.
>
> So the fierce discussion ended
>   And they got up from the ground
> Then someone fetched a bottle out
>   And kindly passed it 'round.

> And we drank to Jack's religion
> In a solemn sort of way
> And the spread of infidelity
> Was checked in camp that day.[53]

Several Plains clergy, however, looked to these range riders as potential converts, and staged "cowboy camp meetings" on an irregular basis during the decade of the 1880s. In 1890 William D. Bloys, the U.S. Army chaplain at Fort Davis, who had come west for his health, introduced a regular "cowboy camp meeting." Bloys had helped establish Presbyterian churches in nearby Fort Davis, Alpine, and Marfa in west Texas, and had also provided regular services for interested ranchers. One of these men, John Means, suggested that Bloys preach at Skillman Grove, a six-thousand-foot pasture located about nineteen miles from Fort Davis. The first meeting there began a tradition. By 1900 the gathering had become interdenominational and had taken on the name of "Bloys Camp Meeting." Bloys knew his audience well. He never tried to force a man to accept a faith he didn't feel he needed. The essence of his message was that God was there for all who would have Him and that a person was not a sissy to declare a faith and live by it.[54]

Locally, the Bloys camp meetings became known as "the Spiritual Hitchin' Post of West Texas." They were so successful that the Baptists eventually established a permanent camp meeting of their own. As C. Kenneth Smith recalled in a later interview, the influence of the frontier women and W. B. Bloys provided the main forces for stability on the west Texas frontier.[55]

Religious life on the Great Plains did not change appreciably until the automobile became common property. As an early twentieth-century Wyoming Episcopalian remarked, "In no part of the world does the automobile play a more important part in the Church's work. To reach the people the missionary must visit. To bring the tender, healing, redeeming ministery of Jesus to distant cattle and sheep ranches, lumber camps, mines, and oil fields, summer and winter, required a mobile ministry."[56]

Gradually, the evangelists exchanged their Gospel Wagons and matched pairs of "missionary colts," with names like "Mark and Barney" or "Luke and John," for Model T Fords. James F. Walter, W. H. Schureman, L. R. Millican, and Brother Van all "pensioned their broncos." Brother Van, however, made the change with reluctance.

A good horse could always find its way home in a snowstorm, he once noted, but his Ford frequently broke down. Millican found the change even more dramatic. Although he had ridden thousands of miles on horseback without incident, he broke a rib when his car misfired.

The spread of the automobile, however, was to mark the end of an era for the itinerant minister and the rural church. As people could drive into town more easily, there seemed less need for the clerics to be on the road to visit them. In addition, the new ease of travel meant that the rural church lost its role as the social focus for the community. The rural churches suffered, for the farmers and ranchers could now go to a larger and more fashionable church in town. The automobile permanently altered the religious history of the Great Plains.

Chapter Five

Conflict and Cooperation on the Western Frontier

The crusade to "tame the New West" often found the mainline ministers jostling one another for control of the same terrritory. Consequently, it provided opportunities for both denominational conflict and interdenominational cooperation. There are numerous examples of each type of activity.

The antebellum frontier had established a firm precedent for theological controversy. The first four decades of the nineteenth century produced a rash of church quarrels, schisms, and public confrontations. The religious leaders of the day disputed with even more vehemence than did the political spokesmen. A good antebellum frontier minister was expected to denounce deism, antinomianism, Universalism, Unitarianism, millennialism, Shakerism, Mormonism, and Roman Catholicism. The Calvinist Presbyterians and Congregationalists also bitterly attacked the Arminian Methodists and Baptists. Disciples of Christ clergymen seemed particularly argumentative. Elder John Smith spent most of his long life at loggerheads with the Methodists, Calvinists, and Spiritualists. Disciples founder Alexander Campbell raised these disputes almost to the level of art. In 1829 he staged a week-long public debate with free thinker Robert Owen, and in 1837 he took on the Roman Catholic Bishop of Cincinnati, John B. Purcell, in another popular exchange. Both debates later appeared in book form.[1]

The Disciples clerics carried their interest in public dispute to the trans-Mississippi West. From 1874 forward, several Disciples debaters toured Texas to stress the differences between themselves and all the other Protestant churches. Disciples pastor T. R. Burnett conducted several public debates with Methodist and Baptist spokesmen. On the other side, Methodist W. M. Price was called the "Campbellite Killer of Texas." In 1889, a small Texas community was thrown into consternation when a Disciples minister and a Bapitst minister held an extended public theological debate. Disciples advocate T. W. Caskey also took on the Seventh Day Adventists, Spiritualists, and Christian Scientists in public disputation. When he ended his debating career in 1896, Caskey boasted that he had driven out of Texas "the host of false teachers who have her borders filled, as the locusts filled the land of Egypt."[2]

Occasionally the Disciples' orators had their speeches printed, thus inaugurating a modest pamphlet war. Joe S. Worlick authored tracts with titles like "My Reasons for not Being a Methodist," and "Methodist Dynamite Exploded." His pamphlet "Some Baptist Blunders" began, "It would indeed be impossible to mention all the Baptist blunders in a small booklet."[3] Clearly, Worlick was a polemicist who would have been more at home on the antebellum frontier.

The antebellum frontier also set precedent for the creation of new sects and denominations. Indeed, the first years of the nineteenth century produced a rash of dissident religious groups who broke from their parent bodies over a variety of causes. The most important of these included the Disciples of Christ, the Stonites, Cumberland Presbyterians, New School Presbyterians, Republican Methodists, Primitive Methodists, Free Methodists, and countless varieties of Baptists. The ferment of the antebellum religious world also provided fertile ground for new prophets such as Joseph Smith, Jr.[4]

By contrast, the theological frontier of the New West appeared relatively quiet. Excluding the Protestant–Hispanic Catholic and the Protestant–Mormon clashes—cultural confrontations that will be discussed in the next two chapters—there was a minimum of public acrimony and church division in the trans-Mississippi West. The chief reason for this probably lay with the fact that no theological issue of the post–Civil War period offered the democratic appeal of those issues debated by the antebellum world. The earlier Protestant concerns over the "restoration" of the early Christian church (Stonites, Disciples), sexuality (the Mormons, the Shakers), church polity (Republican Methodists), and education of the clergy (Cumberland Presbyterians) seemed to have been resolved. After the Civil War, few religious quarrels of the day spoke directly to the heart of the average person. National debates over such items as evolution, higher criticism, and comparative religion appeared far away, indeed, to residents of the Great Plains and Mountain West. Consequently, discussion of these issues remained the prerogative of scholars and theologians, most of whom resided in the East. As Silver City, New Mexico, Episcopal rector Edward Cross observed in 1895, "It is a 'far cry'—to use a Highland phrase—from theology to New Mexico."[5]

The only schisms that western Protestantism witnessed, therefore, emerged as regional components of nationwide movements: the departure of the holiness advocates from the ranks of American Methodism; and the division of the Christian church into the liberal Disciples of Christ and the conservative Churches of Christ.

The idea of a "second blessing," "entire sanctification," or "personal holiness," formed a large part of John Wesley's original teachings. These concepts had faded, however, until their revival by New Yorker Phoebe W. Palmer (1807–1874), who held a series of meetings to keep Wesley's thoughts alive. During the 1880s and 1890s a large number of Methodist ministers, especially in the South and West, adopted this position. When their Bishops declined to support them, they were either driven out of the denomination or they left on their own accord. These groups directed their appeal largely to the rural poor, both those who remained on the land as well as those who had migrated to the cities. Eventually, these sects joined together to form the Church of God (Anderson, Indiana), Church of God (Holiness), and the Pentecostal Holiness Church. From 1893 to 1907, perhaps twenty-five separate holiness groups emerged and several holiness liberal arts colleges were established. By 1910, most of the outspoken advocates of these ideas were no longer members of the Methodist Episcopal Church. Here were issues—the need for a "second blessing," the prospect of living one's life in "personal holiness" and (for some) speaking in tongues—that did reach the ordinary citizen. Followers of these ideas formed a distinct subculture in many western regions.[6]

By themselves these splinter groups were relatively unimportant. Their significance increased, however, when several combined in 1907–1908 to form the Church of the Nazarene. The formation of this church added another strong conservative voice to the states of Oklahoma, Idaho, Texas, and California.

The holiness movement also produced several western experiments in communal living. Drawing on the *fin de siècle* "back to the land" movements, in 1897 the Salvation Army (really a holiness group) established a colony named "Amity," in the Arkansas River Valley of western Colorado. Amity tried to transform the urban poor of the eastern cities into farmers raising crops of sugar beets and alfalfa. While it began boldly, Amity settlers soon found themselves plagued by salt buildup in the soil and declining profits. By 1906 it had collapsed. Several spokemen viewed the Amity experiment as a variety of the social gospel—a concrete program of "applied Christianity."[7]

Sunnyside, Arizona, the utopian vision of converted barroom tough Samuel Donnelly, lasted a little longer. In 1887, Donnelly took over the Copper Glance Mine in the Huachuca Mountains. Thought to be worthless, the mine soon began producing a large amount of copper and silver, and even a little gold. In 1890, Donnelly sought converts for his group and found them mostly among the holiness advocates of western Methodism. About fifty people joined him in the experiment. In 1896, the Los Angeles *Times* described Sunnyside as "the abiding place of some new-fangled creed. The people live on a communistic plan and the whole is presided over by a queer genius who gives away his money."[8] About fifty to eighty people lived in Sunnyside between 1890 and 1901, the year of Donnelly's death. Afterwards, the community scattered throughout the region. But in the 1970s a few members returned to live once again in their childhood home.[9]

Colorado Methodist Alma White established one of the most successful of the western holiness groups. Wife of a Montana Methodist minister, White eventually began preaching on her own. During the 1890s, she moved to Denver to work among the slum areas. In 1901, she appointed herself "Bishop," and established her own church: The Pillar of Fire. The church proved successful and eventually it purchased Denver's declining Westminster College from the Presbyterians. This sect is still active in the Colorado area.

Alexander Campbell's Christian Church also suffered a major division during this period. Like the Methodist–holiness controversy, the difficulties of this denomination also proved national, but since the Disciples were so prevalent in Oklahoma, Kansas, and west Texas, the dispute had considerable impact on the New West.

The controversy had been brewing ever since the middle of the nineteenth century. The issues were complex, but the major ones included the order of worship services, the need for organized mission activity, the propriety of Sunday Schools, and the use of literature other than the Bible. The item that proved the most volatile, however, was the question, Should musical instruments (chiefly organs) be used during worship? Like the question of personal holiness, the issue of church music proved very democratic. Everyone could voice an opinion on it. Thanks to several bitter debates and a minor pamphlet war, these quarrels also reached the public realm. Eventually over one hundred congregations divided. Feelings were so intense that in 1893 the Texas "progressives" baptized their followers on one side of a river while the "non-progressives" baptized theirs on the opposite bank.[10] The division was formally recognized in 1906, with the Church of Christ acknowledged as separated from its parent body, the Disciples of Christ.

Such controversies and denominational divisions, however, did not typify church life in the New West. A far more common mode of conflict came in the realm of interdenominational jostling for regional dominance. The private correspondence of the home missionaries reveals a distinct undercurrent of denominational nationalism. For example, in his letters to his mother, Montana Congregationalist Rollin L. Hartt termed the Helena Unitarians "refined rationalists," and the Episcopal church "a church of St. Judas."[11] The letters of the Congregational Home Missionaries are full of complaints that the Baptists, Disciples, and Presbyterians were encroaching on their territory.[12] Northern Methodists, especially in Montana, often viewed their southern counterparts with a jaundiced eye. Once Henry Kendall, secretary of the Presbyterian Home Mission Board, warned Sheldon Jackson that Episcopal Bishop J. Mills Kendrick was planning to "take New Mexico. He evidently thinks the Cannonicals and vestments will do it! Well, let him try."[13] Such denominational rivalry formed a distinct part of the western religious world.

Viewed solely from the standpoint of efficiency, the persistence of denominational rivalry involved considerable waste. The Kansas Cumberland Presbyterians, for example, lost 43 of their 54 churches before the early twentieth century. By 1930, 29 of 79 Rocky Mountain Northern Presbyterian churches had disappeared. Of the 69 Congregational churches established in the Southwest, only 40 survived into the twentieth century. From 1868 to 1904, 180 Nebraska

Congregational churches went under.[14] The rivalry of the era meant that the churches often spread themselves too thin.

Contemporary observers were appalled at the excessive number of churches. One individual noted that the hamlet of Balfour, North Dakota, with five hundred people, held Episcopal, Catholic, Methodist, and Baptist services on a regular basis. Hillsboro, a nearby Red River Valley community, boasted eight churches for its 1,400 people. Episcopal rector F. A. Shore saw so many spires in Kulm, North Dakota, that he dubbed it "a city of churches."[15] "Do we need a Baptist Church?" asked the editors of the *Cheyenne Leader* in 1877. They concluded that under the American system of voluntary support, the success of a church depended not on the size of the town but on the zeal of its adherents.[16] And so the Baptists came.

For better or worse, denominationalism was the mold into which the American religious experience was cast, and it dominated the West as well. The settlers brought their denominational preferences with them. They gave them up only with the greatest reluctance. Here lay one area where eastern "cultural baggage" proved far more important in shaping life than the impact of the frontier. Many a clergyman must have agreed with the Congregational home missionary who surveyed the hamlet of Fayette, Idaho, in 1893. There were already four active churches there, but as he wrote to his home board, "There is work which must either be done by our church or left undone."[17]

Circumstance, however, occasionally dictated otherwise. During the course of settlement, several ministers of the New West began unique experiments of interdenominational cooperation. During the 1860s and 1870s they established what was, in effect, a "union" of churches. During the "organizing" period, the itinerant clergymen sought out not just their coreligionists but all those who were "interested." Many of the early churches contained people from several different denominations.

Most of the Sunday Schools were also "union" at the time of founding. The school in Silver City, Nevada, for example, contained several Catholic members. The Episcopal choir at Bland, New Mexico, consisted of two Episcopalians, one Catholic, one Mormon, one Presbyterian, and one Congregationalist. When Jacob Adriance held prayer meetings in the Colorado mining camps, he found members of all the major denominations. After some hesitation, Bishop Tuttle gave communion to all Christians, regardless of affiliation. When his choir added three new members, Tuttle wrote his wife that one was "a Russian, one a Jew(!) and one the leader of the band at the theater."[18] In Utah, the ecumenical position reached epic proportions. It was everyone against the Mormons.

Since this early ecumenicism never derived from any deeply held position, however, it seldom lasted. Most of the early "union" churches splintered into their denominational components within a decade. After each denomination had established its own church, interdenominational cooperation became much more formalized. It seldom varied from the combined support of revivals or social crusades; pastoral exchanges; union Thanksgiving or Easter services; and helping dedicate one another's church buildings or synagogues. Consequently, Protestant ecumenicism never took firm root in the western cities. It was not until the early twentieth century that the "union" idea reemerged. Because of falling enrollment, the El Paso Northern and Southern Presbyterian churches joined in 1934—forty-nine years before their parent bodies reunited. In the same community, the Unitarians and Congregationalists smoothed over one hundred years of controversy when they united the following year. In Flagstaff, Arizona, and Logan, Utah, the Methodists and Presbyterians joined forces in a "Federated" church. Such actions, however, came more from economic necessity than from conviction.

In the more rural areas, however, the ecumenical idea had longer life. Here, the West produced numerous examples of cooperation that would have been unheard of in the more settled regions. When the Congregational minister of Silverton, Colorado, left in the spring of 1885, the local newspaper observed that the resident Catholic priest was "fully competent to minister to the spiritual wants of our population until the new pastor arrived."[19] The lack of other clergymen in early Montana led its residents to consider Bishop Tuttle as their pastor, regardless of denomination. Wyoming Episcopal rector Samuel West alternated services one summer with a Presbyterian theological student on a summer pastorate. Each preached every other Sunday, sharing the same choir, Sunday school, and congregation.[20] When home missionary John Hoskin began his work in Deer Lodge Valley, Montana, in 1884, he preached at every school and stopped at every ranch house along the way, without exception.

The Presbyterian minister who served Evanston, Wyoming, during the early 1880s was dubbed "everybody's pastor." The Dubois, Wyoming, Episcopal church really functioned as a "community church." Whenever Episcopal Bishop Frank Spalding visited the isolated western Colorado community of Atchee, he called on every family in town and baptized all infants, regardless of affiliation.[21] The Boulder, Montana, school served as home for Methodists, Presbyterians, and Episcopalians, on a rotating basis once a month from 1878 to 1882. Ranchers and lumbermen in the community of Elk Mountain, Wyoming, built a "people's church" in 1912. They did so with the understanding that any minister of any denomination could hold services there. When Frank L. Moore pastored in Livermore, Colorado, he found eight denominations and eight nationalities in his congregation. They chose to worship not as a denomination but as part of the "invisible church."[22] Thus, in the more isolated areas, the denominations downplayed their theological differences.

Although denominational lines usually remained intact, the years after the Civil War produced a lessening of theological distinctions within them. All the mainline Protestant churches experienced a theological shift toward a common ground of a generally biblical, Arminian Christianity. The antebellum disputes over Calvinism versus Arminianism—limited salvation as opposed to a (potentially) universal salvation—never really reached the trans-Mississippi West. Congregationalist Zachary Eddy recalled how the New England Calvinists, once the dominant religious force for much of the East, had begun to falter. Even though no Arminian could match the Calvinists in argument, their rigorous logic and harsh doctrines had won them few converts. They never reached the masses. "Arminianism has prevailed everywhere," Eddy complained, "in spite of logic."[23]

After the Civil War, Arminianism even crept into the stronghold of the enemy. In 1871, the National Council of Congregationalists formally declared that Arminianism had as much right to recognition within their denomination as historic Calvinism. "It has become a common saying," noted Presbyterian James D. Moffatt in 1889, "that the Calvinist preaches like an Arminian, and the Arminian prays like a Calvinist."[24] Except for the Dutch Reformed churches, certain Baptist groups, and the Southern Presbyterians, Calvinism seemed to be in full retreat. The more democratic Arminian position had prevailed: through the Incarnation of Jesus Christ, a basically loving God had given His Grace to all humankind. Each person had the capacity to accept this offer on his or her own volition.

Moreover, God desired the salvation of the race. The story of this gift could be found in Scripture and could be easily understood. "The Bible is a plain book, addressed to the common sense of man," a Methodist minister had remarked in 1851, "and the arrogant pretense that the common people cannot be trusted with its mysteries is an insult to its author."[25] While this position always retained denominational overtones, a basic Arminianism began to spread through all the western Protestant churches.

There were several reasons why this denominational leveling occurred in the New West. One of the most crucial lay with the general poverty that characterized much of western life. Privation underscored the lives of numerous settlers. The wife of Arizona Baptist minister R. A. Windes remembered how the breaking of a china cup became a major family disaster. Daily life on the Great Plains, especially during early settlement, proved a full-time job. Settlers made their mittens and shoes from grain sacks and wore their real shoes only on Sundays. They roasted ground corn into coffee and turned dried sunflower leaves into tobacco. They ate bread with lard so that the butter could be sold for cash. When Oklahoma was opened, most families lived in tents, as virtually everybody arrived without finances and with only a few household goods. One settler remembered a daily diet that consisted of bread, sorghum molasses, and coffee.[26]

In some areas the poverty continued well into the twentieth century. In 1905, Pacific Northwest Methodist W. W. Van Dusen discovered conditions among his parishioners "quite as primitive as it is possible to conceive."[27] When Claton Rice worked among the settlers of northeastern Utah during the years 1911–1918, he found homes where prairie dog and biscuits provided the only food and quilts and blankets the only covering. When Episcopal priest Samuel E. West taught in the mining town of Hanna, Wyoming, from 1912 to 1913, the area lacked even the rudiments of civilized life. Only one tree existed in the community and the mine superintendent had fenced it in his own yard. On Sundays, for a special treat, West took his students to the superintendent's home so they could look at the tree.[28] Such circumstances left little room for theological disputation.

Second, many settlers of the New West displayed scant knowledge of religious themes. The itinerant ministers were frequently dismayed at the people's lack of familiarity with the basic elements of the Judeo-Christian tradition. While virtually all settlers owned Bibles, the lack of organized religious services had often precluded their use. In the more isolated regions, many settlers became complete strangers to organized religious activities. One Baptist Sunday School missionary met a twenty-year-old Granger, Wyoming, youth who had never seen a minister before. When Episcopal priest Putnam B. Peabody held services in 1903 in a Wyoming ranch house, his congregation included a diverse group, ranging from a decadent Englishwoman, who had once moved in royal circles, to a cowboy who had never attended a church service. Bishop Talbot once met applause after speaking to a group of soldiers. When James F. Walker served as a superintendent of a mining company in Colorado, he sat down to a meal and offered grace. Several miners told him that this was the first blessing they had ever heard.[29] When Methodist Bishop Matthew Simpson visited Virginia City, Nevada, he asked a Cornish miner, "My Friend, are you a laborer in the vineyard of the Lord?" The man replied, "No mon, I be working in 'ee Savage [mine], lower level." Wyoming pastor W. D. B. Gray taught the story of the "good Samaritan" in a biblical context, but the children recalled it as "The Holdup in Jerico Canyon."[30] Another Wyoming minister delivered a sermon on the text of John 3:8: "The wind bloweth where it listeth." Afterwards, a youth politely told him that in Wyoming the wind usually came from the north. This level of ignorance encouraged the clerics to restrict their message to only the basics of Christianity.

Moreover, many of the most successful ministers in the New West had received only modest theological training themselves. When a friend asked Brother Van why he wished to go to frontier Montana, Van replied, "To preach, sing, and encourage people to be good."[31] Van's sermons rarely varied from his standard theme: a simple offer of God's universal salvation. Methodist Henry W. "Preacher" Smith of Deadwood, South Dakota, simply tried to "recall the wandering sinner home."[32] Colorado's Father Dyer shared the same outlook. On his death in 1901, the Denver *Post* described his faith as that of a "vigorous, practical nature." Presbyterians George M. Darley and Ralph Hall were both somewhat embarrassed about their meager theological training. Congregationalists J. D. Stewart and James F. Walker also complained about their lack of formal education. Kansas Cumberland Presbyterians frequently criticized their candidates for ordination as not meeting the denomination's educational standards. Nonetheless, they usually recommended that "under the circumstances" the Presbytery ordain them anyway.[33] Occasionally, this lack of training was even celebrated. A Presbyterian on the prairie frontier of western Canada declared that he would rather have a minister "know less Latin and more horse."[34] Congregationalist James F. Walker remarked that nothing taught in the schools, colleges, or seminaries of the day could have prepared him for the conditions he faced in his isolated southwestern Colorado parish.[35] "The constant ring of the doorbell of the pastor of the west may have spoiled the literary value of his sermons," noted one pastor, "but it has punctuated his addresses with human need and it has filled his discourses with the practical appeal of the heart cry of humanity."[36] While this may be true, it also detracted from his concern over theology.

Consequently, much of the Christianity in the New West reached for the lowest common denominator. Methodist William B. Goode resolved never to use his sermons to condemn but always to look for the goodness he could find on the frontier. Presbyterian Chalmers Martin prayed before each sermon that "the Lord help me to say a fit word—to console the bereaved, to warn the living." Idaho Methodist T. W. Atkinson tried to show Jesus as one who lived the ideal life, and to urge his listeners to pattern themselves after Him. Congregationalist James Walker tempered the prevailing ethic of "self-made men" by noting that all actions were played to a backdrop of supernatural Providence. North Dakota Methodist Harvey S. Randall stressed that the purpose of life was to lose oneself in service to others. Montana Methodist Jacob Adamson based most of his sermons on John 3:16. He operated on the assumption that there were no people so bad that he could not do them some good. Southern Methodist Cyrus Rice had a standard text: "For I have determined not to know anything among you, save Jesus Christ and Him crucified." Presbyterian Ralph Hall always prayed before he began a sermon that he might inaugurate the work of building God's kingdom. Baptist Romulus A. Windes confessed that when he gave a sermon he simply tried "to get people to do better."[37]

Even the more formal Episcopalians had to bend to the prevailing winds. They discovered that many of their parishioners seemed oblivious to the differences between their Church (they always wrote it upper case) and the other denomnations. Traveling rectors often bemoaned the lack of prayer books. They also discovered that their congregations had forgotten when to sit and when to stand during the Litany. Several priests learned that they had to shorten the more lengthy prayers as their congregations were not used to them. Both Colorado Bishop John Franklin Spalding and his South Dakota counterpart, William Hobart Hare, confessed that they had to learn how to speak extempore.

The ministers reflected an increasing flexibility as they discovered the need for adapting their sermons to the situation at hand. Father Dyer once likened himself to a prospector seeking "pay dirt" amidst his congregation of Colorado miners. When Rev. Melton Jones preached in a Clifton, Arizona, saloon in 1899, he compared the images on a deck of cards to the great religious figures of the past. Another variation of this theme, "The Prayer Book in Cards," related each playing card to a biblical theme (the ace, one God; the deuce, Adam and Eve; the trey, the three wisemen; the four, the four evangelists; and so on). This idea also became a popular cowboy ballad.[38] Bishop William H. Hare once likened the problems of his South Dakota Sioux congregation to a horse tangled in its harness.[39] Montana Baptist John Spencer was told at one service that he could "shoot with my canon [a large Bible] or, if you prefer, you may fire with this little pistol [a pocket testament]."[40] When Thomas Uzzell served a Leadville, Colorado, congregation, he denounced the people who stole from the miners as "the lowest skunk[s] in Christendom." A Southern Methodist camp meeting leader in Phoenix in August 1898 compared the climate there to what the sinner might expect in the next world.[41]

The role of music during these western services assisted this theological leveling. In fact, music and singing often played a significant part in western church life. From the earliest days forward, the frontier ministers had realized the power of music as an aid to faith. In 1859, Colorado Methodist William B. Goode discovered that the most effective way of gathering an audience was to "sing them up." "There is a power in song," Goode observed, "and perhaps nowhere else more felt than here among those so long absent from religious associations."[42]

In places that lacked a minister, the people often gathered for a religious songfest. In some isolated areas the leaders would actually "line out" the hymn. Baptist R. A. Windes recalled his first song service in the Lone Star Baptist church in Prescott, Arizona, in 1880.

Six members shared one hymn book, and, as Windes remarked, "we didn't lack anything but the tune."[43]

A Leadville, Colorado, Episcopal priest who stressed music during his services in 1880 found that this innovation drew large crowds. When Congregationalist Rollin L. Hartt staged a song service in Helena in 1896 (that is, without a sermon), he drew one of his largest audiences.[44] After the first pipe organ in Arizona arrived in 1897, a standing-room crowd gathered in the Methodist Church to hear the initial performance.

Rousing hymns formed an integral part of the nineteenth-century western services. Some of the most popular songs included:

> On Jordan's Stormy Banks
> Lead Kindly Light
> Bringing in the Sheaves
> Come Thou Almighty King
> Oh, Worship the King
> Holy, Holy, Holy
> When Morning Gilds the Skies
> Oh Happy Day (When Jesus Washed My Sins Away)
> The Old Time Religion
> Come to the Church in the Wildwood
> Will There Be Any Stars in My Crown?
> Shall We Gather at the River
> Sweet Bye and Bye
> Let the Lower Lights Be Burning
> Jesus, Lover of My Soul
> Children of the Heavenly King
> Nearer My God to Thee
> Amazing Grace
> I Will be a Worker for the Lord
> What a Friend We Have in Jesus
> There Is a Fountain Filled with Blood
> How Firm a Foundation

Episcopal Bishop Frank Spalding was once riding the stage to Yampa, Colorado, when his driver asked him to "give me one of them religious songs."[45] Spalding complied.

Hymn writers Isaac Watts, Charles Wesley, Fanny Crosby, Ira D. Sankey, and others played a major role in forging the western religious outlook. Hymn singing not only provided the chief means by

which lay people participated in public worship, the hymns themselves served as theological textbooks for their congregations.

The more popular songs, with easily memorized choruses, provided an effective means of conveying abstract theological positions. "Praise God from Whom All Blessings Flow" ("The Doxology")
stressed both God's providence and the doctrine of the Trinity. God's
majesty found emphasis in "The Heavens Declare Thy Glory,"
"Before Jehovah's Aweful Throne," and "All Hail the Power of Jesus'
Name," with its popular chorus: "and crown Him Lord of All." Virtually all of Charles Wesley's approximately nine thousand hymns
similarly stressed the love of God for mankind and the joy of a personal relationship with Him. The doctrine of the Incarnation is well
presented in "Hark, the Herald Angels Sing" and "Joy to the World,
the Lord Is Come," while the Resurrection is set forth in "Christ
the Lord Is Risen Today." Those seeking comfort in time of trouble
could turn to "In the Cross of Christ I Glory" or the ever popular
"Rock of Ages."[46]

The impact of the hymns did not end with the church door. When
Rev. George W. Mowbray rode across the Oklahoma prairie, he often
heard a lone cowboy singing a hymn to himself. Ranch hands riding
herd at night discovered yet another use for church music. They
found that singing hymns to the cattle served to prevent stampedes.[47]

Interestingly, the Mormons also emphasized hymn singing in their
worship, but the Saints bent their hymns to emphasize their distinctiveness. Many of the favorite Mormon songs presented Mormon
theology. Several referred to the early persecution of the Saints,
such as "Praise to the Man," which told of the martyrdom of Joseph
Smith, Jr. Still others celebrated the Mormon Zion in Utah, as in
"Oh Ye Mountins High," "In Our Lovely Deseret," and "Beautiful
Mountain Home." Even the best known of all the Mormon hymns,
"Come, Come, Ye Saints," the powerful song of the westward trek,
never crossed denominational lines.[48]

The importance of music accents what might be termed the
"performance" aspect of many a western religious service. While
their counterparts elsewhere might have been surrounded with sol-
emn dignity, services in isolated frontier settlements often served
as a form of "entertainment." When Father Joseph Machebeuf said
Mass in a Central City, Colorado, theater, the audience consisted
of two hundred Roman Catholics "and others." The synagogue at
Grand Forks, North Dakota, often hosted Gentiles who had dropped

in to see how Jews worshiped.[49] One summer Father Dyer alternated his services with a traveling theater troupe on his Colorado mining camp circuit, with Dyer complaining that "the Devil was traveling the circuit as well as myself."[50] In 1883, Episcopal Reverend J. S. McCann actually set up his pulpit in the Bird Cage theatre of Tombstone. A 1900 Gillette, Wyoming, cardboard sign in a saloon bore the message:

> Preaching at 7:30 P.M.
> Dance at 9:00 P.M.
> After Dance, Big Poker Game[51]

The miners frequently shared this view of religious services. Whenever an Episcopal bishop visited in full vestments, he was certain to draw a large crowd. On Daniel Tuttle's arrival in Rocky Bar, Idaho, a small boy offered to get a bell and ring it through the town to alert the people, as he had done for a previous traveling road show the week before. When Episcopal Bishop John F. Spalding spoke in Rico, Colorado, a miner named Brownie Lee passed the plate, gun in hand. When one man dropped in only a quarter, Lee announced, "Take that back. This is a dollar show."[52] In 1873, the Cheyenne *Leader* urged the town's ministers to make their sermons entertaining as well as instructive. A Congregational minister complained from Webster, Idaho, in 1893 that "the people seem to regard preaching services in general as sort of a free beer fight for the entertainment of the people."[53]

The arrival of religious stereoptican slides by 1900 added yet another dimension. In 1919, Methodist Joyce Stanley Kendall recalled how he received stereoptican slides from the Methodist Book Concern but could not use them because so many of his Idaho stations lacked electricity. So, he rigged a conversion kit to his Ford and, with a fifty-foot cord, utilized the battery of his Model T to run the slides. His service consisted of the slides, a short sermon, and prayer. With those, he boasted, "I could get an audience any night of the week."[54]

Thus, while denominational lines may have remained basically intact, there was distinct theological movement within them. Many of the inherited eastern frameworks of understanding underwent subtle shifts of emphasis. Churchgoers who lived on the Great Plains, for example, always viewed the deity as intimately involved in the world of nature. Historians Austin and Alta Fife have shown how cowboys often conceived of God and heaven as extensions of their western experience, with God becoming the "Herd Boss," "Great Owner," or "Boss of the Riders." Heaven, in turn, became "The Last Round Up."[55] Metaphors of the plagues of Egypt dominated the Kansas settlers' explanations of the grasshopper devastation of the 1870s. Some groups proposed a Fast Day as the most appropriate response.[56]

Evidence from surviving sermons suggests that the western clerics preached a democratic, biblical, and Arminian Christianity. Not only were the scriptures an open book, one could find a passage therein that spoke to every human situation. Jesus was less a reconciler between a distant God and sinful Man than a "friend" to people in need.

The western sermons did not dwell on the themes of sin and damnation. Rather, they stressed the fact that God's Grace was freely given for all who wished it. The ministers also emphasized the theme of God's concern for each individual. One senses the believers' deep faith in the working out of Divine Providence in their own lives. This was true even in the face of tragedy. When an Oklahoma woman lost her son to drowning on the Sabbath, she feared him lost in hell; but a voice from the sky assured her that he was safe in heaven. The popular Mormon legend of the gulls that ate the plague of grasshoppers to save the community was not far from the norm of the western Christianity. The Lord moved in mysterious ways, to be sure, but He ever held His people under special, providential care.

New Mexico Archbishop Jean Baptiste Lamy. A strong opponent of the Protestant ministers, Lamy also tried to "Europeanize" the native Hispanic Catholic traditions. Collection of the author.

Matilda Allison, Presbyterian
missionary to northern New
Mexico and founder of the
Allison-James school for girls in
Santa Fe. Courtesy of the Menaul
Historical Library, Albuquerque,
New Mexico.

Alice Hyson, Presbyterian
missionary-teacher to the Hispanics of northern New Mexico.
Courtesy of the Menaul Historical
Library, Albuquerque, New Mexico.

Students at the Allison-James school in Santa Fe in the early 1890s. Allison-James Collection. Courtesy of the Menaul Historical Library, Albuquerque, New Mexico.

Reverend Ralph Hall, Presbyterian "cowboy preacher" of the southern
Great Plains. Courtesy of the Menaul Historical Library, Albuquerque,
New Mexico.

Reverend Gabino Rendon, Hispanic Presbyterian minister, on the road from Santa Fe to Chimayo, c. 1902. Courtesy of the Menaul Historical Library, Albuquerque, New Mexico.

Rev. and Mrs. Romulus A. Windes, pioneer Baptist missionaries in Arizona.
Courtesy of the Arizona Historical Society/Tucson. Photo accession number 1715.

Reverend William Wesley Van Orsdel (1848–1919), "Brother Van," probably the most famous Protestant minister in Montana. Courtesy of the Montana Historical Society, Helena.

Wyoming and Utah Episcopal missionary Bishop Ethelbert Talbot, c. 1891. Talbot was the model for Owen Wister's bishop in *The Virginian*. Courtesy of the Archives of the Episcopal Church USA.

The most celebrated western Episcopal missionary bishop, Daniel S. Tuttle, on one of his many stagecoach rides. Courtesy of the Archives of the Episcopal Church USA

Walter Rauschenbusch, Baptist theologian of the social gospel. Courtesy of the American Baptist-Samuel Colgate Historical Library, Rochester, New York.

New Mexico and Arizona Episcopal Bishop John Mills Kendrick (1836–1911). Photo by J. E. Purdy, 1904. Courtesy of the Archives of the Episcopal Church USA.

Rev. and Mrs. John Roberts, Episcopal missionary to the Arapaho and Shoshone of the Wind River Reservation in Wyoming. John Roberts Papers, #37. Courtesy of the American Heritage Center, University of Wyoming, Laramie.

First Indian Presbyterian Church, Kamiah, Idaho; founded in 1871 by Sue McBeth.

Sue McBeth (1833–1893), Presbyterian missionary to the Nez Perce Indians of Idaho. Courtesy of the Presbyterian Historical Society, Philadelphia.

"Father" Jacob Mills Ashley, pioneer Congregational missionary to New Mexico. Courtesy of Jane Ashley Elmer.

Reverend Sheldon Jackson (1834–1909), Presbyterian missionary to the far West and Alaska. Courtesy of the Presbyterian Historical Society, Philadelphia.

Cowboys going to Sunday school at the Glendo, Wyoming, Congregational church. W. B. D. Gray Papers, #1053. Courtesy of the American Heritage Center, University of Wyoming, Laramie.

Blanchard, Arizona, Sunday school (Bible study class), 1903. Courtesy of the Sharlott Hall Museum, Prescott, Arizona.

The Congregational church's "Utah Gospel Mission." Locally termed "the department of theological controversy," this team carried its evangelical message into the smaller towns of Utah until the 1930s. Courtesy of the Center for Archival Collections, Bowling Green State University, Bowling Green, Ohio.

(*Facing page*) Congregational missionary W. B. D. Gray fording a Wyoming river. W. B. D. Gray Papers, #1053. Courtesy of the American Heritage Center, University of Wyoming, Laramie.

The famous Episcopal Cathedral Car of North Dakota (above), and its interior (below). Courtesy of the Archives of the Episcopal Church USA.

Shoshone Episcopal Mission School on the Wind River Reservation in Wyoming, with Rev. and Mrs. John Roberts and Rev. Sherman Coolidge, an Arapaho. John Roberts Papers, #37. Courtesy of the Western Heritage Center, University of Wyoming, Laramie.

Episcopal church, Rock River, Wyoming.

First Episcopal church in Wichita, 1869. Courtesy of the Kansas State Historical Society.

First Presbyterian church, Phoenix, 1879. Courtesy of the Arizona Historical Society/Tucson. Photo accession number 588.

The first Protestant church in the Pecos Valley of New Mexico: Old Methodist Episcopal Church, South, Roswell, New Mexico, 1888. Courtesy of the Historical Center for Southeast New Mexico.

First Congregational Church, Salt Lake City, Utah. Courtesy of the Utah State Historical Society, Salt Lake City.

First Presbyterian Church, Salt Lake City, Utah. Courtesy of the Utah State Historical Society, Salt Lake City.

St. Michael's Episcopal Cathedral, Boise, Idaho, built within the shadow of the state capitol.

St. Mathew's Cathedral, Laramie, Wyoming. The various denominations
seemed to challenge each other to see who could build the most impressive
structures in the fledgling western towns. American Heritage Center
Collections, #21903. Courtesy of the American Heritage Center, University
of Wyoming, Laramie.

The Exceptional Populations

I: The Hispanics of the Southwest

In 1870 the Roman Catholic Bishop of Arizona invited seven Sisters of St. Joseph of Carondelet to Tucson. The Bishop asked the Sisters to help establish a parochial school system and the institution that eventually became St. Mary's Hospital. The diary kept by Sister Monica revealed how the group was received. On the train near Omaha, the nuns fell into conversation with four Protestant ministers and their wives, all on their way to China. It was not long before the chief topic of conversation turned to religion. "Everyone maintained his own opinion," Sister Monica recalled, "and proved it from the Bible, agreeing only in [that] one point."

The nuns traveled by rail to California and then backtracked by caravan across the Colorado River to Arizona. As they approached Tucson, four priests rode up on horseback to bid them welcome. Soon the entire community had joined the procession.

> Before we reached the city [she observed], their number increased to about 3,000; some discharging firearms, others bearing lighted torches, all walking in order and heads uncovered. The city was illuminated, the fireworks in full play.
>
> Balls of cumbustible matter were thrown into the streets through which we passed; at every explosion, Sr Euphrasia made the sign of the cross. All the bells in the city were pealing forth their merriest strains. On reaching the convent, we found our good Bishop in company of several ladies and

Presbyterian parochial schools among the Hispanics and Pueblo Indians. The Northern Presbyterian church viewed its mission to the Southwest largely in educational terms. During the late nineteenth and early twentieth centuries, the church established primary or secondary schools in numerous small towns throughout the region. (Not all were in operation at the same time.)

Map by Carol Cooperrider from materials provided by Mark Banker and Timothy Banker.

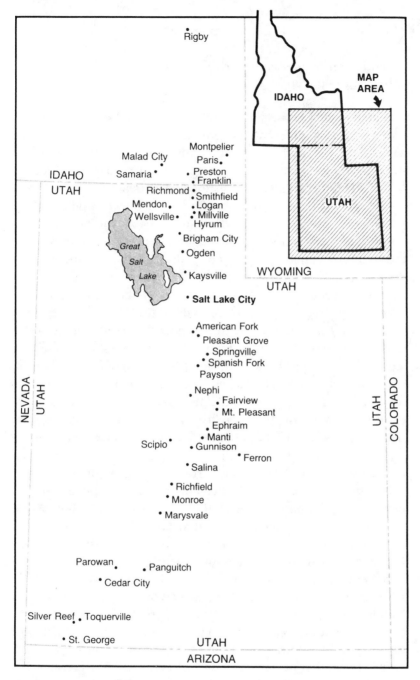

Presbyterian parochial schools among the Latter-day Saints. The church attempted to establish a school in virtually every town of size in the region. (Not all were in operation at the same time.)

Map by Carol Cooperrider from materials provided by Mark Banker and Timothy Banker gentlemen, awaiting our arrival. The crowd then fired a farewell salute and dispersed.[1]

When the first Protestant ministers arrived in the Southwest, they received a very different reception. Unsung and unnoticed, they labored for years with minimal results. Like the Sisters, however, their efforts to introduce schooling and to improve health conditions had important and long-lasting consequences.

Historically, the American Southwest had offered a difficult challenge to each of its successive conquerors. As the northernmost outpost of the Spanish colonial frontier, and later under Mexico, the area had been long neglected. Under the United States, the vast realm was split into New Mexico and Arizona territories. The two territories eventually developed along different lines. Arizona boasted a significant Hispanic population only in the Tucson and Phoenix areas; for most of the nineteenth century, it resembled the other mining frontiers of the northern Rocky Mountain states. New Mexico, however, supported a Hispanic population of over forty thousand residents, scattered in small, isolated communities throughout the Rio Grande Valley and in the mountainous northern half of the territory. In addition, both territories contained a significant number of Indians. Thus, when the first Protestant clergy arrived in the region, they provided yet another dimension of the cultural mix that has characterized the region from the time of initial contact.

Northern Baptist Hiram W. Read has the distinction of being the first Protestant minister to reach the Southwest. From 1849 to 1852 Read served as auxiliary chaplain at Fort Marcy, the army post established on the hill overlooking Santa Fe. While there, he established the first school to teach English. In 1854, Read left the territory. Less than a decade later, he served in the Civil War, where he was captured and eventually exchanged. In 1863, President Abraham Lincoln appointed him postmaster, first in Tucson and later in Prescott, Arizona. Read was a confirmed southwesterner. In 1865 he moved to California, but after a stint in Nevada during the early 1880s, he settled permanently in El Paso in 1883. Described as a "Bible Missionary," Read spent the rest of his life working with the Hispanic population. He adopted the title of "Bishop" (although the Baptists have no bishops) to increase his influence. When he died on February 6, 1895, the El Paso *Times* noted:

Bishop Read was one of the old landmarks of El Paso. He was one of the first Protestant ministers to locate in El Paso and in the early days he did good work here. Peace to his aged ashes.[2]

In the 1850s, when Hiram Read began his work in the Southwest, the residents were little acquainted with his message. There were no Baptists within a thousand miles of Santa Fe, and both the soldiers and Hispanics viewed him as a curiosity. In 1852, he explained to a ministerial convention (attended by four other itinerant Baptist missionaries) how he worked:

> I take my Spanish Bible and go to a house. I tell the family what a choice Book I have and ask them if they would like for me to read a little of it to them. Their consent being readily obtained, I proceed to read two or three chapters and then go on to another house and so on as time will permit. This is the only way by which the great masses of the people can become acquainted with the Scriptures, as it is now well known here that not more than one in 200 can even read or write or tell their own age.[3]

Read and other early Protestant missionaries to the Southwest confronted a unique situation. Although New Mexico was officially Catholic, the vast distances and rugged terrain meant that the Catholic Bishop of Durango, Mexico, had never exercised tight control over the region. As Read observed, "the religion of this country is Catholic, not Roman, but Mexican, for the Pope has no jurisdiction over the country."[4] After the United States gained sovereignty over the region, some Mexican priests expressed an interest in the new Protestant faith. On June 9, 1850, Read accepted the invitation of the local Catholic priest to preach in his adobe church. A crowd of about two hundred gathered to hear Read's talk, delivered in English. Afterwards, several people translated his main points into Spanish. This address was probably the first American Protestant sermon ever delivered in an American Catholic church.

Read also carried on a brief correspondence with the well-known Padre José Martínez of Taos. An eccentric genius, Martínez had introduced the first printing press into New Mexico in 1835. This enabled him to publish a newspaper, *El Crepúsculo* (The Dawn), numerous tracts, and parts of the Bible. A rebel, Martínez attacked traditional Catholic church tithes as excessive. He also wrote a tract that touched upon religious toleration. When Read sent him several religious books, Martínez replied with a gracious letter of thanks. The Protestant missionaries to New Mexico concurred that Martínez was "almost" a Protestant because of his advocacy of religious toleration and his firm reliance on the Scriptures. In 1863, Episcopal Bishop Joseph Cruickshank Talbot held a long conversation with Martínez, probably about his joining the Episcopal church.[5] Later, Presbyterian John Menaul utilized some of Martínez's writings for his own tracts. The interest expressed by Martínez and other Hispanics encouraged the Baptists. They were convinced that New Mexico was ripe for the Protestant message.

Early converts, however, were sparse. A hopeful sign occurred when dissatisfied priest Benigno Cardeñas became a Protestant in 1854. But he later recanted and returned to his native faith. His quarrel seems to have been more with his Bishop than with the tenets of Roman Catholicism. But José S. Señon of Laguna Pueblo, along with several members of the Chavez family of San Antonio, New Mexico, did join the church and remained Baptists. They were the first of what would become a small, but significant Hispanic–Indian Protestant community.[6]

When the Civil War broke out, the Baptists abandoned their missionary efforts in New Mexico. Afterwards, the Methodists and Presbyterians arrived to build on the foundations they had laid. Encouraged by Colorado pioneer Father Dyer, Thomas and Emily Harwood moved from Wisconsin to New Mexico in 1869. They were to spend their entire lives in the area. In fact, the story of Methodism in New Mexico is largely the story of the two Harwoods.

Settling first in the northeastern part of the territory, Emily established a school there, and Thomas began learning Spanish. Thomas also crisscrossed the region in an effort to anticipate the route of the railroad. Later, the Harwoods moved to Socorro and, finally, to Albuquerque, where they founded a Girls' School and a Boys' School. They also established a Spanish–English Methodist newspaper, *El Abogado Cristiano*. Circulation of the paper itself remained small, only about three hundred copies per issue, but the Harwoods' press also published thousands of pages of tracts and other religious booklets.[7]

Thomas Harwood became widely known in the region. A staunch Republican, he was mentioned as a possible candidate for surveyor general and even as governor. In 1900, during his seventy-first year, he traveled fifteen thousand miles by rail, and two thousand by team, preaching 213 times. For Harwood, this was not unusual. He had followed this rigorous schedule consistently from his earliest years forward.

Like Read, the Harwoods fell in love with the Southwest. When the perennial issue of New Mexico's fitness for statehood (achieved only in 1912) was raised, they always defended the territory from attacks by outsiders. Hispanics were not the "voting cattle" that their enemies charged, Harwood insisted. Rather, they were law abiding, quiet, industrious, and clean. Spanish society produced no orphans and few tramps. Moreover, the Hispanics had remained loyal to the Union during the Civil War. At the end of his career, Thomas Harwood observed that "It is a wonder that I am not the most hated of men in the territory because of my leadership in the Mission, but I am thankful to be able to believe that there is hardly a Roman Catholic family in the territory into whose house I would not be courteously received."[8]

The Presbyterians had arrived in the Southwest at about the same period. David McFarland moved to Santa Fe to begin a church and school in 1866, and John Annin served the Las Vegas church from 1869 to 1880. Later, Matilda Allison supervised the popular Santa Fe school from 1881 to 1903. Scottish missionaries John and James Menaul worked among both the Indians and the Spanish settlers in the central Rio Grande Valley during the last decades of the century. They left their legacy in Albuquerque's Menaul School (founded 1895).[9]

If early Spanish converts were few, the "Anglo" segment of the southwestern population proved equally unreceptive to the Protestant message. When Hiram Read moved to Arizona in 1862, he faced a society that flaunted its independence from social convention and organized religion. In 1863, the Arizona legislature rejected a plea to elect a territorial chaplain who was a member of an organized church. Instead, they chose an aggressive freethinker. After the vote, the "chaplain-elect" invited all his supporters for a drink. In Tombstone, gambler Sam Danner, an ex-Southern Methodist, decided to hold the first "church" service in his house. Admission was a "ticket" (a playing card with Danner's initials), and Danner's prayer read:

Oh, Lord, we pray for full forgiveness for all the sins we have
committed, but what we most repent are those we have
omitted.[10]

Arizona maintained this free-wheeling image for years. When Baptist R. A. Windes arrived there in 1879, he complained that the territory had fewer than eight churches and over five hundred saloons.
Three years later, the editor of the Arizona *Weekly Star* located
forty-one places on a single Phoenix street where a person could
buy retail liquor. When a local resident, William Bladen Jett, joined
the Phoenix Methodist church in 1887, his fellow workers taunted
him as "Old Salvation." A 1902 report listed only 6,698 Protestants
(compared with 40,000 Catholics) for all of Arizona.[11]

Presbyterian Thomas F. Ealy and his wife, who served five months
in Lincoln County, New Mexico (from February to July 1878), had
an even more traumatic experience. Sent there as a medical missionary, Ealy and his family found themselves in the midst of the
Lincoln County war. Ealy consistently maintained that he had come
only to teach, preach, and practice medicine. Because he was invited there by one faction, however, he became part of the conflict
anyway. In five months, Ealy held funerals for thirty residents, only
one of whom had died a natural death. "Great danger of being shot"
read a typical recording in his diary. Finally, in October 1878, the
Ealys moved to Zuni Pueblo, where they spent their next two years
in equally frustrating, but at least more peaceful circumstances.
The Ealys surely would have agreed with territorial Governor Lew
Wallace, author of *Ben Hur,* when he said, "All experience gained
elsewhere fails in New Mexico."[12]

Generally speaking, the southwestern Protestant ministers experienced only modest success until the railroad arrived in 1880–81.
With more convenient transportation facilities, thousands of eastern settlers began migrating to the area. Most of the major denominational efforts really began with this influx of new settlers. As
Congregationalist Robert West observed in 1881, "I believe that
next to the Christian church and the Christian school, there is not
an agency that is doing more to evangelize New Mexico than the
thunder of the locomotive."[13]

In spite of the increase in overall population, however, the southwestern denominations experienced a slow growth. In 1890, the
New Mexico Methodists reported about 2,300 members, while the

Presbyterians and Congregationalists listed only a little over 1,000 each. As late as 1900 New Mexico had only fourteen Baptist churches. Baptist population did not expand appreciably until Texans began to homestead the eastern plains of New Mexico during the first two decades of the new century. Then their numbers multiplied rapidly. As the *Southwest Baptist* put it, "The Lord is simply filling this country with Baptists."[14]

Of all the southwestern towns, El Paso initially appeared to be the most inviting. The churches viewed this border town as an obvious jumping-off point for the evangelization of Old Mexico. Thus, many denominations established missions, schools, or settlement houses there. Although they secured relatively few converts (a 1916 survey found under a thousand Mexican Protestants), they did provide needed social services. In addition, the Southern Baptists chose El Paso as the location for their large Spanish publication house. Baptist J. E. Davis founded and directed the Baptist Spanish publications for over forty years. Beginning his work in Mexico in 1905, Davis moved to El Paso in 1916 in the wake of the revolution. By 1925, he had translated over seventy religious books and was printing eight periodicals. The Spanish Baptist publishing house soon became the largest in the world. It supplied literature for all the Spanish-speaking evangelical missions.[15]

From Hiram Read forward, the Protestant missionaries in the Southwest all expressed dismay at the conditions they found. New Mexico supported few schools and had no hospitals. The 1880 census reported an illiteracy rate that approached 65 percent. Travel was difficult, as there were few roads and fewer bridges. While educational facilities existed for the wealthy, they had not filtered down to the masses. The missionaries seized on a single cause for this situation: they blamed everything on the Roman Catholic church.

Catholicism in New Mexico contained many facets, however, and the ministers soon seized on one aspect of the church as their *bête noir*. This was the religious order of "Contradia de Nuestro Padre Jesus," or the Penitentes. The Penitentes were a group of lay brothers who lived in the mountainous villages of northern New Mexico and southern Colorado. During the centuries of Spanish and Mexican rule, they had kept the Catholic faith alive in areas where the church had sent few or no priests. In so doing, however, they had adopted religious practices that were unique to the region. During Holy Week, the brothers flagellated one another. On occasion, they even crucified one of their members.[16] Moreover, the order was shrouded in secrecy. In 1888, when journalist Charles F. Lummis succeeded in photographing their rites, he had to fight off an attempt on his life.

The hierarchy of the Roman Catholic church also viewed Penitente activity with a jaundiced eye. In 1833, the Bishop of Durango, Mexico, banned some of their ritual, but his ruling had little effect. By the 1880s, the Archbishop of New Mexico had also expressed his stern disapproval, but this too was largely ignored. It was not until 1935, when some of the excesses had been moderated, that New Mexico's Archbishop granted the group official church recognition.[17]

If the Catholic hierarchy was embarrassed by the Penitentes, however, the Protestants were horrified. They seized on their activities as the ultimate symbol of the provinciality of New Mexico. Almost all missionaries described Penitente rites as "medieval superstition." Several of them exaggerated wildly. One Episcopalian claimed that the Penitentes actually buried people at Easter. A Congregationalist estimated the Penitente strength at between fifteen and twenty thousand; a Baptist suggested thirty thousand. A Presbyterian guessed that two-thirds of all New Mexicans had somehow been connected with the order.[18] As one observer noted, "I never saw anything, in horror, to equal the worship of the Penitentes."[19]

The home mission literature provided a steady diet of Penitente stories for eastern readers. These included lurid accounts of Holy Week marches, which accorded a prominent role to the macabre "death cart," and wild tales of threats to Protestant missionaries in the area. Some accounts suggested that priests encouraged this behavior, and that sexual excesses formed a part of Passion Week. A representative example of such literature is the 1893 publication by Presbyterian Alexander Darley ("apostle of the Colorado Mexicans"), *The Passionists of the Southwest.* Few could equal Darley's tales of Penitente life.

Had the Protestant missionaries been able to read the Catholic literature, however, they would have discovered that American Roman Catholic church officials were equally troubled over the state of the faith in New Mexico and Arizona. One of the most important events in the religious history of the Southwest occurred in 1850, when Pope Pius IX appointed Jean Baptiste Lamy as Vicar Apostolic of the territory. A French-born ascetic, Lamy also was appalled at the conditions he found when he reached Santa Fe in 1851. Less than one month after his arrival, he described the native Hispanic priests as "either incapable or unworthy," and declared that New Mexico had "20,000 heretics and 40,000 infidels."[20]

During his long term in office (1850–1885) Lamy did his utmost to improve the religious and social conditions of the region. Drawing on the support of several religious orders, he attempted to bring the long-established local Hispanic Catholic faith into the orbit of Euro-American Catholicism. He also faced the added problems posed by the unique Pueblo religious outlook. Over the centuries, Roman Catholicism had been tenuously grafted onto the religious beliefs of the Pueblo Indians of the Rio Grande Valley. Elsewhere, among the Navajo, Apache, and Comanche, the church had been even less successful. Lamy corresponded with the Jesuit Pierre-Jean de Smet, who was widely known for his accomplishments among the Indians of the Pacific Northwest. Lamy urged de Smet to come to New Mexico and work among the Pueblos, Comanches, and Navajos, but nothing came of it.

The Protestants regarded Lamy's reforms with dismay, for they realized that he would reinvigorate the historic strength of Catholicism in New Mexico. Indeed, he did. By the mid-1860s, Lamy had increased the number of New Mexico priests from under ten to over fifty. By 1912, New Mexico boasted seventy Catholic clerics. Interestingly enough, however, these new arrivals included only one native Hispanic priest. The rest were Belgian, German, French or Italian.[21] This was not mere accident. Lamy's personal enemy was not the Penitentes, or even the Protestants. It was the native Hispanic clergy.

The majority of the native-born clerics resisted Lamy's reforms. About half returned to Mexico and of those who stayed, Lamy eventually deposed two: Padre José Manuel Gallegos and Padre José Antonio Martínez. Gallegos accepted the judgment, but Martínez rebelled. When Lamy replaced him with a Spanish-born priest, Martínez refused to submit and established a Catholic schism in Taos. He erected his own private chapel and continued to minister to the perhaps five hundred people who followed him. When he died in 1867, he remained unrepentant. Lamy also tried to replace the native New Mexican folk art—the *santos, bultos,* and *retablos* (which he considered "primitive")—with European imports. In the process, he destroyed many irreplaceable native artifacts.

In her novel *Death Comes for the Archbishop,* a fictionalized account of Archbishop Lamy, Willa Cather has distorted this cultural clash. Historian Paul Horgan has also downplayed the conflict in his biography *Lamy of Santa Fe.* It has taken the efforts of other historians, such as Thomas Steele, S.J., and Ray John de Aragon to revise these interpretations. These authors have emphasized the popular, folk nature of New Mexican Catholicism, with its devotion to Mary and the numerous celebrations in honor of the various patron saints. They have also stressed the central role that religious folk art played in the culture of this region of the Spanish Borderlands. Aragon has suggested that Lamy's removal of the native New Mexican clergy was "tragic."[22]

During Lamy's tenure, the Protestants remained wary. Nonetheless, they continued to fish in troubled waters. They borrowed Bishop Read's technique of going from house to house and reading from Scripture to the Hispanic families. They also donated Spanish Bibles to anyone who would accept them. These unique Bibles have entered into Protestant Hispanic folklore as the Madrid Bible, Gomez Bible, Chimayo Bible, and others—named for the families that became Protestant because of them. The Presbyterians claimed success in converting several former Penitentes. They also found fertile ground in the Taos region among the former followers of Padre Martínez. The Presbyterians maintain that many of Martínez's parishioners, including, some say, a son of the priest, became active Protestants.[23]

Such activity produced inevitable Protestant–Catholic clashes. Socorro Baptist missionary John M. Shaw reported a rash of broken windows, and in 1854 he was attacked by a crowd who stoned him when he preached in Lemitar, New Mexico. A Methodist minister was shot at in Peralta in 1880, and a Hispanic Methodist evangelist was wounded the same year. A decade later, a crowd threw stones at Thomas Harwood and Eustaquio Barela while they were preaching in La Mesilla. Missionaries in south El Paso were similarly mistreated. Lamy once termed the Baptist literature "heretic books," and the European priests he imported did not dissuade local mob action when the Protestants claimed that they might have stopped it.[24]

The Protestants realized the importance of training Hispanic evangelists to reach the native population, but these converts were especially harassed. Priests allegedly followed them from town to town, and a lay group once disrupted Silvestre García's sermon in Doña

Ana by sitting in front of the building and shouting "Amen" and "Halellujah."[25]

Over the years, however, these Hispanic missionary converts became vital to Protestant success among the people of the Southwest. They became "cultural brokers" between the native culture and the incoming Anglo way of life. Initially the mainline denominations seemed reluctant to ordain Hispanic clergy, but they gradually changed their mind. In 1880 the Presbyterians ordained José Ynes Perea. Perea, his wife Susan, and his colleagues, Gambino Rendon and Acorsinio Lucero, helped spread the evangelical Protestant message to the Southwest in the decades flanking the new century.[26]

The majority of the Protestant–Catholic clashes in New Mexico, however, were effected with the pen rather than the sword. In 1873, several Jesuits moved to Las Vegas, New Mexico, where under the able hand of Donato M. Gasparri, S.J., they began publication of the weekly newspaper, *Revista Católica.* The paper was later described as "saving the Faith of the Spanish-speaking peoples of the Southwest and those of Latin American countries."[27]

The presence of a Catholic journal roused the Protestants to action. Presbyterian John Annin founded a short-lived *Revista Evangélica,* also in Las Vegas (the first Protestant newspaper published in the area). It was soon joined by Alexander M. Darley's brief *El Anciano* (Trinidad, Colorado) and later *La Hermandad* (Pueblo, Colorado) which lasted from 1889 to 1908. The most consistent Protestant voice of the state, however, remained with Thomas and Emily Harwood's *El Abogado Cristiano.* None of these local newspapers, however, had the impact of Sheldon Jackson's earlier *Rocky Mountain Presbyterian.*

The Catholic and Protestant papers criticized each other on a regular basis. *Revista Católica* poked fun at prominent national clergymen such as Henry Ward Beecher and Catholic-baiters like Tom Watson. They termed the Hispanics who had become Presbyterians as *faroles apagados,* "blown out lanterns." They criticized both Harwood's theology and his knowledge of Spanish. Father Gasperi suggested that if everyone had open access to the Scriptures, the result would be like the "tower of Babel of American Protestantism." *Revista Católica* also warned its readers that Protestant missionaries posed a threat not only to the Catholic faith but to Hispanic culture as well. In addition, the Jesuits also opposed the proposed plans for New Mexico's system of public education.[28]

The Protestant papers responded in kind. Thomas Harwood placed the blame for New Mexico's poverty and illiteracy squarely on the centuries-old domination of the Catholic church. Other New Mexican editors and politicians joined the fray with severe attacks on the Jesuits. In 1890, Governor Samuel B. Axtell termed them "Neapolitan Adventurers."[29]

The fiercest Protestant–Catholic battleground, however, rested with the issue of the school system. Educational opportunities in New Mexico Territory during the nineteenth century were abysmal. Both Catholics and Protestants agreed on this. Illiteracy remained high, especially among women, and until 1889 there was not a public high school or college in the entire region. In 1880, only 162 schools existed, and they were of varying quality. A few years later, Governor Lionel A. Sheldon reported that "in some localities there are fair schools and in some phantom schools and in others none."[30] Most Protestant and Catholic clerics were well educated for their day, and it was not long before each side began a program of parochial education.

Bishop Lamy inaugurated the process when he invited the Sisters of Loretto at the Foot of the Cross to Santa Fe in 1852. Their small boarding and day school in the capital city formed the first of what would eventually become an extensive Catholic parochial school system. Soon the Sisters expanded their schools to Taos, Mora, Las Vegas, Bernalillo, Socorro, Albuquerque, and Las Cruces. Their Las Cruces school, the only boarding school for southern New Mexico, drew a large enrollment.[31] Most of these schools flourished and when the public school system was finally introduced in the early 1890s, the Sisters' schools simply *became* the public schools. This was true in Mora, Taos, Socorro, Bernalillo, and several other places.[32] While other Sisters came later—the most prominent being the Sisters of Charity, who opened St. Vincent's Hospital in Santa Fe in 1865—the Sisters of Loretto were New Mexico's most successful Catholic educators during the Gilded Age.

Bishop Lamy also invited the Brothers of the Christian Schools (Christian Brothers). Arriving in Santa Fe in 1859, they soon began boys' schools at Taos and Mora. Their fledgling college of Santa Fe—St. Michael's—was on the verge of collapse when Brother Botolph (Peter Joseph Schneider) arrived from the East Coast in

1870 to turn things around. When he died in 1906, Brother Botoph had been president of St. Michael's for thirty-six years. He had shaped it into one of New Mexico's most important institutions of higher learning for the period.

In 1867, Bishop Lamy invited the Jesuits, the premier educational order of the Catholic church. The Protestant missionaries, needless to say, were not pleased at their arrival. Congregationalist Jacob Ashley worried that the Jesuits would soon assume complete control of the "blind Catholics." "They come in flocks," Thomas Harwood complained in 1874, "like blackbirds to a cornfield, twenty-five or more can be seen in a single village."[33] The Jesuits, however, were never as successful as the Sisters of Loretto or the Christian Brothers.

For reasons not fully understood, the Jesuits did not receive full support from the Catholic community of New Mexico, with the exception, perhaps, of Albuquerque. Several Hispanic Catholic spokesmen attacked the Jesuit opposition to the formation of a public school system. Other Catholic clergymen criticized them openly, and Brother Botolph could not have been pleased when the Jesuits opened Xavier College in nearby Las Vegas in 1875. Perhaps the fact that most of the parish clergy came from France, while the Jesuits all came from Italy, made a difference, too. Be that as it may, in 1884, the Jesuits moved their Las Vegas school to Denver, where it became Regis College. In 1917, they transferred *Revista Católica* to El Paso. In effect, they had decided to leave the state to others.[34]

The educational contributions of the various Catholic orders to the territory can hardly be underestimated. Gilded Age New Mexico was a world of vast distances, poor transportation, and scattered settlements. The Catholic schools provided opportunities not found elsewhere. Soon almost every important community supported its parochial school. As late as 1940, members of religious orders operated thirty of the state's public schools, a situation that ended only in the early 1950s.

The various Protestant denominations, however, were equally active in establishing parochial schools. They dismissed the Catholic schools as catering primarily for the elite. They were very critical of the convent schools, accusing them of teaching painting and music rather than self-reliance. Protestant missionaries also expressed general dismay at the lack of concern over the education of young Hispanic women.

Consequently, the Congregationalists' New West Education Commission established academies in Albuquerque, Las Vegas, Santa Fe, and Trinidad, Colorado, and in eleven other isolated New Mexico towns. In El Paso they operated a school for several years before they formed a church. At one time the Congregationalists had almost three thousand children under their school supervision, over ten times as many people as they had in their churches. The Methodists established Hispanic training schools in Tucson, Albuquerque, and El Paso. Their Lydia Patterson Institute in El Paso, which opened in 1914, provided a wide array of social and educational services. Other denominations, such as the Lutherans and Baptists, also began parochial schools, but on a much smaller scale. "We have often said," remarked Thomas Harwood, "that the church that educates will surely win."[35]

The Northern Presbyterians probably carried the main brunt of Protestant parochial education in the region. Shortly after the Civil War, the Santa Fe Presbytery resolved that a school was essential to their mission work. They noted that Catholic opposition to all forms of Protestantism had made such efforts necessary. They got nowhere, however, until the mid-1870s when Rev. George G. Smith of Santa Fe wrote to Sheldon Jackson with a new idea: "Send ladies to this point."[36]

Thus began the intense Presbyterian effort to educate southwestern children. During the late nineteenth and early twentieth centuries, this denomination sponsored over sixty "plaza schools" throughout northern New Mexico and southern Colorado.[37] These schools were established in such isolated Catholic enclaves as Mora, Taos, Capulin, Las Cruces, Cordova, and Truchas, as well as in the larger towns of Santa Fe and Albuquerque.

The Protestants also made two attempts to establish colleges, but these met with only limited success. Congregational minister Horatio O. Ladd established "The University of New Mexico," in Santa Fe in the late 1870s (not to be confused with the present state university, founded by the legislature in 1889). Beset with financial problems, the "old" UNM operated chiefly as a secondary school until it closed in 1893.[38] Congregationalists complained of Santa Fe that "in very few cities or towns of the West has benevolence been extended so generously, and, if the truth must be told, probably in no other are the permanent results so few and disappointing."[39] In 1884, the Presbyterians began the Presbyterian College of the Northwest in Del Norte, Colorado. Its purpose was to train Hispanic youth to teach and preach to the surrounding community. After several years of modest success, the school closed its doors in 1901.[40]

The Protestant primary and secondary schools, however, were far more successful than their colleges. Like the day-to-day operation of the western churches, they became largely a woman's prerogative. In 1878, Presbyterian Mrs. Richard Haines helped form a denominational Woman's Home Mission Society with special responsibility for schools among the "exceptional populations" of the land. The church had discovered that male evangelists sent into the region generally got nowhere. As Sheldon Jackson observed, "They won't come to hear preachers; send us a teacher."[41]

In response to this appeal, hundreds of young women teachers boarded the train to serve in the Protestant parochial schools of the Southwest. Most of them were single. Some stayed a year or two and then returned East; several married locally; but a significant minority spent their entire lives in teaching and/or assisting in the local medical centers.[42] Alice Hyson, Ora Slater, Alice Blake, Leah Thompson, and Matilda Allison are just a few of these women who devoted their careers to such service.[43] As one writer put it, "Christ's command, 'go preach,' is not more obligatory on man than his command, 'go teach,' is on woman."[44]

The Presbyterian plaza schools were invariably shoestring operations. Isolated, accessible only by horse and wagon, with mail delivery twice a week, they would have folded overnight without the dedication of the teachers. In 1895, for example, the tuition at the Allison-James Presbyterian High School in Santa Fe was paid as follows: eleven strings of chili; one sack of cornmeal; a sack of onions; fifteen dollars worth of wool, beans, and chili; one Navajo blanket; five chickens; one box of grapes; and two dozen eggs. One teacher at Aqua de Lobo looked at her borrowed desks and scant supplies and wrote, "I am *determined* to manage in some way to accommodate all who may come." Obviously, one needed a headmistress with a large number of wealthy eastern friends to enable such an operation to survive. There was no question as to the purpose of the schools. As Mrs. J. V. Dilley of Mora wrote in 1889, "However, prejudiced the people may be at first against Protestant *religion,* they soon learn the value of a Protestant *education*; then the religion follows in due time."[45]

Not only did the women supply the personnel for the schools, they also helped produce the necessary funding to keep them going. Sheldon Jackson's exaggerated claim that the Southwest contained no virgins over twelve led to a greater emphasis on "women's work for women." From their initial task of packing missionary boxes, the Women's Board of Home Missions expanded their role to assume the task of supervising the scattered Presbyterian educational activity in New Mexico and Utah. They viewed the regions as similar to foreign mission areas. "Young woman," advised a speaker in 1887, "go West."[46]

Although a nominal public school law passed the New Mexico legislature in 1872, very little was effected for almost twenty years. It was not until 1891 that the public school system really began in earnest. Within a decade, however, it was operating with marginal effectiveness over most of the territory. The Protestants responded to the new situation by gradually phasing out their private schools. Some continued until the 1920s, but today only the Presbyterian Menaul School of Albuquerque is still active. The Congregationalists always maintained that the state public school system had been modeled on their New West program of schools and academies.[47]

The Protestant parochial schools provided a much-needed educational service. They helped "Americanize" hundreds of children. Hispanic youth who began in the plaza schools often went on to Allison-James or Menaul high schools, and from there to the University of New Mexico. Their descendants today are doctors, lawyers, and teachers around the state.

Although the young women who taught at these schools would probably have been shocked at the comparison, they might be viewed as "Protestant nuns." Mostly unmarried, deeply committed to their faith, more than a little suspicious of other churches, underpaid, overworked, and often very isolated, these Presbyterian, Methodist, and Congregational teachers resembled the Sisters of Charity or the Sisters of Loretto far more than they ever realized.

The presence of the rival school systems occasionally caused religious tension. Teachers at the Presbyterian plaza schools complained of opposition from the local priests, who countered by establishing parochial schools of their own. Sometimes the priests threatened families with excommunication if they sent their children to the Protestant schools. Whenever a child decided to enroll in a Catholic school instead of the Protestant one, they were understandably delighted. Occasionally, the local Hispanic residents would insult or harass the Protestant women. One teacher considered it a major victory when she finally got a longstanding opponent to doff his hat when she walked by.[48]

The Roman Catholic leadership, on the other hand, felt equally strong about the matter. While they had no objection to Protestants ministering to their own people, they considered the Hispanics and Pueblo Indians "theirs." Thus, they deeply resented the attempts to wean Catholic children away from the faith through Protestant schooling. The church looked to the Jesuit *Revista Católica* to expose the Protestant "errors" and to hold to the true principles of the faith. In 1912, Benjamin M. Read praised the Jesuits of the territory as being of great assistance to the local priests, "firstly in defending and maintaining the Catholic faith of the Mexican people and secondly in opposing Protestant fanaticism and bigotry."[49] As late as 1946, a church pamphlet praised the Jesuits for doing "yeoman's service in combatting a menace which had become rampant at that [particular] period."[50] In 1912, the *Catholic Encyclopedia* concluded that the New Mexican Hispanic population had largely kept the faith, "despite the poverty of the people and the moneyed competition of the Presbyterian and Methodist missions, which have selected New Mexico as a field of operation."[51]

In terms of numbers, the *Catholic Encyclopedia* was surely correct. In 1890, New Mexico had about 100,000 Catholics and 5,000 Protestants. In 1906, the figures were 122,000 Catholics and 13,000 Protestants. None of the statistical compilations distinguished between Anglo and Hispanic Protestants, so these figures must be estimated. Thomas Harwood noted that the Spanish Methodist work grew from 15 people in 1870 to 1,743 in 1900. In 1884, the Methodists divided their work into Spanish and English language divisions, with Harwood assuming responsibility for the former. In 1906, they claimed 3,100 Spanish Protestants. If one assumes that the Baptists, Presbyterians, and Congregationalists had approximately the same number, that would make around 9,000 people, or about half the state's Protestants in 1906.

The figure is probably too large, however. Harwood was more honest when he observed that "the extent of the influence of the Mission cannot be put into figures."[52] Even though accurate figures do not exist as to the number of Spanish Protestants, a safe guess might be around 5 percent of all southwestern Protestants.

The majority of New Mexico Hispanics have remained Catholic, but the state did produce an active Hispanic Protestant contingent.

The most significant aspect of Protestant–Catholic tension in New Mexico (and to a lesser extent in Arizona and west Texas) was what did not happen. The potential for violence always existed and, indeed, in 1875 a Methodist minister, of Elizabethtown, New Mexico, was shot and killed. The murderer was never apprehended, but since the Methodist cleric was involved in politics as well as religion, the motive remains unclear.

In spite of the harassment on both sides, however, New Mexico did not become another Northern Ireland. When General Stephen Kearny gave his initial speech from the rooftop of the Las Vegas plaza in 1846, he spoke judiciously:

> My government will keep off the Indians, protect you in your persons and property, and I repeat, will protect you in your religion. I know you are all great Catholics; that some of your priests have told you all sorts of stories; that we could ill-treat your women and brand them on the cheek, as you do your mules on the hip. It is false. My government respects your religion and allows each man to worship his Creator as his heart tells him best. Its laws protect the Catholic as well as the Protestant; the weak as well as the strong, the poor as well as the rich. I am not a Catholic myself; I was not brought up in that faith, but at least one-third of my army are Catholics and I respect a good Catholic as much as a good Protestant.[53]

The separate functions of church and state, as established by the Constitution, paved the way for eventual tranquility.

Another reason for the relative peace can be traced to the fact that New Mexico did not really have a single Protestant–Catholic clash. On the one side lay the New Mexico folk Catholicism of José Antonio Martínez and José Manuel Gallegos; it confronted the Lamy-backed Euro-American Catholicism. In addition, the Jesuits complicated the issue, since they never really got along with the other religious orders. On the other hand, the Protestants themselves were split into several competing denominations—Presbyterians, Congregationalists, Methodists, and so on. While they usually put forth a united front against the Catholics, when the issue of possible public financing for parochial schooling arose, the old tensions (especially between the Presbyterians the Methodists) invariably resurfaced.

Lastly, the theme of the vast spaces in New Mexico came into play. In spite of all the schools—both Protestant and Catholic—hundreds of young children went without education. The reason lay in the isolation and distances of the territory. If a school did not exist within, say, ten miles of a home, formal education was really not feasible. Thus, there was enough work for both Protestant and Catholic in the vast terrain of the American Southwest.[54]

Chapter Seven

The Exceptional Populations

II: The Latter-day Saints

By the time the first Gentile (that is, non-Mormon) ministers arrived in Utah in the mid-1860s, the main body of Saints had lived in the Great Basin for almost twenty years. During that time they had forged a new identity based on several themes. These included the martyrdom of Joseph Smith, Jr.; new revelations in the *Book of Mormon* and Smith's other writings; polygamy, a "peculiar institution" that gave the group international notoriety; Brigham Young, who would rule the region until his death in 1877; and the isolation afforded in the valley of the Great Salt Lake.

The Saints had arrived in Zion via a journey—that most powerful of all mythological vehicles. The great Mormon trek from Missouri and Illinois to Utah ranks as one of the country's paramount folk epics. It involved about sixteen thousand people whose suffering and heroism have become legendary. Nonetheless, the trek has failed to become part of the national mythology. Instead, it is seen as the provenance of a single, sectarian group. Historian Jan Shipps has argued that Brigham Young's leadership of this journey to Utah provided the pivotal point of Mormon history. In their move out of the Missippi Valley to the West, the Mormons recapitulated the flight of the ancient Hebrews from Egypt.[1] Through this "reenactment" of the Exodus, they forged themselves into a "peculiar people," as described in I Peter 2:9: "a peculiar people, a holy nation, a royal priesthood." The city of Salt Lake had become to the Saints what Jerusalem had symbolized for the Jews.

In denying the legitimacy of all other Christian denominations, the Mormons developed such a strong sense of identity that they considered themselves a separate nation. In 1857 they spoke seriously of seceding from the Union. In 1860, English traveler Richard Burton noted that the Saints treated the Fourth of July "with silent contempt."[2] Abraham Lincoln's wise "hands off" policy toward the Mormons during the Civil War helped prevent such action.[3] The Saints even devised a separate alphabet with a unique orthography—"The Deseret Alphabet." Ostensibly created for better communication with the Indians, it also served to isolate the Mormons from mainstream American culture.

Thus, when the Protestant ministers arrived in Utah in 1864, they met a distinctly hostile environment. Except for a handful of Apostates (ex-church members) in Salt Lake City, perhaps five hundred scattered Gentiles, and the contingent of soldiers at nearby Camp Douglas, the forty thousand Saints dominated the entire region. In the 1860s, the missionaries in Utah were as isolated as if they had been serving in Asia or Africa.[4]

Reverend Norman McLeod was the initial Protestant home missionary to arrive in Utah. Sent from Denver by the Congregational Home Mission Society, McLeod organized the first Gentile church in Salt Lake City in February 1864. The next year he supervised the construction of a building, "Independence Hall," where he held regular services. According to Episcopal rector Thomas W. Haskins, however, these "services" were actually anti-Mormon tirades, directed chiefly against polygamy.[5] "Your campaign against Mormonism opens brilliantly," a supporter wrote McLeod from Denver, "and will end, I am confident, gloriously."[6]

Independence Hall was owned by the Congregational Church. Nonetheless, all the Gentiles in town soon became involved with it. The hall served as the locus for both church services and a Sabbath School. From this location, McLeod also wrote his editorials for a local anti-Mormon newspaper. The Methodists used the hall for six months in 1870, and virtually every evangelical denomination in Utah, as well as the Jews and the Woman's Antipolygamy Society, held their initial organizational meetings there. In addition, the hall entertained a steady stream of anti-Mormon speakers. The son of the prophet, Joseph Smith II, also spoke there. In 1869 Smith charged Brigham Young with distorting his father's teachings.

The superintendent of McLeod's Sunday School was Dr. J. King

Robinson, an army surgeon who had married an attractive woman of Mormon background and had accumulated some property in downtown Salt Lake City. In October 1866, Robinson was assassinated and the property gutted. The pretense for this action lay in the argument that it had been the home of immoral activities. Nonetheless, the attack was obviously directed at the Gentiles in general. McLeod later discovered a carved message on a fence post near Robinson's grave that read: "Damn the Gentiles. We did this."[7]

Since a Catholic priest named Kelly proved to be the only Gentile cleric in the area, he read the last benediction over Robinson. The next day, he too received a death threat. Kelly, however, sought out Brigham Young and showed him the warning, and Young assured the priest that he would be safe. As it turned out, Robinson's murder was the last religiously motivated death in nineteenth-century Utah.[8] However, for many years the Congregationalists continued to commemorate the anniversary of Robinson's murder.

McLeod, who had already survived one attempt on his life, was in the East lecturing against the Mormons when the assassination occurred. Warned by the commanding general of Fort Davis not to return, the minister spent the next several years in touring the nation with his anti-Mormon message. He even had an interview with President Rutherford B. Hayes on the matter. In his speeches, McLeod pulled no punches. He termed the Saints "anti-Christian, anti-republican, and so utterly repulsive to humanity and the spirit of our Government, as to demand action of Congress."[9]

During McLeod's absence, the Utah Congregational work collapsed. In May 1867, however, the Episcopalians arrived in Salt Lake. The fledgling Gentile community quickly turned to them for support. The Episcopalians, however, adopted a tack that differed from McLeod and Robinson. They ignored the Mormons and held their services as they would have in any other part of the land. As Rector Thomas Haskins noted, "It was not to antagonize evil by direct assault, but to plant and maintain a positive good."[10] Another Episcopal Bishop later claimed that his church was out to convert not "Mormons but Mormonism." His successor maintained that the chief goal of the Episcopal church was to "bring to bear upon the Mormon community those influences which would slowly eat away its peculiar tenets and bring it little by little, closer to normal Christianity."[11]

The Episcopalians continued this policy of politely ignoring the

Saints until the early years of the twentieth century. Instead of polemics, they concentrated on establishing numerous institutions throughout Utah, including Salt Lake City's St. Marks hospital, founded in 1872, and several educational centers. The Episcopal rectors seldom mentioned Mormon doctrine or practices in their schools or services. The other denominations accused them of cowardice, but this policy of détente (one that the Roman Catholics also adopted), enabled them to become the best liked of all the church groups.[12]

In the 1860s and 1870s, Protestant optimism remained high. The churches all were convinced that Mormonism would collapse once the light of Scripture had had a chance to penetrate the region. The early missionaries anticipated a tough fight, to be sure, but they had no doubts that they would eventually succeed. The more astute of them, however, admitted that traditional ways might not work and that "everything has to be new and fresh."[13]

Although muted somewhat by events, this semiofficial optimism prevailed for the remainder of the century. Writing from Ogden in 1876, a Congregational missionary predicted that the spread of an open Bible would soon bring victory. The next year, a Salt Lake missionary admitted that while little could be done until Brigham Young's death, the quest for power afterward would surely produce internal schisms that would bring about Zion's collapse.[14] In 1902, an Episcopal Bishop wrote that Mormonism was but "a passing feature" of American life. Three years later a Congregationalist termed it less a religion than "a gigantic political, commercial, co-operative socialism."[15] Such statements, however, were whistling in the dark.

During these decades, the other mainline Protestant churches— the Baptists, Presbyterians, Methodists, and Congregationalists— chose not to adopt the Episcopal policy of détente. In fact, for over fifty years their clergy carried on a virtual cultural war against the Mormons. The scope and nature of the attacks varied with the person and the denomination, but they differed only in degree. Every denomination had its "Mormon expert" who was eager to share his views with anyone who would listen.

McLeod inaugurated this role for the Congregationalists and served it well until the mid-1870s, when Charles R. Bliss, head of the New West Education Commission, took over. Bliss never ceased warning of the danger to America from the Mormons and the "French

Jesuits." Since he served for thirteen years as editor of the society's newsletter, *The New West Gleaner,* he enjoyed a wide forum.[16]

The chief Baptist protagonists were itinerant evangelist M. T. Lamb and pastors Bruce Kinney and J. C. Andrews. In 1885, Lamb toured throughout Utah lecturing on the "fallacies and absurdities" in the Book of Mormon. The next year, he published his lectures under the title *The Golden Bible; or, The Book of Mormon, Is It from God?* Bruce Kinney, who had served a church in Albuquerque before taking charge of the Utah and Wyoming region in 1903, wrote several works along similar lines. His *Mormonism, The Islam of America* (1912) and *Frontier Missionary Problems* (1919) concentrated on the political dangers inherent in the Mormon faith. He accused the Saints of trying to establish an *imperium in imperio* to control both state and national government. The nation had more to fear from the Mormons, he warned, than from any other group of similar size.[17] Mormonism was not just un-American, he said, it was anti-American. Few surpassed Kinney's anti-Mormon rhetoric: "In fact, the whole Mormon system is based upon a bogus book, rotten revelations, tricky translation, a profligate prophet, a counterfeit creed; it is being propagated to-day by a profiting president, abetting apostles, bigoted bishops and plundering priests."[18]

Perhaps the boldest of the early Baptist ministers was Rev. J. C. Andrews, who pastored churches in the Salt Lake area and in Provo during most of the 1890s. Andrews often stood at the Mormon temple enclosure gate at Salt Lake City, where he handed out Baptist tracts to visitors as they left the temple grounds. In 1897–98, he gave a series of Sunday evening lectures on "Mormon Fallacies." He strongly encouraged the students from Provo's Brigham Young Academy to attend them. When the students did come, they joined him in a heated theological discussion that lasted until midnight. Not surprisingly, Andrew feared to go fishing or hiking without a companion. He lived in constant concern for his safety.[19]

The main Methodist protagonist was Thomas Corwin Iliff, who served as Presiding Elder and superintendent of Methodist work in Utah from 1876 to 1900. Like the others, Iliff produced numerous anti-Mormon pamphlets and sermons. He achieved his main reputation, however, from his opposition to polygamist Congressman Brigham H. Roberts. In 1898, after Roberts had been elected to the House of Representatives, Iliff conducted a nationwide speaking tour to urge Congress to reject him because of his polygamy.[20] When

Congress eventually refused to seat Roberts, Iliff claimed much of the credit. Iliff's successor John L. Leilich, superintendent from 1901 to 1904, continued the anti-Mormon thrust, but with less success. He opposed the seating of Utah Senator Reed Smoot in 1902, but when his charge of polygamy could not be proven, Smoot eventually took his seat. This Methodist attack against Smoot was the last major public tilt over the issue of polygamy. A decade earlier, the church had forbidden the "peculiar institution," and gradually (except for certain isolated areas) it faded away.[21]

The Presbyterians offered the Saints their strongest opposition. Rev. R. G. McNiece arrived in Salt Lake in the mid-1870s, and immediately began to supply eastern periodicals with anti-Mormon articles. McNiece charged that the lives of Presbyterian teachers in Utah schools were in danger. The editor of the Mormon *Deseret News* hotly denied these charges. He was especially indignant over the accusation that the Mormons had set fire to one of the Presbyterian school buildings. "If the Mormons wished to burn every sectarian chapel and school house in the territory," he asked, "what is there to hinder them?"[22] For over twenty years, however, McNiece kept up his attacks on the Saints. He frequently served as host for ministers who had come to Salt Lake for a firsthand view of the opposition. Since Salt Lake City lay on the main route of the east–west railroad, he entertained numerous visitors. McNiece provided much of the anti-Mormon material for the national press.

Other Presbyterian clergy joined the battle. Samuel Wishard who served as Synodical Secretary for Utah and Idaho from 1888 to 1915, often wrote and spoke against the Saints. Rev. G. W. Martin, who spent many years serving a church in Manti, Utah, labeled Mormonism "an organized delusion." Reverend Newton E. Clemenson stated in an 1896 pamphlet that "either Christ or Joseph Smith must go down." The Presbyterian General Assembly and writers in the *Home Mission Monthly* also joined the fray.[23]

William M. Padden, who pastored Salt Lake City's First Presbyterian church from 1897 to 1912 and then worked for the Synod until 1931, was the last of these Presbyterian anti-Mormon crusaders. Padden often attacked the Mormons in his sermons. In 1921, when he heard rumors that the president of Logan Agricultural College was a polygamist, he led a crusade to depose him. This overt confrontation, however, was more characteristic of the nineteenth than the twentieth century. After World War I, most of the evangelical ministers reduced their open attacks on the Saints.[24]

In 1897, the Presbytery of Utah drew up a pamphlet (endorsed by both the state Baptists and Congregationalists) entitled *Ten Reasons Why Christians Cannot Fellowship with Mormons.* The list included items that the early missionaries would have found familiar: the Mormon's claim to be the only true Christian church; a critique of their "anthropomorphic" theology; their priesthood; the writings of Joseph Smith; and a final denunciation of polygamy. Two decades later, the Presbyterians reissued the pamphlet. Things had not changed appreciably in the interim.[25]

The standoff that emerged between the Mormons and the Gentile churches provided what historian John D. Thornley has termed "one of the most remarkable studies in group relations afforded by American history."[26] The majority of missionaries could see nothing good in Mormon society. They displayed little of the Christian charity that they directed toward the ex-slaves, Chinese, and recent immigrants. The closest historical analogy might be the tension produced by the North's reconstruction of the South from 1865 to 1877. But reconstruction lasted only twelve years and eventually came to an end. The same could not be said for Gentile–Mormon tensions. They are still very much alive today.

Victorian spokesmen denounced the Latter-day Saints with regularity. Contemporary novelists poured forth such a stream of vitriol that modern historians have been able to discover only five nineteenth-century Gentile novels that could be classified, even vaguely, as "pro-Mormon."[27] Periodic gatherings of national church bodies added to the rhetoric. The following resolution adopted by the Centennial Methodist Conference (1884) conveyed this depth of feeling:

We believe that Mormonism is contrary to the Word of God, irrational, out of harmony with the civilization of the 19th century, and hostile to the peace, prosperity, and perpetuity of the American government. It fosters immorality and defies law; it robs the poor; has paved the roadways of its power with carcasses of the helpless; calls lechery by the name of love, and slavery of women by the divine name of marriage. Its fingers drip with the blood of massacre, and its purse has become plethoric by robbery.[28]

Urged on from many sides, the federal government began to marshal its attack against "that twin relic of barbarism," the polygamous practices of the Saints. In 1882, Congress passed the Edmunds Act, and five years later the Edmunds–Tucker Act, to force the Saints to end plural marriage. The new legislation forced many polygamists into hiding; those who were caught ended in jail.

The Utah Saints blamed the nearby missionaries for these eastern denunciations and far-off congressional decrees. Since the Mormon faith has no "ministers" per se—virtually every male over twelve is admitted to the priesthood—the Mormons developed a special dislike toward the denominational clergy.[29]

One Mormon spokesman bitterly remarked that "[The ministers] have declared war on us and are therefore legitimate targets for counter attack. Unable to agree among themselves on tenet and doctrine, they have yet found, deep in their spiritual bosoms, a common bond of union, hatred of the Mormons."[30] Because of this antagonism, the home missionaries generally played an insignificant role in Mormon community life. Although they were seldom mistreated or ostracized, they simply "didn't belong." "Some of the fault for this," confessed a former Baptist missionary to Utah, "may lie with the attitude of the minister toward Mormons."[31]

Mormon culture as a whole, however, proved unsuitable for general assault. Consequently, the clergy began to seize on certain aspects of it for emphasis. Soon, two themes emerged as the chief items of denunciation: the practice of polygamy and the Mountain Meadows Massacre of 1857. These items played the same role for Utah's Protestants as the rites of the Penitentes had served for their counterparts in New Mexico: each provided a stark symbol of the dangers inherent in the opposition.

Ever since its official announcement in 1852, the concept of plural marriage had both shocked and titillated the Gentile world. Within a few years, the doctrine of polygamy had given the Saints a worldwide reputation. As part of their crusade against plural marriage, the denominational clergy made special efforts to enlist the aid of the Protestant women. American women had helped drive slavery from the land, they said; now, they needed to turn their attention to the plight of their sisters in Utah. Although the majority of the plural wives acquiesced in their status as part of God's will, the revolt of the few—especially Brigham Young's recalcitrant wife Ann Eliza Young—became steady grist for their mill.

The story of the Mountain Meadows Massacre proved equally powerful as a symbol of the foe. In the fall of 1857 a group of Arkansas and Missouri immigrants, known as the Fancher train, were making their way through southern Utah on their way to California. Unfortunately, they chose an awkward time to pass through Zion, for an American army battalion was then marching on Utah. On the morning of September 7, a group of Mormon militiamen and their Indian allies attacked the caravan without warning. One hundred and twenty people were killed in what still ranks as the worst incident of religious violence in American history.

Afterward, the Gentiles maintained that the attackers had operated under direct orders from Brigham Young. The Mormons, however, exonerated Young and placed the sole blame on the Indians. Twenty years later, the government tried, convicted, and executed Mormon John D. Lee for the crime, but he clearly served only as a scapegoat.

But the story of the massacre did not fade with Lee's execution. Over the years it was continually refurbished through song, folklore, and legend. Few missionaries to Utah remained unfamiliar with its basic theme. "It is hard to realize that such a horrid slaughter of human beings could have taken place in this free land," remarked the Presbyterian *Home Mission Monthly*, "and in the name of religion."[32] Even the most recent book on the event is subtitled "a monumental crime."[33] Current sentiment is still so sensitive that the site of the catastrophe receives no official recognition from the state of Utah.[34]

When the Gentile clergy began to arrive in the Salt Lake Valley in the 1860s and early 1870s, Brigham Young occasionally allowed them to speak in Mormon facilities. He opened the Salt Lake tabernacle to both Presbyterian and Methodist speakers, and he allowed a Catholic priest to celebrate Mass in the tabernacle at St. George. Methodist Bishop Calvin Kingsley once spoke to a large Salt Lake tabernacle audience on the theme of "The Kingdom of Heaven." In the course of his discourse he mentioned dying and "going to Abraham's bosom." After the sermon, Brigham Young brought down the house by observing that if Bishop Kingsley did as planned, "he will go to the bosom of an old polygamist."[35] Young seemed to have a special regard for the Methodists. When two of their visiting ministers introduced themselves to him on the street, he extended his hand with a smile saying, "I am glad to meet you, I was once a Methodist myself."[36] Young, however, clearly had a motive with his ecumenical stance. He wanted to show the Saints how much better off the Mormons were when compared with other denominations.

The mainline clergy readily availed themselves of every opportunity for public debate with the Saints. To their dismay, they discovered that the Mormons rather enjoyed this theological jousting. Young must have seen these public disputes as yet another means of strengthening the faith of Zion. Once he boasted that "our elders can outpreach them all."

Perhaps the most dramatic of these public exchanges came during June 12–14, 1870, when Methodist minister J. P. Newman, chaplain of the United States Senate, debated Mormon Apostle Orson Pratt in the tabernacle at Salt Lake. The issue of the debate was polygamy. Both men drew on a wide knowledge of Scripture to argue their position. Newman maintained that the main biblical statement on marriage could be seen in the first marriage of Adam and Eve. Since it was monogamous, God had obviously intended this as the ideal for mankind. Pratt countered by citing all the numerous Old Testament patriarchs who had several wives.[37]

This exchange was widely attended. Ten thousand people heard the third debate. It also received national attention through *Harpers Weekly,* which covered it thoroughly. Fourteen years later, Baptist Richard Hartley and Elder Ben E. Rich held another major public debate in the Ogden tabernacle.[38] These debates could best be labeled as standoffs, for each protagonist clearly held his own in the search for proof texts from the various books of Scripture.

Around the turn of the century the Protestant missionaries shifted their strategy. They began to rely on history and literature rather than Scripture as their battleground. Episcopal Bishop Franklin Spalding led this change in emphasis. Convinced that reliance on isolated biblical proof texts was unsatisfactory, Spalding shifted the argument to include psychology, biblical criticism, and a reexamination of the Mormon historical sources. This can best be seen in his 1909 pamphlet "Joseph Smith, Jr., as a Translator." In this essay, Spalding sought to expose what he termed the mistakes in Smith's "translation" of the Egyptian *Book of Abraham.* The clear implication, of course, was that Smith was also in error with his *Book of Mormon.* Spalding must have touched a nerve, for over thirty replies

to his work appeared in the *Deseret Evening News,* all defending
the accuracy of Joseph Smith's version.[39] The Bishop also had plans
to introduce a new series of similar anti-Mormon pamphlets. Only
his untimely death in 1914, when he was accidentally struck and
killed by one of the few autos in Salt Lake, prevented this step. But
his "Joseph Smith, Jr., as a Translator" signaled the shift of the opposition from a biblical base to a historical and literary one. There it
has remained to this day.[40]

When the Protestant ministers arrived in Utah in the 1860s, the
situation there seemed as formidable as New Mexico had appeared
to their counterparts in the 1850s. Only Salt Lake, Ogden, and
Corrine—founded when the railroad entered the valley in 1869—
held any Gentiles. Two decades later, in the community of American Fork Canyon, for example, only twenty of two thousand people were not Saints. Paralleling their New Mexico experience, the
denominations turned primarily to schools, and later to itinerant
evangelists, to undermine the Mormon hierarchy.

The missionaries often charged that the Mormons had no schools
before the Protestants arrived to establish them. This is not quite
accurate. The Mormons did open some schools while they were
alone in the region from 1849 to 1864. The University of Utah was
chartered in 1850; and the Saints also tried to establish "fee schools,"
where the local communities taxed themselves for the buildings
but left the expenses and teachers' salaries to the parents of school-
aged children.[41] Under this system, the teachers utilized the main
public buildings in town for classes and spent Saturdays in visiting
the students' homes to collect their pay. Payment usually came in
kind: grain, flour, pigs, or whatever the family could afford. Brigham Young had grown up under this system in Vermont and he
could conceive of no other. Young's strength lay in the realm of
practical matters rather than theory. As late as 1873 he declared
that "I am utterly opposed to free schools." He also stated that "I
will not give one dollar to educate another man's child."[42]

Hence, the early Mormon schools were few and unsatisfactory.
Although the University of Utah existed on paper, it had no campus, faculty, or students until much later. In the early years few
Utahans were qualified to go on to college, let alone teach. No public lands were set aside for education and the Mormon community, comprised largely of humble people, resisted such taxation. As
one observer wrote in 1869, "Most school masters in Utah are Gen-

tiles, as there are very few intelligent men among the natives."[43] Many of the Mormon converts who had emigrated from Europe came from similar backgrounds. One English-born settler marveled at the "learnin'" of young photographer W. H. Jackson (who had an eighth grade education).[41] Clearly, the majority of the Gilded Age Mormons lacked formal education. Lack of education, however, did not necessarily mean a lack of intelligence.

Most early Mormon teachers could not devote full time to the task. As books were rare in Utah, the teachers often used the Mormon Scriptures as texts, for copies of these were found in every home. This meant that the religious message of Sunday and the secular message of the week proved almost identical. Some schools even insisted on using the Deseret alphabet. The early Mormons did establish schools, then, but these were essentially Mormon parochial schools.[45]

As soon as they reached Utah, the Protestant ministers began their rival educational program. Within two or three days after the Episcopalians had arrived in 1867, they had opened a school. The Methodists began theirs in 1870; the Presbyterians in 1875; the Congregationalists in 1880. All were convinced that the schools would serve as the most effective way to crack Zion's stronghold.

The Protestant churches devoted much of their energies to educational endeavors. Baptists and Methodists together established about thirty schools, while Episcopalians founded several highly regarded academies, located in such places as Reno, Salt Lake, Ogden, and Logan. They also established several smaller mission schools in outlying districts. The Utah Protestant mission schools were so well known that President Grover Cleveland praised them in his 1884 message to Congress. It was estimated that twenty thousand children went through the Congregational schools and perhaps fifty thousand through the Presbyterian system.[46]

As in New Mexico, the Congregationalists and Presbyterians proved the most zealous advocates of schooling. In both areas, the Congregationalists utilized their New West Education Commission. Spearheaded by Charles R. Bliss, the denomination spent about three-quarters of a million dollars and sent 720 missionaries to teach in thirty-six schools in Utah and New Mexico. Aided by Colorado College, they also established academies in Salt Lake, Ogden, and Provo, as well as other places. At one point they administered twenty-nine schools scattered throughout rural Utah. "The Mormon people will send their children to our day schools," crowed one missionary, "and Brigham and his bishops can't prevent it."[47]

The Presbyterians also established an impressive educational program in Utah, all directed by the Women's Board of Home Missions. They built a total of forty-nine schools there, although not all were operating at the same time. Led by Reverend Duncan McMillan of Mount Pleasant, they devised a scheme to place an elementary school in the main town of each of the six great valleys of Utah: Cache, Salt Lake, Utah, Sanpete, Sevier, and Iron County. They hoped that each school would eventually grow into an academy, fed by a satellite system of primary schools in the outlying regions. A Presbyterian college in Salt Lake would cap the system. From 1875 to 1915, the church may have invested as much as 1.5 million dollars in the operation.[48]

The Protestant churches realized that the people of Utah could be reached by no other means. "I am confident that this is *the way*," remarked a Congregational missionary, "and the only way." In 1891, the Episcopal Bishop of Nevada and Utah called the schools "the cheapest and most efficient missionary agents we can employ in these towns."[49]

Numbers seemed to bear this out. In 1883, the Presbyterians had enrolled about two thousand students in thirty-three schools in Utah and Idaho. An 1887 statistical breakdown of students showed that 26 percent were from Mormon homes, 11 percent from half-Mormon homes, and 40 percent from Apostate homes. In 1890, about 67 percent of Utah's children were enrolled in Protestant mission schools.

Generally speaking, these mission schools were of high caliber. The New West Education Commission hired only college graduates, and a few even held master's degrees. Teachers who proved inadequate were quickly dismissed. The teachers, many of whom were from New England, obtained their maps, bells, organs, and curriculum materials from the East. They bolstered their classroom techniques with annual teachers' institutes. Rejecting the Deseret Alphabet, they introduced McGuffey Readers and graded instruction. Several academies offered music and Latin, college preparation, and pedagogy for those who planned to teach. In addition to the Ten Commandments, the Sermon on the Mount, and Bible reading, the mission teachers also emphasized the celebration of Thanksgiving, Christmas, Washington's Birthday, Easter, Memorial Day, and Independence Day.

The Protestant emphasis on Bible reading and "Americanization" had considerable long-term impact. Their celebration of the traditional holidays also helped bring the Mormon children into the cultural mainstream. Prior to this, the Mormon schools had observed only their own holidays: April 6, the birthday of the Mormon church; July 24, Pioneer Day; December 23, the birthday of Joseph Smith, Jr.; June 1, the birthday of Brigham Young; and various Jubilees.[50]

Duncan McMillan urged the Presbyterians to select women for their teaching positions, and this policy was adopted by all the denominations. Protestant women had access to Mormon homes in a way that the men did not. The Baptists, too, always saw the women teachers as paving the way for the missionary.[51]

While no accurate statistics have survived, perhaps as many as a thousand women were involved in the Utah program of Protestant parochial education. Most of them were single, and the turnover proved rapid. Some married locally, occasionally even Mormons, but the majority returned to the East after a year or two. Of the 279 teachers listed in a New West history, for example, only 183 served for at least two years.[52]

Mormon farmer William H. Henry, Jr., recalled how Virginia Dix, a highly cultured middle-aged woman, won the heart of Oxford, Idaho, by her skill in the classroom and her gracious personality. She introduced a literary society, a class on Spenserian writing, poetry, and Bible memorization. Another Mormon student recalled, "They were New England teachers and believe me, they dwelled on that stuff."[53]

The women in rural areas did not limit their work to school hours. One of them, a widow by the name of Mrs. M. M. Green, lived and worked in Gunnison, Utah, for over eight years. After school Mrs. Green began a sewing school, a "kitchengarden" and a cooking school. On Wednesday evenings, she staged a popular lecture, musical, or debate, or held an evening with a historical figure. She also opened a reading room. Since she had some acquaintance with medicine, Mrs. Green gave a series of lectures on public health laws, and occasionally advised families on proper medicines. The local Mormon bishop praised her efforts in the realm of public health.

In 1890 Utah passed its first comprehensive public school law. It was to prove a harbinger of change. While the Protestant parochial schools did not decline immediately, the handwriting was on the wall. Three years later, the Episcopalians closed their Logan academy and threw their support behind the public schools. In 1897, Thomas Iliff recommended that denominational budget cuts be made in the school program rather than in the churches. The Presbyterians began to phase out their primary schools in order to concentrate on the academies and the proposed college in Salt Lake City. Today, only the Presbyterian Watsach Academy in Mount Pleasant remains in operation.

The proposed Protestant college always served as a bone of contention, as each of the three evangelical denominations—Congregationalists, Methodists, and Presbyterians—had plans for a Salt Lake institution of higher education.[54] After some bitterness, the Presbyterians won out. Their victory was assured through the largesse of Sheldon Jackson. In 1894, Jackson met Duncan McMillan in New York to discuss how to dispose of a fund that Jackson had inherited. Jackson had hoped to establish a Presbyterian college in Santa Fe, but McMillan convinced him that Salt Lake City had more potential for success. The school was to become the "Princeton" of the region, but financial problems continued to plague its operation. In 1911, the college—renamed Westminster—opened its doors at the present location. Five years later, the college held its first large graduating exercises. All the major Utah denominations—Methodists, Congregationalists, Presbyterians, and Episcopalians—contributed financially to its operation. Their cooperation was touted as a model of interdenominational efforts but, actually, it was a cooperation of necessity rather than a blueprint for the future.

As an adjunct to their program of education, the Protestant churches also relied on the efforts of itinerant missionaries. One of the first of these was Methodist H. D. Fisher who, in 1883, made a six-month tour of Utah for the American Bible Society. Fisher carefully avoided controversy and concentrated on simply distributing free Bibles. He received modest cooperation from Mormon authorities and even set up a few joint Gentile–Mormon Bible reading groups. When one Mormon objected that Fisher was trying to get his people "mixed up," Fisher replied, "You Latter-day Saints are going to heaven, and as we Gentiles want to go there, too, I thought it would be well to get acquainted beforehand."[55] The Protestant clergy felt confident that if the Bible were distributed widely enough, its light would undermine the Mormon reliance on Joseph Smith's teachings.

After the 1890 school law went into operation, the Protestants offered further encouragement to their itinerant evangelists. From the late 1880s onward, Congregationalists, Methodists, Presbyterians, and Baptists all expanded their Utah itinerancy programs. Methodist Emil E. Mork began his itinerant work in 1885 and spent his entire thirty-nine year career in the state, moving his gospel tent from town to town on a regular basis. Presbyterians Samuel Wishard and George Martin carried so much apparatus with them that they resembled a traveling carnival. In 1898, the Baptists established a "Gospel Wagon" that eventually distributed over twenty-thousand free tracts and Bibles.[56]

Probably the last important representatives of these polemical itinerants were Presbyterian George P. Peacock, Jr., and Congregationalist John D. Nutting. An 1895 Mormon convert to Presbyterianism from southern Utah, Peacock was educated at the Manti Mission School. After several years of working on a farm, he began his travels in 1899. Ordained in 1909, Peacock's denominational sanction was removed in 1931; nevertheless, he carried his evangelical message across Utah until his death in 1950.[57]

John D. Nutting arrived in Salt Lake City in 1892 and organized the "Utah Gospel Mission" eight years later. For the next fifty years, he and a team of "wagon missionaries" also traversed the state. He headed what became informally known as the "Department of Theological Controversy." As late as 1927 he complained that the other churches had dropped their theological challenge to the Saints. While the other denominations had decided to work *with* the Mormons, Nutting worked primarily to convert them. Although his converts were few, Nutting left a remarkable legacy. His contemporary photographs are preserved in over one hundred glass negatives that depict life in Utah from 1900 to the 1930s.[58]

Perhaps the most perceptive Utah missionary accounts may be found in *Ambassador to the Saints* (1965) by Presbyterian missionary Claton S. Rice. A student at Princeton, Rice arrived in St. George, Utah, in 1908. He spent much of the next ten years in ministering to the Saints. He was initially greeted with hostile stares and indifference. One sheepman told him that he spoke without authority and that he should not try to lead their young people astray.

Rice's account of his life with the Saints is unique in two respects. First, he found himself caught in the emerging liberal–conservative theological split in his own Presbyterian denomination. Thus, he developed theological doubts of his own. In 1909, he left Utah for further study. Whenever he had the chance, Rice queried other Protestant leaders about their beliefs. Accused by the Mormons of being "without authority," he also remained suspicious of the various Presbyterian statements of creed. He developed doubts that led him to question whether he could rely on his own reading of Scripture to understand God's absolute truth.

Even more important, Rice learned to appreciate the virtues of Mormon society. He grew to admire their loyalty to the group, their willingness to tithe, their extensive recreation program, and their desire to give each person a standing in their community. When he transferred his work to northeastern Utah, he observed how the Mormon community of Roosevelt was able to establish irrigation successfully, while the nearby Gentile community at Myton was unable to agree on a program and failed. In 1930, he expressed this appreciation by publishing a collection of *Songs of "The Mormon Way."* "I found much to admire in the Saints," he confessed.[59]

Rice was a versatile man. During his years in Utah, he trained debaters, taught violin, coached sports, and played baseball. When the Dixie Academy began in St. George, he introduced both baseball and tennis. His chief entry into the community, he discovered, came through his athletic skills. "Although my theology might be heterodox," he noted, "they soon discovered that my baseball was orthodox."[60] While the Mormon community was willing to use Rice's skills in a myriad of ways, he later confessed that he had little impact on the region in terms of converts. But his appreciation of the virtues of Mormon life makes his memoir unusual.

In 1914, after years of frustration, the Gentile churches adopted what they termed the "Utah plan." This called for a consolidation of rural mission work in the larger centers of population. During the same year, the churches established the Utah Interdenominational Commission and the Utah Home Mission Workers Council. Gradually, the churches agreed among themselves to vacate areas if another denomination had a mission in the region. These pragmatic adjustments were made in nineteen places across the state. As another example of ecumenical cooperation, this method, like the founding of Westminster College, was born of necessity rather than conviction.

From the beginning, the Mormon leadership viewed this Protestant crusade with a jaundiced eye. The Protestants themselves anticipated this reaction. As Bishop George Randall wrote to Bishop Tuttle in 1867, "I suppose that an open attempt to convert Brigham Young's followers would be followed by very unpleasant consequences."[61] After the Mountain Meadows Massacre of 1857 and the death of Robinson, however, the Saints turned to simple harassment rather than violent opposition.

The harassment assumed several different forms. In the early days, for example, no Mormon would sell land or water rights to a Gentile. Those Saints who traded at the Gentile stores were warned to desist. An occasional document shows disfellowshipping of those parents who sent their children to the Gentile schools.[62] One missionary reported in 1886 that "the most opprobrious title which children on the street can apply to our children is 'Presbyterian.' "[63]

Missionaries in the isolated settlements were especially vulnerable. When Emil E. Mork arrived in Santaquin in 1885, no one would tell him where the post office was located. After Presbyterian Edward Murphy moved into St. George in the 1880s, he attended a Mormon service and heard himself denounced from the podium. At the end of the service, the bishop proclaimed a curse on the Presbyterian work in St. George.[64] When Duncan McMillan arrived in Ephraim, Utah, he was greeted by Bishop Knute Peterson, who said, "Are you that damned Presbyterian devil who is preaching at Mount Pleasant?" When Brigham Young visited the area, he called McMillan a series of names. Young urged the Mormons of Mount Pleasant to depose McMillan, depicting him as "a wolf who enters the corral and begins to destroy the sheep."[65]

Even the women teachers were occasionally harassed. When the mission school opened in Fillmore in 1880, the Bishop denounced all the Presbyterian women who came to teach there. Unless Apostates lived in the region, many had difficulty finding lodging. Some were insulted by the Mormon men. A Baptist teacher complained from Provo in 1899 that little children had thrown mud and stones at her and that verbal abuse was commonplace. Perhaps the most serious incident, however, occurred in Spanish Fork when someone fired a shot through the window of the school. The teacher, Lucy Perley, allegedly remarked, "Children, there is no reason to be afraid of a man who can't shoot straighter than that."[66] The schools and their teachers always lay at the heart of the Mormon–Gentile conflict.[67]

All things considered, however, the situation remained relatively peaceful for most of the period. McMillan's policy of sending the women to the West proved a very wise one for both sides. While the Mormon parents might disapprove of their presence, many of the Mormon children grew to know and admire their teachers. Victorian sensibilities, moreover, dictated that no man would harm a woman, regardless of her faith.

In 1907, a Mormon asked Methodist E. E. Mork if he were still preaching the gospel. When Mork replied that he was, the man noted, "Well, we Mormons are hard cases; you can not catch us very easy; you don't make many converts."[68] Generally speaking, this was true. Although the Protestants made a few prominent converts, their numbers were never large. The Gentile percentage of the population of Utah showed little increase over the years. The 1870 census, for example, noted 730 Protestants out of 100,000; 1884 accounted for 1,848 out of 169,000; 1890, 4,645 of 208,000; 1906, 7,423 of 335,000; and 1914, 8,767 of 404,000. The Protestant population continued to rise, but only in the same proportion as the Gentile immigration to Utah. This meant that few Mormons were turning to the Gentile churches for their spiritual welfare. A financial assessment of the Protestant effort is also revealing. An 1895 circular estimated that it cost the Baptists 177 dollars for each Utah convert, Methodists 500 dollars, Congregationalists 880 dollars, and Presbyterians 1,028 dollars.[69] By 1895, of the eighty Protestant churches in Utah, only eight had become self-supporting. A 1950 census listed only 17,500 Protestant church members out of a state population of 620,000.

What limited successes the Protestants had came when they were able to draw on existing dissension within the Saints. They established their strongest toeholds in areas which attracted Apostate immigrants. The Benjamin, Utah, Presbyterian church (1886–1916), for example, was composed almost entirely of three disfellowshipped Mormon families. The Apostates welcomed Duncan McMillan's attempt to set up a parochial school in Mount Pleasant in 1875; they told him he could preach (and they would even attend), "but they would not believe anything I might say about religion; as they were done with all that kind of stuff."[70] Claton Rice enjoyed the

company of several Apostates in Dixie, but noted that they often
found themselves unable to trust any church. Rice knew of one
young man who had decided to reject the Book of Mormon. Nonetheless, he had also decided to remain within the church because
"the Mormon church is a good clan to belong to."[71]

The Utah missionaries, therefore, dealt with failure on a daily basis.
The Episcopal Missionary Bishop of Nevada and Utah reported in
1897 that he had determined not to visit most small towns, because
they were solely Mormon, and attempting to work in them meant
spending money with no results. In 1912, Bruce Kinney reported
that ninety out of four hundred Utah towns had no Protestant work
at all.[72] A woman teacher from Malad City wrote in 1888 that the
conversion of the Mormons seemed almost hopeless. One missionary observed in 1913 that "it seems like I have been beating my
head against a stone wall." The rapid turnover in both mission school-
teachers and Utah clergymen probably reflects this frustration. In
1882, Methodist Superintendent Thomas Iliff called Utah the most
difficult mission field on the entire globe.[73]

A considerable part of the Protestant failure to convert the Mormons, however, may also be traced to the Saints' aggressive response
to their crusade. Beginning in the 1870s, the Mormons inaugurated an alternative educational program of their own. Brigham Young
Academy opened in Provo in 1870, and Brigham Young College in
Logan two years later. After 1887, the Saints began to establish a
system of church-supported academies and junior colleges in all of
their major settlements. From 1890 to 1929 they instituted after-
hours weekday training classes for elementary school children. In
1912, they began their plan to establish several hundred seminaries for young adults adjacent to the public schools.[74] All of these
programs were clearly aimed at countering the Protestant school
network. In the end, they were successful.

Ironically, the Protestant schools helped provide training that the
Saints eventually bent to their own needs. Over the course of his
life, the prophet Joseph Smith, Jr., made several statements con-
cerning education. In 1833 he said, "the glory of God is intelligence";
ten years later, he remarked, "It is impossible for a man to be saved
in ignorance," and "If a person gains more knowledge and intelligence in this life through his diligence and obedience than another, he will have so much the advantage in the world to come."[75]

Thus, Mormon educators eventually drew on Smith's observations to construct their own system of instruction.

The Saints also thwarted the Protestant efforts through their open appreciation of the need for recreation. Young and his successors demonstrated a much better understanding of human nature in this regard than did the Protestant clergy. While the nineteenth-century ministers never actually opposed fun, several of them walked rather close to the edge.[76] The Methodists, Baptists, and some Presbyterians tended to view dancing with a jaundiced eye. From the earliest days, however, the Mormons leaned the other way. At the January 1847 encampment near Council Bluffs, Brigham Young observed, "If thou art merry, praise the Lord with singing, with music, with dancing, and with a prayer of praise and thanksgiving."[77]

The Saints maintained this emphasis on social celebration after they reached Utah. Unlike the other religious leaders of his day, Young encouraged both the theatre and social dancing. As one visitor marveled in 1862, "The Prophet dances, the Apostles dance, the Bishops dance."[78] Indeed, the Saints danced with vigor. They performed square dances, quadrilles, the Varsouvienne, Virginia Reel, Berlin Polka, Heel and Toe Polka, the Schottishe, the Waltz, the Two Step, and the "polygamy dance." The festivities usually opened and closed with a prayer and often lasted all day or all night. A dance climaxed every celebration or festival of importance. Such social dancing served much the same role for Utah as the camp meetings provided on the southern Great Plains. They brought isolated people together for a combined secular and religious occasion.

It is interesting to speculate why the Protestants were relatively more successful with the Hispanics in New Mexico than with the Mormons in Utah. One would postulate that it might have been the other way around. The Hispanics reflected a lengthy tradition of Roman Catholicism, while the Mormons remained very close to both the theology and the polity of the major evangelical Protestant churches. Yet this very similarity may have been the reason for the Protestant lack of success.

One key difference between the Hispanics and the Mormons lay in their response to the open Bible. The words of the Old and New Testaments carry a power that can move the scholar in his study as well as the farm wife at her daily chores. In both New Mexico and Utah, the Protestants spent much time in emphasizing the words of Scripture. In fact, most Hispanics who joined the Protestant churches did so because of their individual reading of the Bible. But the Mormons already had an open Bible. The Saints considered Scripture as part of their canon, and it was daily fare in many Mormon homes. The Mormons never denied the Old and New Testaments, nor doubted their worth as sources of revelation. They simply *added* to them with the *Book of Mormon, Pearl of Great Price, Doctrines and Covenants,* and the official statements of the current prophet of the church. Consequently, they never argued against Scripture. This unique situation blunted the main thrust of the Protestant missionary. As Bishop Tuttle once observed, the scriptural arguments of the evangelists could never quite find their mark.[79]

As with New Mexico, the overall result of the Protestant effort in Utah does not lend itself well to measurement. Presbyterian spokesman Herbert W. Rehard once listed the main Protestant accomplishments in Zion as follows: the destruction of polygamy; the conversion of several Mormons; the inauguration of a school system that eventually laid the basis for effective public schools; the achievement of toleration for the other Christian churches; and the increasing Mormon loyalty to the United States.[80]

Bishop Tuttle credited the Protestant efforts with changing "the fanatical, oligarchic community of 1867 into the American Utah of today [1900]."[81] Some clerics even suggested that all they had ever wanted to do was to draw the Mormons more closely into the mainstream of the Christian tradition, but this was clearly after-the-fact reasoning. Yet by World War I, the 'mainstreaming' of the Mormons had occurred. In 1883, Henry Ward Beecher had observed that the Mormons were "not altogether strange." He praised them for their sound morality and for their faith in Scripture. It was a deeper faith, he noted, than one found in many a church audience.[82] In 1917, Methodist Superintendent John J. Lace noted that he heard many Mormons proclaim a more orthodox version of the Gospel than some professors in the Methodist theological seminaries.[83] The rise of the Fundamentalist–Modernist controversy of the 1920s was to accelerate this process. As the mainline churches found themselves divided into liberal and conservative wings, the Saints began to appear more and more like another "conservative" denomination.[84] Three generations of Protestant missionaries had played a distinct role in this transformation.

Chapter Eight

The Exceptional Populations

III: The Native Americans

The third group of the "exceptional populations"—the Native Americans—provided the western ministers with perhaps their greatest challenge. The Protestant missions to the Indians proved very different from the parallel mission programs to the Mormons and the Hispanics. Church mission efforts to the latter groups were relatively new; both began in earnest only after the Civil War. Missions to the Indians, however, drew on a heritage that reached back over 250 years. Virtually all of the Gilded Age missionaries knew of the exploits of their celebrated predecessors: John Eliot, John and David Brainerd, Samuel Kirkland, the Mayhew family, Francis LeJau, Samuel Worcester, Marcus and Narcissa Whitman, Henry and Eliza Spalding, and Father Pierre Jean de Smet. Moreover, from the first cultural exchange to the 1920s, mission goals remained basically the same: to "Christianize" and "civilize" the American Indians.[1]

Protestant missions to the Mormons and the Hispanics, of course, drew funding solely from the denominations involved. But the church missions to the Indians relied on a partnership with the federal government. Although the Constitition sundered the bonds of church and state in 1787, this separation had never really applied to Indian affairs. Beginning with George Washington's administration, the government worked hand-in-glove with the churches in a joint attempt to solve the "Indian problem."[2]

The missionaries to the Indians often found themselves at the forefront of the cultural confrontation between Anglo-American and native ways of life. Generally speaking, the missionary goals were all-inclusive: "to make them English in language, civilized in habits, and Christian in religion."[3] Thus, they demanded that Indian converts reject all the trappings of native life. This position often accelerated the disintegration of Indian culture. But the cultural confrontation between the two groups was always multidimensional. The missionaries formed but one part of a wide variety of influences simultaneously bearing down on the Native Americans. These included a complicated treaty system, hunger for Indian land, corrupt traders and Indian agents, the presence of the army, the destruction of the buffalo, and the pervasive popular belief that the Indian was a wild beast who would soon disappear.[4]

By the close of the Civil War, American Indian policy had reached a point of crisis. Numerous confrontations by the Great Plains tribes brought forth harsh responses from the United States Army. The Bureau of Indian Affairs had earned the dubious reputation as the most corrupt of all federal agencies. Several reformers, such as Oregonian John Beeson and Minnesota Episcopal Bishop Henry Whipple, increasingly called for a change in national policy. In 1865, the Senate inaugurated its own two-year investigation of Indian affairs.[5]

President Ulysses S. Grant had prior firsthand acquaintance with Indian issues. Early in his administration, he launched his only claim to statesmanship, the famous Grant's Peace Policy. As historian Francis Paul Prucha has noted, this program proved "almost as many-faceted as the Indian problem it hoped to solve."[6] Viewed in the broadest sense, Grant's proposals established the basic framework for Indian–white relations for the next three generations. The Peace Policy ended the old treaty system, which viewed each tribe as a separate "nation"; it encouraged the government to direct its attention to the individual Indian as much as the tribe, a program that culminated in the Dawes Act of 1887; and it restricted the nomadic tribes to specific reservations, either by persuasion or force, as well as promising to provide sufficient rations, tools, seeds, and other benefits. In addition, the federal government promised to establish schools for Indian children. The ultimate goal of this effort was to prepare the Indians for complete assimilation and eventual citizenship.

From the churches' point of view, the most challenging aspect of Grant's new program was the opportunity to select the federal Indian agents who would serve on the various reservations. In effect,

historian Henry Fritz observed, Congress reacted to the demand
for reform by unloading the whole Indian problem onto the American churches.[7]

Thus, Congress appointed a Board of Indian Commissioners which
assigned the approximately seventy Indian reservations to the major
American churches. Prior mission work with the tribe was to be
the main criterion for selection. After considerable deliberation,
the board awarded the Northern Methodists fourteen agencies with
54,473 Indians; the Northern Baptists five with 40,800; the Congregationalists three with 14,476; the Episcopalians eight with
26,929; the Northern Presbyterians nine with 38,069; and so on.
Nobody sought the Indians' opinion on the matter.[8]

Much to the board's surprise, the decision brought forth cries of
protest that the distribution had been unfair. Several denominations
found themselves completely left out of the process. The Mormons,
for example, had accomplished a great deal of prior missionary work,
but their theology and practice of polygamy made them totally unac-
ceptable. Although Moravian missions dated from the early eighteenth century, they too were bypassed. The Southern Baptist,
Southern Methodist, and Southern Presbyterian churches probably
had the largest numbers of Indian members. But the Civil War was
far too fresh for the board to allow them to "Christianize" any Indian groups.

The greatest objection to the board's distribution policy, however, came not from the Protestants but from the Roman Catholics. Initially, the Catholic church claimed prior rights to forty-two
agencies, but the board awarded them only seven, which they
accepted. Since the board included no Catholic member, church
spokesmen claimed discrimination. As a counter action, the Catholics then established their own Bureau of Catholic Indian Missions.
In the process, through a system of contract schools, they secured
considerable aid from the government.[9] Thus, the Peace Policy unex-
pectedly introduced a forty-year religious struggle among the
nation's churches that recalled some of the quarrels of sixteenth-
century Europe.[10]

The church appointment of federal reservation agents, sometimes
called the "Quaker Policy," lasted approximately ten years. Virtually all historians who have studied this decade conclude that it produced no appreciable improvements in Indian–white relations. The
rapid turnover of the new Peace Policy agents—the average stay

was only 2.3 years—certainly contributed to this stagnation.[11] The lack of accomplishment clearly showed that the dilemmas of American Indian policy extended much further than mere administrative malfeasance.[12] Even the appointment of "good people" did not alter the situation.

The "Quaker Policy" of the 1870s, however, did have a significant impact on American church life. It firmly propelled the major denominations into the arena of Indian affairs. Within a decade, the churches lost their power to appoint Indian agents, but they never really lost their interest in Indian work. From the 1870s until the present day, the mainline denominations have generally maintained a concern for "their" tribes and reservations.

Consequently, from the 1870s forward, hundreds of missionaries and their families traveled west to serve on Indian reservations. Some stayed six months, others remained sixty years. Regardless of their length of service, they formed an integral part of the western religious experience.

Throughout the late nineteenth century, the turnover in Indian mission service remained high. The majority of missionaries, therefore, probably had minimal impact on their tribes. For example, the Methodists terminated their 1879 mission to the Comanche after less than a year. Presbyterians William Truax and James Roberts worked diligently to establish mission schools for the San Felipe and Santo Domingo pueblos, but the Indians wanted no part of them. A German Lutheran missionary to the San Carlos Apache remained less than a year because he could command neither English nor Apache. Dr. Taylor S. Ealy and his wife spent four years (1877–81) at Zuni Pueblo in total frustration. As Presbyterian Corrie Pond said of her Indian mission work: "It is like throwing rubber balls against the wall. . . . They bounce back into our faces."[13]

Others, however, had considerably more endurance. Scores of missionaries spent their entire lives in working with the tribes of the Great Plains and Mountain West. Many of them left behind a significant local legacy. Among the most important figures were John Roberts with the Arapaho and Shoshone of Wyoming; Sue L. McBeth with the Nez Perce of Idaho; William Hobart Hare with the Sioux of South Dakota; Charles H. Cook among the Pima of Arizona; and John J. Methvin and Joseph Samuel Morrow among the western Oklahoma tribes. Their impact on these Indian groups often resulted from the blending of the personality and message of the missionary with the specific needs of the Indians themselves.

In February 1883, Welsh-born John Roberts arrived in Wyoming to open an Episcopal mission among the Arapaho and Shoshone of the Wind River reservation. He remained among his "adopted people" for over fifty years. After learning the languages of these two long-term enemies, thrown together on the same reservation through the vagaries of American Indian policy, he tried to ease their way into modern society.

Shortly after his arrival, Roberts and his wife opened a pair of schools for Indian boys and girls. Their girls' boarding school (1889–1945) enjoyed a wide following because Roberts ran it in a creative fashion. Roberts relied on bilingual education, using both English and Indian languages in his curriculum. In recognizing the cultural dislocation that often beset the girls, he built a circular log cabin for them on the school grounds. Constructed in the fashion of a tipi, he encouraged the girls to practice their native songs and dances there.

Over the years, Roberts became fully acquainted with the Arapaho and Shoshone ways of life. The Department of the Interior recognized him as an expert on both Arapaho and Shoshone language and customs. He also gained a modest national reputation by maintaining that the one-hundred-year-old woman whom he buried in 1884 was Sacajawea, the famed Shoshone guide of Lewis and Clark.

Roberts's impact on the Arapaho (he was less successful with the Shoshone) relied on several items. First, the missionary struck up a deep and lasting friendship with Chiefs Washakie and Black Coal, eventually baptizing the former into the Episcopal church. Both chiefs wanted the tribe's young people to be educated in the white man's ways. Thus, they aided Roberts's schools whenever they could. Roberts declared that Washakie and Black Coal were "two of the greatest men" he had ever known, "regardless of color, race, or nationality."[14] In addition, Roberts's missionary efforts benefited from a curious overlapping of Arapaho and Old Testament legends. Although the Indians lacked the Christian concepts of sin and grace, they shared stories of a benevolent creator, a flood, and a resurrection. Roberts baptized numerous Arapaho into the Episcopal church. There is no question that he and his family aided the Arapaho in their adjustment to the Anglo-American world.[15]

While Gilded Age women seldom became ordained Protestant

ministers, in effect they assumed those duties when they entered
the mission field. Surely, Presbyterian Sue L. McBeth was a minister in everything but name in her work with the Nez Perce of Idaho.
Born in Scotland, Sue McBeth grew up in Ohio, where she early
developed a fascination for Native American ways. After her initial
mission efforts to the Choctaw were interrupted by the Civil War,
she tried city mission work in St. Louis. Then in 1873, she arrived
in Kamiah, Idaho, to teach the Nez Perce. Six years later, her sister
Kate joined her. They, in turn, were succeeded by their nieces, Mary
and Elizabeth Crawford.[16]

Like most nineteenth-century missionaries, Sue McBeth viewed
Nez Perce culture as hopelessly inferior to mainstream Anglo-
American civilization. But she also viewed the individual Nez Perce
as potentially equal to the best that the nation could offer.[17] A purist,
she rejected any blending of Nez Perce "heathenism" with Christianity. Thus, she insisted that all converts adopt Anglo-Protestant
ways completely. For years she warned the Nez Perce of numerous dangers: the nearby Catholic mission, ungodly soldiers, horse
racing, and whiskey.[18] More importantly, she also tried to restructure tribal society along Presbyterian lines. She appointed her own
Indian friends as elders (often bypassing traditional tribal leaders
in the process) and urged the Nez Perce women to create special
groups of their own. Drawing on the legacy of popular social gatherings, a tradition among the Plateau people of the Northwest, she
established an annual Nez Perce camp meeting. Touted as an alternative to the traditional Fourth of July debauch, the Nez Perce camp
meeting flourished well into the 1930s. Its motto read: "first, religious; second, educational; third, social."[19] Hailed as "a theological
seminary by herself," Sue McBeth devoted many years to her school
for training Nez Perce preachers. Over the years she instructed several Nez Perce in Christian doctrine, including members of the well-
known Lawyer family and Rev. James Hayes. Hayes, in turn, took
the Presbyterian message to the neighboring Shoshone and Bannock.
While she communicated initially in sign language, it was not long
before McBeth had mastered the Sahaptin language of the Nez Perce.
By 1879 she had compiled a Nez Perce grammar that approached
fifteen thousand words. Eventually, she published both a grammar
and a dictionary.[20]

If Sue McBeth helped restructure the Nez Perce world, she also
received much in return. A frail woman beset with a series of ail-

ments, McBeth battled ill health throughout her life. During much of her stay in Idaho she had great difficulty walking. Yet she left her St. Louis city mission work with a determined resolution: "I will go to the Nez Perces; with such work to do for Christ I can rise to life again." In large measure, this proved true. Over the years she developed an intense love for her Indian "boys," as she called them. They returned the affection, calling her "Pika," or "Mother." The entire tribe grieved when she died. Thus, in her twenty years of service to the Nez Perce, Sue McBeth both gave and received the innumerable gifts of the spirit.[21]

South Dakota Episcopal Bishop William Hobart Hare probably achieved the widest reputation of his nineteenth-century missionary contemporaries. Born into an aristocratic Pennsylvania family, throughout his career Hare retained his entrée into eastern establishment circles. Once he even attended a special meeting at the White House to discuss American Indian policy. Under the auspices of the powerful reform group, the Indian Rights Association, Hare wrote articles and delivered countless speeches on Indian issues. In addition, he became a national spokesman for stricter South Dakota divorce laws. He also attracted considerable (and unwelcome) publicity when he became embroiled in a nine-year high-church–low-church controversy that eventually resulted in an embarrassing court trial. These activities combined to give Hare a high profile on Indian mission matters. By the end of his long life, he had become almost an institution. On his seventy-first birthday, the Sioux Falls city officials declared him "one of the great missionaries of America."[22] His biographer later dubbed Hare "the John Eliot of the nineteenth century."[23]

Hare had considerable impact on the lives of the Indians of South Dakota. From his appointment in 1872 until his death in 1909, he worked tirelessly on their behalf. Thanks largely to his efforts, South Dakota had the most extensive Episcopal mission program in the nation.[24] Like his contemporaries, Hare viewed the various Indian cultures as marching up the social ladder toward "civilization." While he deemed contemporary Indian life as inferior, he considered the individual Indian as potentially equal to anyone. As he wrote in 1873: "The sum of the whole matter is this: the Indians are Men. We differ from them in *degree*, not in kind. Exactly where, or nearly where they now are, we once were; what we are now, they will (if not absolutely, yet according to their measure) by God's blessing become."[25]

Like Roberts, Hare emphasized education. He hoped that educated Sioux children might, in turn, teach their parents. Accordingly, he established four Indian boarding schools, the most important of which was St. Mary's for Indian Girls at Springfield, South Dakota. Because of his interest in Sioux education, he became a staunch advocate of the federal government's minority schooling programs at Hampton, Virginia, and Carlisle, Pennsylvania.

Termed *Zitkana Duzahan*, "Swift Bird," by the Sioux, Hare spent a great deal of time in overseeing his vast diocese. Realizing the need to bring the Indians together, in 1873 he inaugurated the first Indian Episcopal Convocation. Like the Nez Perce and the Pima camp meetings, this Indian convocation brought Indian people in from all parts of the region. For years it proved an important social and religious gathering. It also helped foster a sense of Sioux tribal identity.[26] In addition, Hare confirmed perhaps seven thousand Indians in the rites of the Episcopal church. Several of these later went on to enter the priesthood, including Amos Ross and Philip Deloria. As the 1890 annual Episcopal report observed: "It is safe to say that no religious body has accomplished more valuable and permanent spiritual results among the Indians than has this Church."[27] Much of the credit for this lay with the efforts of Bishop Hare.

Born in Germany, Charles H. Cook was over thirty years of age when he accepted an assignment in 1870 to become a Methodist teacher to the Pima and Maricopa Indians of southern Arizona. In 1881, Sheldon Jackson recognized his accomplishments and arranged for the Presbyterians to assume Cook's support. A few years later, when many Pima converted to Christianity, most of the new converts joined the Presbyterian church.[28]

Like the other missionaries, Cook shared all the cultural assumptions of his age. He insisted that Pima converts cut their hair, adopt western clothes, assume western surnames (many chose "Cook"), and learn English. For a generation, reservation visitors noted that several Pima spoke English with a German accent. To accelerate acculturation, Cook established several schools that emphasized such practical skills as household duties, carpentry, and, especially, techniques of irrigation. Cook spent over forty-three years with the Pima in Arizona. His impact on Native American life equaled that of any missionary of his generation.

When Cook arrived in the Southwest, he found that white pressure on Pima life had brought their culture into complete disarray. The band was beset with controversy and factionalism. By introducing the Presbyterian church hierarchy to the Pima, Cook helped to reinvigorate Pima cultural traditions. Cook appointed several tribal leaders as Presbyterian elders and thus refurbished their traditional moral and ethical role.[29] In 1906, Cook inaugurated the annual Pima revival meeting. For perhaps the first time, this gathering brought Pima from all the separate villages together. The revival meeting proved crucial in molding a genuine "tribal" outlook. Cook's concern over such practical economic issues as water rights—during one year Arizona whites took all the Pima water—helped push the tribe toward redress through the court system. Anthropologist Edward Spicer concluded that no example of constructive tribal transformation through Protestant mission work compares with Cook's efforts among the Pimas.[30]

In 1887 Methodist John J. Methvin arrived in Indian Territory to work among the "wild" or "blanket" Indians of the West. He remained in this work for fifty-four years. Making his headquarters at Anadarko, he began by walking from teepee to brush arbor to explain the Methodist version of the "Jesus Road."

Initially, the tribes greeted him with indifference or hostility. Shortly after his arrival, To-hau-sin, a Kiowa chief, came to his cabin and inquired why he had come there. Methvin told him that "I was not here to make money or engage in business, or to persuade the Indians to adopt the white man's ways. I had come to bring a message of love from our Great Father above, and He was the Great Father of all, both Indians and whites, and that Jesus His son came down into this world to reveal the Father's love to us."[31] Methvin eventually converted To-hau-sin and his wife. After this, several other Kiowa also joined the Methodist church.

Methvin dealt with about ten Indian dialects (none written) in his initial evangelistic efforts. While sign language, pidgin English, and broken "Indian" sufficed for most business purposes, he felt frustrated in attempting to explain the Gospel message through such means. Consequently, he urged all of these young Plains Indians to learn English. In the meantime, he relied heavily on several Native Americans as his translators: Etalye, a young Kiowa who had spent a year at Carlisle; Tsait-kop-ta, an Apache who had lived with a Christian family in New York after his imprisonment at Fort Marion in

St. Augustine; and Andreas Martínez, a Mexican who had been stolen and sold as a youth to the Kiowa. All three became essential conduits for Methvin's Methodist message.[32] In fact, Methodism spread through western Indian territory less by organized churches than by such itinerant Indian preachers.[33]

Joseph Samuel Murrow began his Southern Baptist missionary career in 1857 with the Seminole Nation in Indian Territory.[34] After the Civil War, he moved to Atoka to work with the Choctaw Nation. Over his long life—he lived to be ninety-four—Murrow founded over seventy-five Baptist churches in Indian Territory. He built many of the wooden frame churches with his own hands. Over the years he baptized perhaps two thousand people, most of them Indians, and helped ordain over seventy preachers, also mostly Indian. In addition, he organized the Choctaw–Chickasaw Baptist Association— an all-Indian convocation—and helped pioneer the successful Baptist work with the "blanket" Indians of western Indian Territory.

Like Methvin, Murrow worked in a region with numerous tribal languages. Consequently, he never mastered any single Indian tongue.[35] Over the years he continually urged all the tribes to learn English. To aid this endeavor, in 1879 he established a Bible School for native preachers, which later grew into Bacone Indian University (first located at Tahlequah, then moved to Muskogee). Bacone became one of the most important Oklahoma Indian colleges, and for fifteen years Murrow served as president of its Board of Trustees. In 1887 he founded the Atoka Baptist Academy, which later was absorbed by the Murrow Indian Orphan Home.[36] His educational and social efforts made him known to virtually every tribe in Oklahoma. His constant emphasis on English as the *lingua franca* also had important long-term results.

The Presbyterians, Baptists, and Methodists all gained numerous converts in the Indian Territory–Oklahoma region. Due to prior efforts by antebellum missionary Samuel Worcester and his historic Dwight Mission, the Presbyterians established their influence in Indian Territory during the period of removal. After the Civil War, however, the Baptists and Methodists proved even more successful. They grew rapidly because they downplayed formal theology. Rather, they emphasized a sincere call to the gospel ministry. Moreover, all three churches stressed a literal reading of an open Bible, a position that appealed to a wide native audience. Finally, and most important, they all utilized the talents of the Native American preachers.

In the post—Civil War years, a considerable number of Indians served as ministers to their people. Stephen Foreman worked forty-six years for Presbyterianism among the Cherokees. Charles Journeycake, the last Chief of the Delawares, became the first Delaware Baptist minister. Journeycake delivered his two-hour sermons only in Delaware, but his successor, John Sarcoxie, preached in both Delaware and English.[37] John Jumper, a Seminole chief, resigned his position in 1877 to work full time as a Baptist minister. Cherokees Jesse Bushyhead and Assistant Chief Samuel Smith also served as Baptist ministers.[38] Methodist Indian ministers included Coweta Micco, James McHenry, and William Oakchiah. The Presbyterians enlisted the services of Thomas W. Perryman, Joseph Smallwood, and Frank Hall Wright. By 1917 the Protestant churches claimed 150 full-blood Indian clergymen.[39]

The Oklahoma Indian groups also adapted easily to such frontier institutions as the camp meeting. Drawing on a legacy of prior gatherings, the Indian camp meeting often became an important time of social celebration. Choctaw Samuel Czarina recalled that the Indian women cooked for days to prepare for these "big eats." Deer, turkey, beef, and pork were either roasted over barbecue pits or boiled in gigantic pots. Everyone was welcomed at the gatherings, and they often lasted over a week. Many camp meetings were exclusively Indian, but at times they were integrated. A white evangelist recalled that when he exhorted at such a gathering, eight interpreters translated his sermon into eight different tribal languages. One translator relied on sign language.[40] Like the Pima and Nez Perce camp meetings, the Oklahoma convocations remained significant social institutions.

In addition to the camp meeting, the white missionaries to the Indians established two other institutions that had long-term impact on Native American life. These were the Indian hospitals and Indian schools. Eventually, the federal government assumed the responsibility for both Indian health care and Indian education. But for much of the period under consideration, the government shared these tasks with the American churches.

Both the Presbyterians and Episcopalians built modest Indian hospitals. The former established operations in Ganado and Indian Wells, in Arizona, while the latter built hospitals in the Choctaw Nation and among the Navajo at Fort Defiance, Arizona.[41] Miss Eliza W. Thakera ran the Fort Defiance hospital for over a decade during the early twentieth century. Episcopal Bishop John Mills Kendrick praised Thakera as "one of the two best women in the world." Unfortunately, her hospital enterprise suffered from both personnel antagonisms and underfunding; it never achieved major status.[42] Bishop Hare established no similar Indian hospital work in South Dakota because, as rumor had it, he could never find people who would work well together in such isolated and improverished circumstances.[43]

Of all the missionary institutions, however, the Indian schools proved the most vital. In the long run, they provided one of the most lasting legacies of the Protestant–Indian encounter. Moreover, on-reservation education offered the churches their most direct means of influencing American Indian life.[44]

In general, the tribal leaders approved of these church educational efforts. Often, however, they saw the schools as serving their own purposes. As Opothleyohola, an Upper Creek leader, once stated stated to a group of tribal elders: "I have always been opposed to the white man's religion, but I am not opposed to education. We must educate our children and instill in them a love for their race so that they may stand between us and trouble."[45]

By the early 1880s, most Protestant denominations had begun some type of Indian school. Missionaries, wives, and children all joined in to keep these fledgling institutions afloat. Since these efforts were never adequately funded, all members of the "missionary family" had to assist in the day-to-day running of the schools. Church efforts at Indian schooling received a needed boost when the federal government began its own educational program for Indians at Hampton and Carlisle.

In 1878, Captain Richard Henry Pratt selected a group of Cheyenne and Kiowa captives at Fort Marion in St. Augustine, Florida, for an experiment. The young Indians were to be sent back home, but he convinced them to enroll in General Samuel Chapman Armstrong's Hampton Institute, a Black school established in Virginia shortly after the Civil War. In 1879, Pratt began his crowning experiment in Indian education. That year, he welcomed 82 Sioux young people to his newly formed Carlisle School in Carlisle, Pennsylvania. From 195 Indians representing twenty-four tribes in 1882 to 1,200 Indians representing seventy-nine tribes only twelve years later, the success of the Carlisle experiment breathed new life into the concept of Indian education.[46]

In spite of its bold beginning, however, the Carlisle program had its opponents. In 1880, in a celebrated incident, Sioux Chief Spotted Tail withdrew his young people from Carlisle. He demanded that they be educated on the reservation, closer to home. In 1884, the Indian reformers, meeting at the annual Lake Mohonk conference, agreed. They passed a resolution urging the government to establish good manual labor and day schools on the various reservations.[47] The Indian missionaries applauded this effort. As John Roberts recalled, "The Indian colleges sent back the young braves as gents and not gentlemen. The boys and girls who were educated on the reservation in government schools were taught to do the things of life in a practical way, to farm, to take care of stock, and to make a living. That's what I mean between gents and gentlemen. A gent is a beggar and a gentleman works."[48]

Therefore, throughout the 1880s, the federal government continued to contract with the various denominations for this purpose. Both Protestant and Catholic churches became heavily involved with the program of Indian education. Much to the Protestants' dismay, however, they discovered that the Catholic Indian schools had more success in their quest for federal funds. Therefore, during the mid-1890s, the Protestants decided to pull out of this church–state partnership. Instead, they began to advocate a (nonreligious) federal school system for the reservations. As Prucha has noted, the year 1912 marked the last Protestant–Catholic quarrel over Indian schooling.[49]

With the phasing out of the contract school system, the various church schools began to decline. In 1884, for example, the contract and independent mission schools educated over one-fourth of the nation's Indian pupils.[50] After 1900, however, they enrolled less than 15 percent.[51] Although the religious bodies still maintained about fifty schools in 1907, with an enrollment of four thousand pupils, it was clear that the government had begun to assume the basic task of Indian schooling.

By the end of World War I, many of the Indian mission schools had fallen on hard times. Several closed their doors or consolidated with others. Only the strongest continued. Their goals, however, remained unchanged. As the Dwight Indian training school in Oklahoma declared (in 1918): "the training received shall be a solid and sure foundation for any line of useful work and that the educated Indian may be a Christian Indian."[52]

The daily schedule at Cook's Arizona school revealed how the Presbyterians blended the practical with the spiritual. Breakfast began at 6:30, with morning prayer and cleanup lasting until 8:45. Then, half of the children attended class while the rest filed to their stations in the kitchen, sewing room, laundry room, farm, shop, or barn. Lunch came at 12:00; afterwards, the work group attended classes and vice versa. From 4:00 to supper, the children played. After supper they attended chapel and studied; they were in bed by 8:00. This program, the official brochure noted, tried to give the Indians "a Christian education which would fit them for self support."[53]

A hypothetical observer visiting the Indian reservations of the Great Plains and Mountain West in 1915 would have been hard pressed to evaluate the impact of over two generations of Protestant mission activity. The theoretical missionary goals of Christianizing and civilizing the Indians had produced ambiguous results. The Indian cultures had proven surprisingly resilient. They had adopted some aspects of Anglo-American culture, rejected others, and blended still others with more traditional ways. While the *fin de siècle* years boasted several prominent examples of full-blooded Indians who had adopted many white ways—Dr. Charles Eastman, Dr. Carlos Montezuma, Rev. Sherman Coolidge, Rev. Henry Roe Cloud, and Jim Thorpe, among others—they were in the minority.

Yet the Protestant ministers could point to several areas of considerable impact. On a national level, a large number of American Indians had joined the Christian churches. In 1912, about 70,000 Indians (out of 300,000) were reported as churchgoers; four years later the figure had jumped to 97,000.[54] Another estimate of 1917 placed the figure of Indian Christians at 62,000 evangelical church members and 90,000 nominally Roman Catholics.[55]

On a local, reservation level, church statistics proved even more noticeable. Many Nez Perce, Pima, Papago, Sioux, and Cherokee had become Presbyterians. By 1923 the Presbyterians boasted 138 organized churches among the Native Americans. As early as 1875, the Methodists had claimed 775 Indian members in South Dakota alone. Over the years, they extended their influence to the Yakima, Creek, Kiowa, Cherokee, and Chickasaw.[56] In 1885, the Congregationalists listed 45 Indian churches with 3,700 members. They estimated that 100,000 Indians had heard the Gospel because of their Indian mission efforts. In 1895, the Baptists claimed 100 Indian churches. Thirteen years later they listed 4,000 Indian Baptists in Oklahoma and Indian Territories alone. Within a ten-year period, Charles Cook baptized 1,800 Pima Indians as Presbyterians. This was approximately half the tribe. When Bishop Hare died in 1909, of the estimated 20,000 South Dakota Indians 10,000 were baptized members of the Episcopal church.[57] Judged by number of converts alone, the Protestant clergy claimed a considerable impact on American Indian life.

In addition, the missionaries often served as valuable collectors of Indian languages, artifacts, and folklore. The most able men and women became experts in the specific culture of their region. For example, Sue McBeth's pioneering linguistic work with the Nez Perce received praise from Smithsonian anthropologists. Presbyterian Stephen R. Riggs helped translate the Bible into Dakota and also compiled a dictionary of the Dakota language. Franciscan Father Berard Haile did similar valuable linguistic studies with the Navajo language.[58] The Presbyterian Dwight Mission magazine, *Cherokee Gospel Tidings,* printed material in the Cherokee language until it closed in the 1950s.[59] John Menaul translated the McGuffey Reader into the Keres language of the Laguna Pueblo. John Roberts translated several items into Arapaho and Shoshone. Isabel Crawford translated the Lord's Prayer into sign language, and so on. As the years wore on, this gathering of language and cultural data became vital to both anthropologists and historians. Ironically, while the missionaries were engaged in trying to undermine Indian culture, they also provided one means of saving it from extinction.

From the 1870s to the era of World War I, the missionaries invariably voiced the tribal point of view on matters of local and national concern. As soon as he arrived in South Dakota, for example, Bishop Hare denounced the rumor that any white who killed a Sioux would be paid two hundred dollars. Reverend H. L. Morehouse reminded his Baptist audiences that "The Blanket Indian in his simple life is a 'child of nature,' yet withal, with a human nature not radically different in its essential traits from yours or mine."[60] Roberts, Cook, McBeth, and others could always be counted on to present the Indian viewpoint.

The numerous revitalization movements of the late nineteenth century also reflected the impact of the missionaries. These syncretic religious movements blended Christianity and native beliefs in a unique combination. Examples include the peyote religion, the Shaker faith, and the Northwest feather cult. The most dramatic, the Ghost Dance religion of the 1890s, saw the Paiute prophet, Wovoka, evoke the Ten Commandments and the name of Jesus in a crusade to drive the whites from the continent. The Ghost Dance faith found numerous converts among the Plains tribes who had been recently confined to reservations. Wovoka's crusade, of course, culminated in the tragedy at Wounded Knee.[61] Although the missionaries denounced these revitalizing faiths with vehemence, they were, ironically, as much a result of their teachings as were their highly touted lists of Christian converts.

For some tribes in the Great Plains and Mountain West, however, the missionary's introduction of Christianity might almost be viewed as a "revitalization" movement itself. The Five Civilized Tribes of Indian Territory, whose cultures were so disrupted by removal, often responded in this way. Several Cherokee, Choctaw, and Seminole leaders became ordained Protestant ministers, and many members of the five tribes were at least nominally Christian. Historian Angie Debo has observed that Christianity may have helped provide a new social structure for the Creek Nation—a tribe that had lost 24 percent of its people during removal and that faced the imminent collapse of its old community organization.[62] The Pima, Nez Perce, Choctaw, and Sioux also clearly utilized Christianity to help reinvigorate their traditional cultures.

One result of the missionary–Indian interaction, therefore, occurred with the blending of Christianity and traditional native beliefs. The Indian groups accepted many Christian teachings, but they did so with a difference. The tribes drew on their earlier heritage of large social gatherings to transform such innovations as the Indian camp meetings, Indian convocations, and all-Indian churches into their own institutions. The Indian Presbyterian Church at Kamiah, Idaho, for example, heard sermons and sang hymns in the Nez Perce language. The Mount Zion Presbyterian Church in Battiest, Oklahoma, did the same in Choctaw. These all-Indian churches, and others like them, became avenues of religious syncretization. They served as acceptable vehicles, both to incorporate Protestantism into Indian life and simultaneously to refurbish native culture. Thus, the Indian churches and Indian ministers played important parts in the ever ongoing process of Native American–Euroamerican cultural interchange.

If the names Roberts, McBeth, Hare, Cook, Methvin, Murrow, and Riggs have not achieved the national fame of Eliot, Brainerd, or the Whitmans, the cause did not lie with their lack of devotion to the faith. Perhaps their modest reputations may be traced to the basically local nature of their impact. Or perhaps the subsequent generation of historians (which should have written the missionaries' stories) felt uncomfortable with their avowed goals. Whatever the reason, the last great age of American missionary history came to an end with their generation. After World War I, church leaders began the difficult task of "rethinking missions." Yet, as Presbyterian George P. McAfee noted in 1920, "No Indian mission was ever a failure; and no missionary has failed to accomplish God's purposes when he faithfully prosecuted that work, though derided by the world and called in question by the church."[63] But, once again, nobody asked the Indians.

Chapter Nine:

The Social Gospel in the New West

During the period from 1865 to 1896, the mainline Protestant churches maintained a consistent interest in the trans-Mississippi West. In the last decade of the century, however, the churches gradually awakened to a new "threat" to the republic: the rise of the city. Although they never abandoned their efforts in the New West, the demands of urban America gradually drew their attention away from the home mission frontier.

The crusade to save the West had been halted, the secretary of the Congregational American Home Mission Society remarked in 1890, and the battle lines reversed to meet the "inrushing perils from abroad." If Horace Bushnell and Lyman Beecher were alive today, Rev. Thomas B. McLeod noted in 1898, they would be appealing to the churches to save the great cities from "barbarism." As Josiah Strong had suggested in *Our Country*, the city had suddenly emerged as the "nerve center" of American civilization.[1]

The American churches responded to this situation by developing a unique theological emphasis: the social gospel. Reading the scriptures afresh, the clergy tried to apply the social insights of the Old Testament prophets and Jesus to the society around them. Their controlling metaphor was the attempt to usher "The Kingdom of God" into American life.

Every major denomination produced voices for social gospel concerns. Congregationalist Lyman Abbott, Methodist Samuel Parks Cadman, Presbyterian Charles Stelzle, and Episcopal priest William

S. Rainsford all emerged as major denominational spokesmen. But none approached the insights of Baptist theologian Walter Rauschenbusch, especially in his two books, *Christianity and the Social Crisis* (1907) and *A Theology for the Social Gospel* (1917). Rauschenbusch's version of Christianity held that Jesus had come to earth to save not simply the individual soul but the social order as well. Any society that perpetuated grave injustices in its midst, he wrote, was clearly un-Christian and needed to be reformed. In Rauschenbusch's view, true Christianity encompassed the whole of life; it could not be limited simply to individual salvation.[2]

During the *fin de siècle* years, the ideas of the social gospel moved into most denominations. As historian C. Howard Hopkins has observed, however, the social gospel never really became an organized "movement."[3] Instead, the men and women who shared its basic theological underpinnings utilized the existing denominational frameworks to enact their social reform programs. Because of this flexible structure, the ministers varied their social emphasis from region to region.

In the urban Northeast, the Protestant churches directed most of their social gospel efforts toward resolving the problems of the growing immigrant slum areas. Here they emphasized public health measures, free legal aid, employment assistance, and other social services. Recent scholarship has shown that the southern churches also became involved with social concerns. Yet the southern social gospel focus differed considerably from that of the urban northeast. The southern clergy stressed the issues of anti-child labor legislation, prison reform, Sabbath observance, temperance (very much a social gospel item) and Appalachian mountain work. Since the social gospel proved more an "attitude" than a set of prescriptions, regional clergymen could bend the mood to the problems at hand.[4]

The western clergymen did just that. For those New West cities that duplicated eastern slum conditions, the ministers introduced similar social service programs. Other ministers in the polyglot, mining areas also followed suit. Specific circumstances in the West, however, called forth a unique application of the social gospel atmosphere. This regional distinctiveness emerged in three areas: The establishment of Chinese schools; aid for immigrant health seekers to the Southwest; and the popular ideology of social ethics created by Topeka Congregationalist Charles M. Sheldon.

In the urban Northeast, the Protestant clerics relied heavily on the "institutional church" as a means of conveying the new social awareness. Born from the dilemma of how to resolve the needs of urban immigrants, the institutional church began to move beyond traditional church roles. Instead of being open on Sundays only, it extended its ministry over all the days of the week. In addition, the ministers began to increase the variety of services offered. These included gymnasiums, reading rooms, recreation halls, kindergartens, pharmacies, day nurseries, and free legal advice. By the early twentieth century most large institutional churches also utilized the expertise of a registered nurse.

Ministers in the West also drew upon the concept of the institutional church. They especially utilized it in the two western cities that most duplicated the crowded slum conditions of the Northeast, Omaha and Denver. From 1870 to 1920, Omaha grew from a hamlet of 16,000 to a city that approached 200,000 people. In 1880, one-third of the population was foreign-born; by 1910, the figure had risen to 54 percent. South Omaha, dominated by its Swift and Armour packing plants, turned the city into one of the largest meat packing centers of the nation.

Although Episcopalians represented only 1.1 percent of Omaha's population, their priests spearheaded the city's social reform program. In 1891, Rev. John Williams helped mediate a bitter labor dispute and shortly afterwards, his bishop, George Worthington, called in the Sisters of St. Monica to work with the women in the city's red light district. One of the most innovative Episcopal programs came with the establishment of their "Associate Mission"—a group of unmarried priests who lived communally while trying simultaneously to establish schools and missions throughout the city.[5] Other denominations, such as the Methodists, Baptists, and Presbyterians, inaugurated similar social service programs for Omaha. But the Episcopal priests seem to have balanced their social and educational programs with greater foresight and skill.[6]

The Queen City of Denver experienced the same rapid growth. Only 35,000 in 1880, by 1900 it boasted a population of 134,000. Like Omaha, Chicago, and New York, Denver's streets abounded with social misery. Consequently several Denver ministers introduced strong social gospel programs for the city.

In Thomas ("Parson Tom") Uzzell and Myron Reed, turn-of-the-century Denver produced two highly articulate clerical spokesmen for social justice. In 1885, after leaving his pastorate in Leadville,

Uzzell took over Denver's Methodist "People's Tabernacle." He remained there until his death in 1910. In addition to his regular ministry, Uzzell established a free dispensary, with three physicians on duty, and founded a free second-hand store in the church's basement. He also began an employment bureau. Through his connections with the railroads, Uzzell secured half-cost rail transportation for those in distress to any point in the nation.

Uzzell had numerous friends among the city's elite, and he worked with them to establish several municipal welfare programs. The People's Tabernacle regularly arranged free summer camp excursions to the mountains. His church was one of the first to establish night schools and kindergartens, and it also taught sewing, cooking, and English to immigrants. Later Uzzell organized an annual rabbit hunt in Lamar, in the southeastern part of the state. After the rabbits had been dispatched, the hunters shipped the meat to Denver to be given to the poor.[7] When Uzzell died, he was one of the most deeply mourned men of Denver.

His fellow pastor, Myron W. Reed, achieved a similar local reputation. Called to Denver's First Congregational church in 1884, Reed remained a prominent public figure until his death in 1899. Reed's sympathy lay largely with the working class of the region, and he became one of the Mountain West's most articulate spokesmen for the cause of labor. He advocated improved safety devices for the mines and steel mills and worked hard for the enactment of a workman's compensation law. He also attacked the sweat shop and child labor. His sympathy for the working man eventually got him in trouble with his fashionable, middle- class congregation. During a bitter labor strike at the mining town of Bull Hill, he confessed to his church that his heart lay with the miners. Shortly thereafter, he broke with the Congregatonalists and founded a popular nondenominational church that lasted until his death.

Reed also became involved in numerous social crusades. He was a chief mover in the creation of the city's Associated Charities organization, and served as president of the state board of Charities and Corrections. He became so popular that in both 1886 and 1892 he was nominated for Congress. When he died, people stood in line for two hours for a last glimpse of the body. One Denver newspaper compared his funeral with that of a prince.

Unlike several of the other social gospel clerics, Myron Reed was also an excellent pulpiteer. His friends called him "the greatest

preacher west of Brooklyn" (the home of Henry Ward Beecher).[8]
Reed's four-sermon series, "The Evolution of a Tramp" (1886)
achieved such popularity that the Denver *Post* reprinted the talks
several years later. Reed's chief fame, however, rested with his epi-
grams. He had a Mark Twain-like gift of compressing deep thought
into just a few words.

The tramp is a warning to us that our social system has failed.

A man who says he has never had a doubt in matters of faith
wears a No. 6 hat.

It is not a comfortable world while a single soul goes
without.

It costs more to arrest, try, convict and hang a man than to
endow a kindergarten.

I am interested in politics because I believe that every
political question is a social question, and that every social
question is a religious one.

Let us think clear and speak straight.

We have no private right to forgive a public injury. We have
no private right to forgive a private injury to another man. The
duty of forgiveness is wholly personal. Society must not forgive
the smallest injury to the humblest individual.

All the law is boiled down into one word—love.[9]

Baptist Jim Goodheart and Methodist Francesco P. Sulmonetti
inherited Denver's social gospel mantle from Reed and Uzzell. A
former gambler and reformed alcoholic, Goodheart was close to
suicide when he was converted in Denver's Sunshine Mission in
1904. Four years later he returned to Denver to head the mission,
and later, although he had no formal training, was ordained a Baptist minister.

Goodheart made the Sunshine Mission into a major Denver institution. His church provided an employment bureau, offered free
food and lodging for transients, took in orphans, and assisted a segment of the population that few churches were able to reach. In
1918, the Mayor of Denver created the position of city chaplain for
Goodheart (really the director of public welfare). The local Chief
of Police said that if it were not for Goodheart, he would have to
add thirty men to his police force.[10]

In 1910, the Methodists established the Holy Trinity Italian Evangelical Institutional Church. Sulmonetti's sermons in Italian were

supplemented by free medical treatment and free legal advice. In addition, the church opened an evening school to teach English. In 1915, the Methodists also established a Spanish Methodist church that specialized in bilingual classes in sewing and cooking and also sponsored "noonday luncheons" for undernourished children. This church had a library, with a regular "story hour," and taught both music and handiwork. It ministered to about 1000 Spanish-speaking residents.[11]

Other western clergymen also spoke out strongly on social issues. Denver's Episcopal Dean, Henry Martyn Hart, enthusiastically advocated an early version of the income tax.[12] The Episcopal Bishop of western Nebraska, George Allen Beecher, and the Bishop of Salt Lake City, Franklin Spencer Spalding, both gained regional reputations as spokesmen for Christian Socialism. Spalding's successor, Paul Jones continued the social emphasis until he eventually was forced from office because of his opposition to World War I. In rural Oklahoma, Presbyterian Thomas Woodrow edited a short-lived Christian Socialist newspaper during the mid teens.[13]

Outside of Omaha and Denver, however, the Plains and Mountain West boasted few genuine urban areas. The 1900 census revealed that the U.S. had many cities over 25,000 in population, but (excluding the coastal states) only a few fell in the New West. Salt Lake City, Topeka, and Lincoln were around 50,000, but after that the figures fell rapidly: Colorado Springs, 21,000; El Paso, 16,000; Oklahoma City, 10,000; Tucson, 8,000; Tulsa, 8,000; Albuquerque, 7,000; Boise, 6,000; and Missoula, 4,000. As Episcopal home missionary Hugh L. Burleson observed in 1918, the West had "no 'city problem' in the ordinary sense of the term."[14]

Although the clergy in these medium sized cities never confronted the same degree of social unrest, they, too, introduced their own version of the social gospel. Salt Lake City and Topeka could hardly be considered major urban areas, but the Protestant leaders in each town founded the same type of institutional churches or social outreach programs as if they had been located in Denver or Omaha.

In 1915, the Utah Methodists invited an Italian minister from Butte to help establish a mission in the heart of Salt Lake City. Working there with a community of about 2,000 Italians, he inaugurated a series of social programs: immigrant clubs, English language classes, Sunday Schools, night schools, a kindergarten, sewing classes, and several mothers' clubs. Volunteers from the church also helped run the city library.[15]

Congregationalist Charles A. Sheldon began a similar campaign in Topeka. Soon after his arrival in 1888, Sheldon became concerned over the quality of life in nearby "Tennessee Town," the city's black district. By 1892, he had founded a kindergarten training school, which eventually enrolled over 250 children. A church social—admission to which was a book—provided the basis for the Tennessee Town Library. His church members supervised the library on a volunteer basis. One observer, however, noted that, "A man needed a bottle of Paine's Celery Compound to restore his nerves after each experience in the library." A Literary Society, sewing class, Day Nursery, Penny savings bank, Christian Endeavor, Manual training, and a village improvement society rounded out Sheldon's program of social concern.[16]

Even the clergy who served in the isolated western plains drew from the mood of the social gospel. In Hankinson, North Dakota, for example, a Congregational minister organized a gymnasium for the young men in the region. The church in the mining community of Rock Springs, Wyoming proved even more imaginative. Rock Springs contained 47 different ethnic groups and claimed that it was a "New York in miniature." From 1907 to 1912, the local Methodist church functioned as if it had been located in the lower east side of New York City. It organized night schools, reading rooms, and various educational courses. Two women church workers arrived from the East, and at one time they boasted six different classes in operation.[17] Numerous ministers in El Paso also began settlement houses for Mexican immigrants. Thus, the western clergy adopted the framework of the institutional church for a variety of communities, ranging in size from Denver and Salt Lake City to Rock Springs and Hankinson.

The altruism of the social gospel mirrored a widespread concern for the continued survival of the middle class world. The tone of the social gospel statements reflected the same sense of urgency that had animated the earlier calls to "save the West." As an Episcopal rector told a national church audience in 1913: "Our nation is trembling in the balance, we are not far from some great process of reconstruction. Shall it be Christian reconstruction or godless revolution?"[18]

Because of this concern for the safety of society, the western social gospel clerics found ready allies. They picked up much support from the reform politicians of the Progressive Era, and also from the newly emerging class of professional social workers. Few saw any conflict with such alliances. Everyone agreed that the church provided the "inspiration and idealism" necessary to keep the social service agencies from becoming "heartless bureaucracies."

During the first two decades of the century, this spirit of cooperation manifested itself in numerous attacks on the urban vice districts. For almost three generations the western clergymen had denounced the "openness" of western vice, but with minimal effect. By 1910, however, other groups joined the chorus: fledgling health organizations, such as the American Social Hygiene Association, reform mayors and governors, and the emerging women's organizations. This new combination proved irresistible, and gradually the western communities moved to close down their vice districts.[19] By 1910, the opium dens had disappeared from Albuquerque. By 1915, Denver had outlawed its vice region. In 1917, the state of Arizona passed legislation against public prostitution; Albuquerque also closed its red light region at this time. After several ineffective crusades, even El Paso drove the gambling and red light districts underground. By 1920, then, most of the "sporting" element of the western towns had moved their activities behind closed doors. A long-term goal of the early western ministers had (finally) come to fruition. Thanks to the new political alliances, the clergy's middle class version of morality had emerged victorious.

In addition to these reform measures, the western clerics applied the national social gospel atmosphere to the specific needs of the region. One of the most important of these came with the scattered Protestant efforts to aid the immigrant Chinese. The Chinese formed the most striking of all the immigrant groups. Brought in to build the railroads and then dumped when the construction had finished, they were conspicuous by their strange garb, long pigtails, and exotic ways. Moreover, the Chinese population was almost all men. In El Paso in 1900, for example, there were 255 Chinese males and only two females; by 1916, the city claimed 239 males, but the female population had increased to only four. "El Paso is the Chinese mecca of the southwest," boasted the local paper, obviously without asking any Chinese males.[20]

While the majority of Chinese remained in the Pacific Coast states, primarily California, they also made their presence felt in the intermountain West. During the last two decades of the century the inland states of the New West recorded a population of between 300 and 1700 Chinese each. "There is no town on the coast," declared the *Phoenix Gazette* in 1886, "where the Chinese have as strong a foothold as they have in Phoenix."[21] Denver, Tucson, Rock Springs, Salt Lake City, and Albuquerque also listed significant Chinese communities. So many Asians resided in Prescott, Arizona, that everyone in town knew the date of the Chinese New Year. In Evanston, Wyoming, town officials dismissed schools for the Chinese New Year so that the whole town could attend the festive celebrations.

No other immigrant group provoked a more ambiguous reaction than the Chinese. A modern study of American reaction to their presence is titled, *The Unwelcome Immigrant.*[22] The official government response was spelled out in the form of the Congressional exclusion laws of 1882, 1892, and 1902. Historian John Wunder has shown that, over the years, the various western state legal systems also developed a distinct anti-Chinese bias.[23] Unofficial community actions spoke even louder. In 1889, the Flagstaff *Champion* warned that, "All boys that have been in the habit of throwing stones and clubs at Chinamen will take notice that hereafter they will be promptly arrested for any unnecessary assault on Chinamen."[24] Methodist Father John Dyer always felt that he alone staved off an 1880 Breckenridge, Colorado, anti-Chinese riot. When the crowd started to shout "the Chinese must go," Dyer mounted the nearest steps and began singing, "All Hail the Power of Jesus Name." After several verses, he launched into an extemporaneous sermon on the theme that God's love was meant for all humanity, and that all men were brothers.[25] Eventually the crowd dispersed.

Other areas were not so lucky. Anti-Asian violence disrupted many western towns. On September 3, 1885, a riot at Rock Springs, Wyoming, killed 28 Chinese miners. As late as 1905, all the Chinese miners in Silverton, Colorado, were loaded onto box cars and sent to Durango, with orders not to return. In 1910, an aristocratic Chinese visitor observed that no Chinese gentleman would dare send his son to study or travel in America. The son would surely be lumped with the Cantonese coolies and either be scorned or persecuted.[26]

Virtually the only groups that tried to ameliorate this situation were the western ministers and their churches. Numerous Protestant clergy all through the New West organized Chinese schools or special missions as part of their church enterprise. While these efforts were scattered and often short-lived, they should not be discounted. Dealing with the "Chinese problem" formed an important aspect of the western social gospel program.

The Chinese schools rose and fell as the need dictated. In 1881, the Tucson Episcopalians established an English language school for the Chinese and both the Prescott Congregationalists and Methodists followed suit soon afterwards. The women of the Deadwood, South Dakota Congregational church established a Chinese school during the mid-1880s, as did the women of First Presbyterian Church in Omaha.

In 1896, the Baptists established a Chinese mission in El Paso. Denver's First Baptist Church provided weekly English instruction during the early 1890s for about 65 Chinese students. The class was "doing an imperishable work for a greatly neglected and pitiable class—" the official booklet noted, "a class whom the Master loved and saved." The Chinese school of Central Presbyterian Church in Denver lasted well into the twentieth century.[27]

Teaching English and the rudiments of Christianity to this group was not easy. The Chinese population fluctuated constantly. Everyone hoped to strike it rich and then return home. Several of the men resisted the introduction of Christianity and spoke ill of "Melican Religion." One observer felt that the Chinese attended the English classes in spite of the religious dimension rather than because of it. Some of the laborers went to both Protestant and Catholic missions, seemingly without distinction. When the Silverton, Colorado, Congregational Church began a Chinese Christian Endeavor Society in 1891, the *Silverton Standard* cynically noted that its goal was "to convert the Chinese and induce them to handle soiled linen and red checks with more Christian charity."[28]

Chinese and English, of course, share no cognates, and it is unlikely that many of the teachers had familiarity with the Chinese language. Moreover, they had access to few teaching aids. Isolated hymn books or missionary tracts, with parallel columns of text, were all that were available. Thus, the Chinese men often sat down to face the beginning McGuffey readers. One Denver Presbyterian layman journeyed to Shanghai for a full year of language study. One can imagine his reaction when he returned to discover that the tongue of North China, which he had learned, was totally unintelligible to the Canton peasants in his classes.[29]

In spite of the difficulties, however, many Asians learned English and, along the way, several converted to Christianity. One estimate suggests that perhaps 50,000 Chinese had joined American churches by 1910. Several converts became ministers. Christian evangelist Lum Foon pastored up and down the West Coast, while Sia Sek Ong, Gee Gam, and Le Tong Hay (Methodists); Tong Keet Hing and Fung Chak (Baptists); and a Rev. Wong (Presbyterian) were also active. Naturally, both the Protestants and Catholics established the majority of their Chinese missions on the West Coast. The most famous church woman to work with the Chinese there was probably Donaldina Cameron, director of the Presbyterian Mission Home in San Francisco. Cameron and her successor, Margaret Culbertson, devoted their lives to rescuing young Chinese women from local houses of prostitution. The Cameron House is still in operation.

It is difficult to assess the effectiveness of these sporadic church efforts. For those Chinese who remained, the language training must have been invaluable. Most returned to Asia, however, and gradually the letters to their former teachers dwindled. Some, such as Charlie Wann, a product of the Congregational Chinese School in Prescott, retained their contacts. Wann returned to China and became a millionaire merchant. Later he established a Christian hospital in Hong Kong, and he always provided considerable support for Chinese missionaries. Through these Chinese schools, the the western churches established their own version of "practical Christianity."

The West's second unique social gospel effort developed in the realm of health care. By 1900, The White Plague, or tuberculosis, had emerged as the nation's leading killer, far ahead of cancer and heart disease. It claimed over 150,000 people a year, earning the grim sobriquet: "Captain of the Men of Death."[30] No cure existed except for rest and (perhaps) a high, dry climate. Colorado, New Mexico, Arizona, and west Texas were all highly praised in this regard. In the early years of the century, the National Tuberculosis Association estimated that perhaps 7000 people with TB moved to the Southwest every year. By 1920, perhaps 10 percent of New Mexico's population consisted of health seekers. Many of the immigrants came from the moderately prosperous middle class, but a significant number were so ill that they were unable to work after they arrived. The Phoenix and Salt River Valley Immigration Commission warned these newcomers that "persons coming for health

reasons should arrive with sufficient money to pay all living ex-
penseses for at least one year." New Mexico and Arizona spokesmen had to appeal formally to eastern physicians not to send them
tubercular patients who could not support themselves.[31]

A surprising number of ministers first came West because either
they or their families were trying to "chase the cure." These included Albuquerque Congregationalist Jacob Mills Ashley, who moved
chiefly because his son had TB, and Baptist Bruce Kinney, who
accepted an offer to pastor Albuquerque's First Baptist Church
because of an ill wife. The files of Missionary Episcopal Bishop J.
Mills Kendrick are full of requests from seriously ill clergymen seeking a position in the Southwest.

Numerous private sanatoriums had arisen to meet the health seek-
er demand, but their fees restricted them to the wealthy. According to the National Tuberculosis Association, over half of those who
arrived in the Southwest were on the verge of poverty. Moreover,
as the contagious nature of the disease became known, southwestern sentiment began to cool toward the new immigrants. The New
Mexico territorial legislature forbade consumptives from entering
the teaching profession. Arizona ranchers and businessmen often
refused to hire health seekers, and western landlords increasingly
hesitated to rent to them.[32] Thus, many immigrants lived in hastily
constructed "tent cities," partly to be outdoors, but partly because
they could afford nothing better. "If there is one above another
deserving our sympathy," noted a southwestern Presbyterian observer, "is it not that one who is afflicted with tuberculosis, poor in this
world's goods, a thousand miles or more from home and friends,
regarded with fear, and excluded from honest hotels."[33]

The western clergy viewed the dilemma of the health seekers as
a legitimate area of Christian concern. This proved to be a unique
aspect of the western social gospel, and it spread across all denominations. In 1902, the Catholic Sisters of St. Joseph began a hospital
in Albuquerque for those with lung diseases. In 1904, the Baptists
sent a trained nurse to the city to help the growing public health
program. Two years later Presbyterian minister Hugh A. Cooper
(who had himself arrived with TB) opened a five-room cottage for
indigent health seekers. This grew to become the Presbyterian Hospital of Albuquerque. In 1912, the Methodists established a TB
Sanatorium in the nearby Manzano Mountains. The greatest ac-

complishment of Rabbi W. S. Friedman was the establishment of the National Jewish Hospital in Denver. It complemented the city's (Episcopal) St. Luke's. The Baptists established TB hospitals in both El Paso and Tucson; the Episcopalians, St. Luke's in the Desert in Tucson; and the Methodists, what is now Good Samaritan in Phoenix.[34]

At the turn of the century, the answer to TB lay far in the future. No cure was found until World War II. Hence, these sanitariums remained a western social gospel concern for almost half a century. They were widely praised at the time for combining the resources of modern science with the ancient wisdom of Scripture. "Is this not an appealing work?" asked a writer in the Presbyterian magazine *La Aurora* in 1913. "Is it not a humanitarian undertaking? And more is it not Christian?"[35]

The programs for western immigrants, the language schools for itinerant Chinese laborers, and the facilities for southwestern health seekers formed the heart of the western social gospel. Yet in a very real sense, these social programs did not represent a major departure from the overall thrust of mainline Protestantism in the New West. From the earliest days, the frontier ministers had always included a strong institutional dimension to their ministry. Few western clerics saw their task as simply "to preach the old Gospel." Instead, they had often supplemented their sermons with educational, health, and social work. Church worker Lillian D. Ashe realized this when she wrote to the Episcopal Bishop of New Mexico inquiring about a position. She wanted a job, she said, not as a teacher but in "social settlement work in cities—what you would include in your regular mission work."[36]

This institutional dimension of western Protestantism had yet another effect on the religion of the region. It helped erode the earlier criticism of church activity. Organized opposition to the churches seldom gained widespread support in the West for the various denominations were all providing genuine social services. As Bishop Tuttle remarked in his *Reminiscences*, "When the Church takes the lead in beneficent activities for human welfare, sneering at or capricious criticism of her is never heard."[37]

In 1902, the Episcopal Bishop of Boise, James B. Tunsten, remarked that, "The American who is being made on the square mile of the far western country is developing in a quite different way from the American whose life is cast where thousands live to the square mile."[38] Indeed, the theology of the social gospel had arisen largely as a response to the overcrowded immigrant areas of the Northeast. But the writings of Topeka Congregationalist Charles M. Sheldon provided an interesting variation to the norm. In his classic novel, *In His Steps*(1896), Sheldon tried to fit the traditional social gospel concern for the welfare of others into the isolated, more individualistic environment of the New West. Although he was not a deep thinker like Walter Rauschenbusch, Charles Sheldon emerged as the popularizer of social gospel ideas for the West.[37]

Sheldon arrived as pastor of the Central Congregational Church in Topeka in 1888. To bolster his sagging Sunday evening services, he began reading to his congregation from chapters of a novel he had written. Like the later movie serials, he left his audiences hanging in suspense when he broke off his narrative for the night.

This technique worked rather well, and in October 1896 he repeated the process with his most recent story *In His Steps*—the seventh of what would eventually be twenty-five such ventures. As he had done with his six previous stories, Sheldon sold *In His Steps* to a religious magazine, the *Advance*, which later published it in book form. Due to a technicality—the publisher of the *Advance* filed only one copy with the proper copyright department, instead of the necessary two—the copyright was nullified. Thus, the book was thrown into the public domain. There it has remained. It is still in print in numerous editions.[39]

The plot is simple. A poor wanderer (who clearly is not an ordinary tramp)—"not more than thirty or thirty-three years old, I should say"—collapses and dies before the astounded congregation of Reverend Henry Maxwell. This so unnerves the pastor that he asks his congregation to make a vow that for one year they will ask themselves "what would Jesus do?" before they perform any action. The plot then revolves around how a newspaper editor, businessman, singer, college president, and clergyman use their talents in this new light.

The story is a little hard on modern sensibilities, for Sheldon seemed to know just exactly what Jesus would have done in a wide variety of cases: Jesus would run a certain type of newspaper. He would not print accounts of prize fights or society gossip. He would not run liquor or tobacco ads. He would use a girl's beautiful voice for gospel singing rather than opera performances. He would try to bridge social classes and clean up the local slum district. And he would urge the college president to leave the ivory tower to enter the world of politics.

The little book sold incredibly well. Exactly how many copies were sold will probably never be known. In 1930, Bruce Barton estimated 23 million. Sheldon himself claimed around the same figure. In popular parlance, the book became known as "the second best seller to the Bible alone." Literary critic Frank L. Mott lowered the estimate to around six million, which is still a considerable number. *In His Steps* was also published in an English penny edition, produced in a lantern-slide version, acted as a drama, and translated into numerous languages, including Russian and Arabic.

Sheldon continued to write in a similar vein until his death in 1946. *The Narrow Gate* (1903) was a short temperance tract; *The Reformer* (1901), called attention to the housing problem; *The Heart of the World: A Story of Christian Socialism* (1905), and *Jesus Is Here* (1914) followed in succession. None was very important, however, and *Jesus Is Here*, where Jesus is described as someone who "looked like an average man—only different" has to rank as the worst of the lot.

Fads such as *In His Steps* are far easier to describe than to account for. Explaining the enormous success of this book—one which Sheldon could never match in any of his later works—is not easy. Yet surely one reason lay in the universal application of his message. Sheldon called on every person to stop and ask—in modern translation—"Is this a moral deed?"—before acting.

The universal nature of Sheldon's message meant that it could be applied in any situation. As such, it soon traveled around the world. Born in Topeka, his ideas found a ready home all through the New West. From the slums of Denver to the Bloys' camp meeting in west Texas, from the parochial schools in New Mexico, to the Wyoming Cowboy Sunday Schools, *In His Steps* encouraged everyone to ask: "What would Jesus do?"

Charles Sheldon took the heart of the social gospel—moral responsibility for others—and transformed it. He made it applicable to the sparsely settled environment of the Great Plains and Rocky

Mountains. Like Rauschenbusch's message, Sheldon's Christianity included a concern for the whole of life. Through *In His Steps*, Sheldon helped universalize an ideology that united both individual and social responsibility. Along with the TB hospitals and Chinese schools, Sheldon's book ranks as a unique contribution to the story of the social gospel in the American West.

Conclusion

From the end of the Civil War to the beginning of World War I, the mainline Protestant clergy played numerous roles in the life of the New West. For their parishioners, they performed the standard denominational tasks: organizing churches, supervising the construction of buildings, delivering sermons, counseling, providing communion, performing wedding ceremonies, and conducting funerals. Even those westerners who lived outside the bonds of convention usually asked for traditional services at times of marriage or death. For their communities at large, the clergy helped organize public school systems, served as librarians, established parochial schools and colleges, distributed appropriate literature, lectured on a variety of topics, and engaged in social work. The missionaries on the scattered Indian reservations organized hospitals, camp meetings, social clubs, and schools wherever they went. When the social gospel movement emerged, the clergy adapted it to the particular needs of the Great Plains and Rocky Mountains. In addition, for over two generations the ministers served as the foremost representatives of "culture" in the New West.

Moreover, the ministers performed these tasks on remarkably limited means. Throughout these decades, the poverty-stricken western parishes relied heavily on irregular eastern sources for much of their financing. In spite of these stringent limitations, by World War I hundreds of church buildings, manses, schools, academies, colleges and hospitals dotted the Plains and mountain region.

In 1906, the federal government compiled the nation's first special religious census. It revealed that the western territories and states contained approximately the same percentage of churches and communicants as the rest of the nation. Nationally, a little more than one-third (about 39 percent) of the population professed membership in some religious organization.[1] The New West, then, had joined the religious mainstream. The home missionaries had done their job.

However one tabulates western church statistics, the figures demonstrate growth. From 1870 to 1916, the Methodists increased their rolls from 2 million to 6 million. Much of the gain occurred west of the Mississippi. On a regional level, the Congregationalists in the Rocky Mountain area grew from nil in 1865 to 188 churches and almost 14,000 members fifty years later.[2] The individual story of John F. Spalding, Episcopal Bishop of Colorado (1874–1902), brings this growth into even sharper focus. During his tenure, Spalding increased his clergymen from 7 to 93, and his communicants from 500 to 5,150, his church buildings from 7 to 100, and the value of church property from 30,000 dollars to 1,150,000 dollars.[3] As Bishop Boyd Vincent said of him in a memorial sermon: "If one wanted to sum up Spalding's career in a single word, that word would be 'accomplishment.' "[4]

Similar "accomplishments" characterized all the mainline Protestant denominations in the region. As Edwin S. Gaustad's *Historial Atlas of Religion in America* shows, by 1906 they had achieved significant membership in all the western states. The figures revealed that the Methodists were strong in Idaho, Nevada, Colorado, Arizona, and Wyoming; the Baptists in Kansas, Nebraska,, Oklahoma, and West Texas; the Presbyterians in Colorado and New Mexico; the Congregationalists in South Dakota, Nebraska and Colorado, and the Episcopalians in Colorado, Wyoming, South Dakota, and Nevada.[5] In addition, several Indian groups had become Christian. In only four decades, then, the mainline Protestant denominations had "churched" the West.

While it is true that overexpansion and denominational rivalry caused the collapse of many individual churches along the way, even that may not always indicate failure.[6] The frontier churches functioned as flexible and democratic institutions. They rose and fell as the need dictated. If a mine played out or a town disappeared, so too did the church. If a community changed ethnic and social complexion, the church was also likely to change. Buildings could be dismantled or sold and the organization re-formed at another place and time. As late as 1899, the pastor of the First Baptist Church in Colorado Springs complained, "It is the rarest thing in the world to find a family that has made up its mind to stay. . . .Every one talks of 'going back home.' "[7] Few other institutions of western life reflected this mobility as closely as the pioneer churches.

In spite of this statistical growth, however, it was also clear by 1915 that the ministers had not brought the New West "safely into the Protestant camp" as they had initially hoped. Their modest membership rolls and the rapid turnover of both clergy and parishioners weakened their overall impact. Their crusade against western "vice" did not gain widespread public support until the Progressive Era of the early twentieth century. Their much-vaunted campaign against the Mormons and the Hispanic Catholics may have provided needed social services, but it produced relatively few converts. The results of the Indian mission efforts always remained a bit ambiguous. Except perhaps for some regions of the southern Great Plains, the clerics had been unable to shape the "fluid" West in their own image.

The reason for this "failure" lay in the variegated nature of the West itself. An 1881 study of Nevada noted that "[t]here is as great a diversity in the creeds of Nevada as there are varieties in the assay of its ores. The Mosaic character of its population fitly typifies the religion of its people."[8] Frontier photographer William Henry Jackson agreed. As he traveled the prairie west of Omaha during the late 1860s, he met representatives of every language, religion, and ethnic group.[9] Each group, moreover, brought to the West its own religious preference. Although there were inevitable defections, most denominations retained their integrity. The main exception would be the ethnic churches (the Swedish Baptists, Italian Methodists, and so on), which usually declined with the Americanization of the second and third generations. Certainly the Mormons, the Catholics, and certain Indian groups held their own on the cultural battleground.

Thus, as the mainline Protestant groups entered the New West, they confronted the great challenge of their day: dealing with religious diversity. A generation before the eastern churches discovered the heterogeneity of immigration from abroad, the home missionaries dealt with pluralism on a daily basis.[10] Their failure to shape the social order of the New West revealed all too clearly that the mainline Protestant churches did not embody the whole of the national cultural heritage. Other components also jostled for position. While the Protestant ministers formed an integral part of western life, they were not the only force on the horizon. From the earliest years, they shared their religious mantle with rabbis, Catholic priests, Mormon bishops, and other clerics from the vast range of the American religious spectrum. Later they shared their "secular" functions with civic magistrates, physicians, nurses, professional educators, government officials, and social workers. In other words, by 1915 the missionaries in the New West had become but a single component of the ever-shifting social and religious mosaic of the American nation.[11]

Even if they often failed to shape the social order, there can be no denying that the ministers shaped countless individual lives. Scores of memoirs attest to the central place played by regular church services, ministerial visits, camp meetings, song fests, youth groups, church sociables, and Sunday Schools.[12] Pinning down such contributions, however, has become almost an impossible task.

Contemporary observers recognized this situation. Numerous accounts acknowledged the difficulty of evaluating the impact of the Protestant home missionary. As an Episcopal cleric noted at the Bishop William Hobart Hare memorial service, Hare did not irrigate the desert, introduce a new variety of wheat, increase the yield of South Dakota corn, or build a railroad. Instead, Hare concentrated primarily on enhancing the realm of "the spirit."[13] A Presbyterian clergyman made a similar observation at Henry Kendall's memorial service. Although Home Mission administrator Kendall oversaw the distribution of 13 million Presbyterian dollars, his chief monuments were deemed intangible. They lay in the "sustained and viable character of the western settlers."[14]

Other contemporary observers praised the home missionaries in the most glowing terms. An 1881 spokesman for frontier Nevada declared that "no more self-denying labor was ever accomplished than that performed by these heralds of religion."[15] Two decades later, Rev. Newell Dwight Hillis boldly stated that the nation owed its greatest debts to its educators and that chief among these were the home missionaries.[16] President Theodore Roosevelt put it even more eloquently: "It is such missionary work that prevented the pioneers from sinking perilously near the level of the savagery against which they contended. Without it the conquest of this continent would have had but an animal side. Because of it, deep beneath and through the national character, there runs that power of firm adherence to a lofty ideal upon which the safety of the nation will ultimately depend."[17] These are bold statements, impossible to document with any precision. But they do indicate the high regard that contemporaries felt toward the home mission movement.

While the personal impact of the home missionaries will probably always remain elusive, their theological legacy is a bit easier to discern. As Colin B. Goodykoontz has suggested in *Home Missions on the American Frontier* (1939), the primary thrust of the home mission movement was a conservative one. Judging by the surviving sermons, the mainline ministers in the West preached a basic, Arminian Christianity. They spoke of human sin and divine redemption through God's freely given grace. They placed a high value on ethical behavior and on individual moral choice. In general, they presented a simple, biblical Christianity, regardless of denominational affiliation.

The Sunday Schools reinforced this theological conservatism. More prominent than the churches until the turn of the century, these Sunday Schools served the West as democratic religious institutions. A typical Sunday School teacher stressed the fact that any person of intelligence (man, woman, or child) could understand God's word as found in Scripture. The Bible remained an open book. The children memorized random verses, and a "common sense" understanding of the words prevailed. The various religious communes and theological hairsplitting proved short lived. Academic arguments over evolution, liberal theology, higher criticism, and comparative religion seemed far away. This legacy of conservatism may still be seen today in many areas. The national evangelical revival of the 1980s clearly reveals these western roots.

Finally, one comes to the role of the western clerics in the "mythological" West of legend, popular culture, and film. Here, the clergy have fared especially poorly. Millions of people recall the names of Billy the Kid, Wyatt Earp, George A. Custer, Calamity Jane, Belle Starr, Jesse James, and Wild Bill Hickok. Only a handful remember Sheldon Jackson, Brother Van, or Bishop Tuttle. Nonetheless, the social impact of Jackson, Van, and Tuttle far outweighed the contributions of the others. Why have scholars, novelists, and filmmakers given the clergy such wide berth?

Those who would make heroes of the western ministers face a difficult task. Along with the women, the clerics represented convention; they embodied the society's regulations and restraints. The other, more acclaimed members of the western pantheon conveyed a "freedom" from social restrictions. Historian Ray Billington has argued that the continued popularity of nineteenth-century western culture reflects this universal desire to "lessen the controls necessary in today's societies."[18] But the Protestant clergy came to the West as spokesman for *increased* social controls. Their Christianity ended in grace and freedom, to be sure, but it began with original sin and a clarion call for restraint. Thus, the western clergy played the role of Aunt Sally to Huck Finn, or the Sheriff of Nottingham to Robin Hood. This is not the material from which great legends are made. Few mythmakers have even bothered to try.

The constitutional separation of church and state points to yet another reason why the western clergy have never achieved a mythic stature. Regardless of their contribution to the settlement of the West, the clerics all retained a denominational affiliation—Jackson was a Presbyterian; Van, a Methodist; Tuttle, an Episcopalian. Thus, they represented but one aspect of the panorama of America's religious faiths. This "particularization" has made it difficult for the cleric to enter the rich vein of western folklore. Because of their denominational links, the clergy can never be "universalized." The Protestant ministers, therefore, have never really shared in the saga of America's grand epic. It is doubtful if they ever will.

From 1865 to 1915, the New West produced no genuinely "national" religious figure. The region called forth no theologian of importance, such as Horace Bushnell or Walter Rauschenbusch. It created no vigorous crusaders for or against the theory of evolution, such as Congregationalist Lyman Abbott or Presbyterian James McCosh; nor did it produce any religious reconcilers like popular spokesman Henry Ward Beecher. There were no great evangelists to rival Dwight L. Moody, Billy Sunday, or Sam Jones, or song masters to match tunes with Ira Sankey. Instead, the typical western minister proved to be a hard-working and practical (but often anonymous) servant of his church.

Perhaps the life of Rev. John Mallory Bates best sums up the careers of these forgotten clergymen. Bates spent over forty years on the plains of western Nebraska in the service of his parishioners and his Episcopal church. When he died in 1930, an admirer noted in a memorial sermon: "[N]o temples have been erected to honor him, but his memory is enshrined in the hearts of many people."[19] Or, as eighty-seven-year-old Oklahoma Baptist Leon D. Martindale observed in another context, "I wouldn't say I've fought a good fight—them are Paul's words, but I have done my best."[20] Thousands of his compatriots could have said, "Amen."

Notes

Introduction

1. George Allen Beecher, *A Bishop of the Great Plains* (Philadelphia: Church Historical Society, 1950).

2. Frank Bergon and Zeese Papanikolas, eds., *Looking Far West: The Search for the American West in History, Myth, and Literature* (New York: Mentor, 1978). Rodman W. Paul and Richard W. Etulain, eds., *The Frontier and the American West* (Arlington Heights, Ill.: AHM, 1977).

3. James T. Addison, *The Episcopal Church in the United States, 1789–1931* (New York: Charles Scribner's Sons, 1931); Gaius Glenn Atkins and Frederick L. Fagley, *History of American Congregationalism* (Boston: Pilgrim Press, 1942), 155.

4. Ferenc Morton Szasz, *The Divided Mind of Protestant America, 1880–1930* (University: University of Alabama Press, 1982).

5. The best of these transcend mere antiquarianism: see Colin B. Goodykoontz, *First Congregational Church of Boulder: An Historical Sketch, 1864–1939* (Boulder: First Congregational Church, 1939); Gunther Rothenberg and Israel C. Carmel, *Congregation Albert, 1897–1972* (Albuquerque: n.p., 1972); Virginia Cole Trenholm, "Wheatland's First Church," *Annals of Wyoming* 29 (April 1957); Margaret Connell Szasz, *First Congregational Church of Albuquerque, New Mexico, a Centennial History: 1880–1980* (Albuquerque: AVC Printers, 1980).

6. Henry M. Merkel, *History of Methodism in Utah* (Colorado Springs: Dentan Printing Co., 1938); Allen duPont Breck, *The Episcopal Church in Colorado, 1860–1963* (Denver: Big Mountain Press, 1963); Motier A. Bullock, *Congregational Nebraska* (Lincoln: Western Publishing and

Engraving Company, 1905); Carlos Castaneda, *Our Catholic Heritage in Texas, 1519–1936* (Austin: Von Boeckmann-Jones, 1936), 7 vols. Henry W. Caspar, S.J., *History of the Catholic Church in Nebraska,* 3 vols. (Milwaukee: Bruce/Catholic Life, 1960–69); Lewis A. Myers, *A History of New Mexico Baptists* (Albuquerque: Baptist Convention of New Mexico, 1965); Harriet Rochlin and Fred Rochlin, *Pioneer Jews: A New Life in the Far West* (Boston: Houghton Mifflin Company, 1984).

7. Clifford M. Drury, *Marcus and Narcissa Whitman and the Opening of Old Oregon,* 2 vols. (Seattle: Pacific Northwest National Parks and Forests Association, 1986); William Warren Sweet, *Religion on the American Frontier,* 4 vols. (Chicago and New York: Henry Holt, 1931–46); Colin B. Goodykoontz, *Home Missions on the American Frontier* (Caldwell, Ida.: Caxton Printers, 1939; rep. 1971); Robert William Mondy, *Pioneers and Preachers: Stories of the Old Frontier* (Chicago: Nelson Hall, 1980); Ross Phares, *Bible in Pocket, Gun in Hand: The Story of Frontier Religion* (Lincoln: University of Nebraska Press, 1964); William M. Kramer, ed., *The American West and the Religious Experience* (Los Angeles: Will Kramer, 1970); Gary Topping, "Religion in the West," *Journal of American Culture* 3 (Summer, 1980), 330–350. Louisa Ward Arps, ed., *Faith on the Frontier: Religion in Colorado before August, 1876* (Denver: Colorado Council of Churches, 1976). This work also includes a good bibliography compiled by Harold M. Parker, Jr. Norman J. Bender, "Crusade of the Blue Banner in Colorado," *Colorado Magazine* 47 (Spring 1970), 91–118. See also the essays in Ferenc M. Szasz, ed., *Religion in the West* (Manhattan, Kan.: Sunflower University Press, 1984). An excellent study, which arrived too late to be fully incorporated here, is Carl Guarneri and David Alvarez, eds., *Religion and Society in The American West: Historical Essays* (New York: University Press of America, 1987).

8. *The Lutherans in North America* (Philadelphia: Fortress Press, 1975), 264. The book is multiauthored, but Fevold wrote the section on the period 1875–1900.

9. Henry Ward Beecher to Miss Harris, December 21, 1864, Stowe–Day Library, Hartford, Conn. Zachary Eddy, *The Evangelization of Our Country* (New York: American Home Missionary Society, 1877); Helen O. Belknap, *The Church on the Changing Frontier: A Study of the Homesteader and His Church* (New York: George H. Doran, 1922).

10. Edward Laird Mills, *Plains, Peaks and Pioneers: Eighty Years of Methodism in Montana* (Portland: Binfords and Mort, 1947).

11. Stephen R. Riggs, *Mary and I: Forty Years with the Sioux* (Minneapolis: Ross and Haines, 1969; orig. publ. 1880); John L. Dyer, *The Snow-Shoe Itinerant* (Cincinnati: Methodist Book Concern, 1890); Ethelbert Talbot, *My People of the Plains* (New York: Harper and Brothers, 1906); Daniel S. Tuttle, *Reminiscences of a Missionary Bishop* (New York:

Thomas Whittaker, 1906); Samuel E. West, *Cross on the Range: Missionary in Wyoming* (Philadelphia: The Church Historical Society, 1947); George Allen Beecher, *A Bishop on the Great Plains*; Ralph Hill, *The Main Trail* (San Antonio: Naylor, 1971); Cayton Rice, *Ambassador to the Saints* (Boston: Christopher Publications, 1965). Ralph Connor (Charles Williams Gordon) has given a fictional account of the minister in the Canadian West in *The Sky Pilot: A Tale of the Foothills* (London: Hodder and Stoughton, 1899; 1903).

12. Cited in Mark Banker, "Making Haste Slowly: A History of Presbyterian Missions in the American Southwest," (Ph.D. diss., University of New Mexico), 1987, Chap. 1.

Chapter One

1. Edward S. Murphy, "Diary," Idaho Historical Society, Boise.

2. Robert West, *Missouri, Arkansas, Indian Territory and Texas as a Mission Field* (Boston: Congregational Home Missionary Society, 1881), 2. Pamphlet, Congregational Library, Boston.

3. Sidney E. Mead, *The Lively Experiment: The Shaping of Christianity in America* (New York: Harper and Row, 1963).

4. John Henry Barrows, *Spiritual Forces in American History* (Boston: Congregational Home Missionary Society, 1899), 4–5; William Kincaid, *Another Year of Home Missions* (New York: American Home Missionary Society, 1889), 11; J. M. Sturdevant, *American Emigration* (New York: American Home Missionary Society, 1857), 7–8.

5. William N. Sloan, *Spiritual Conquest along the Rockies* (New York: George H. Doran Company, 1913); W. G. Puddefoot, *The Minute Man on the Frontier* (Chicago: Thomas Y. Crowell, 1895); George H. Durand, *Joseph Ward of Dakota* (Boston: The Pilgrim Press, 1913), 71; Ernst C. Helmreich, ed., "Letters of Pastor Christian Helmreich: Establishing a Lutheran Congregation in Weyerts, Nebraska, 1887–1888," *Nebraska History* 58 (Summer 1977), 185; *North Dakota Evangel*, September 16, 1888.

6. Joseph P. Thompson, *The Theocratic Principle; or, Religion the Bond of the Republic* (New York: American Home Missionary Society, 1868), 17.

7. Samuel J. Mills and Daniel Smith, *Report of a Missionary Tour through that Part of the United States which Lies West of the Allegheny Mountains; Performed under the Direction of the Massachusetts Missionary Society* (Andover: Flagg and Gould, 1815), 47; Samuel J. Mills and John F. Schermerhorn, *A Correct View of that Part of the United States which Lies West of the Allegheny Mountains, with Regard to Religion and Morals* (Hartford, Conn.: P. B. Gleason, 1814).

8. Rev. Samuel Parker, *Journal of an Exploring Tour beyond the Rocky Mountains* (1838; rpt., Ross and Haines, 1969), 83–85; Frank Bergon and Zeese Papanikolas, eds., *Looking Far West: The Search for the American West in History, Myth, and Literature* (New York: Mentor, 1978), 144ff.

9. Horace Bushnell, *Barbarism the First Danger: A Discourse for Home Missions* (New York: American Home Missionary Society, 1847), 26, 23; Lyman Beecher, *A Plea for the West* (Cincinnati: Truman, 1835); see also, Edmund Norris Kirk, *The Church Essential to the Republic* (New York: American Home Missionary Society, 1846). Pamphlet, Stowe–Day Library, Hartford, Conn.

10. *Fifteenth Annual Report of the American Home Missionary Society* (New York, 1841), 73, as quoted in Robert E. Riegel, *Young America, 1830–1840* (Norman: University of Oklahoma Press, 1949), 257.

11 Charles R. Bodo, *The Protestant Clergy and Public Issues, 1812–1848* (Princeton: Princeton University Press, 1954); Charles I. Foster, *An Errand of Mercy: The Evangelical United Front, 1790–1837* (Chapel Hill: University of North Carolina Press, 1960; Clifford S. Griffin, "Religious Benevolence as Social Control, 1815–1860," *Mississippi Valley Historical Review* 44 (1957), 423–44. There is a good critique in Lois Banner, "Religious Benevolence as Social Control: A Critique of an Interpretation," *Journal of American History* 60 (1973), 23–41; Colin B. Goodykoontz, *Home Missions on the American Frontier* (Caldwell, Idaho: Caxton Printers, 1939), 369–75. Elizabeth Twaddell, "The American Tract Society, 1814–1860," *Church History* 15 (1946), 116–32.

12. Colin B. Goodykoontz, *Protestant Home Missions and Education in the Trans-Mississippi West, 1835–1860,* 72–74. Pamphlet, University of Colorado Special Collections, Boulder; Polly Welts Kaufman, *Woman Teachers on the Frontier* (New Haven: Yale University Press, 1984), xvii–49; cf. Anne M. Boylan, "Evangelical Womanhood in the Nineteenth Century: The Role of Women in Sunday Schools," *Feminist Studies* 4 (1978), 67–80.

13. Edward Beecher, *The Question at Issue* (Boston: T. R. Marvin, 1850), 23.

14. E. B. Smith, *An Address* . . . (Concord: Eastman, Webster and Company, 1834), 1–5. Pamphlet, Andover Newton Theological Seminary, Newton Center, Mass.

15. Others would include Allegheny (Methodist), DePauw (Methodist), Knox (Presbyterian and Congregational), Carleton (Presbyterian), Otterbein (United Brethren), Kenyon (Episcopalian), Hanover (Quaker), and Wittenberg (Lutheran).

16. John B. Hill, "Timothy Hill and Western Presbyterianism: A Review of the Life and Letters of a Superintendent of Missions" (unpublished typescript, Kansas Historical Society, Topeka, c. 1926), 705–6.

17. Joseph B. Clarke, "One Year of Home Missions," in *Papers Read at*

the Fifty-eighth Annual Meeting of the American Home Missionary Society (New York: American Home Missionary Society, 1885), 6.

18. Storrs, as cited in Joseph B. Clarke, *Leavening the Nation: The Story of American [Protestant] Home Missions* (New York: Revell, 1903; 1913), 341.

19. Walter Prescott Webb, *The Great Plains* (Boston: Ginn and Co., 1931).

20. John M. Waddell, *Christian Education in Its Principles* (Philadelphia: C. Sherman and Son, 1858), pamphlet, Presbyterian Historical Society, Philadelphia.

21. Bruce Kinney, *Frontier Missionary Problems* (New York: Fleming H. Revell, 1918), 85.

22. Josiah Strong, *Our Country* (New York: American Home Missionary Society, 1885; rev. ed., 1896). In 1963, Harvard University Press reissued Strong's book with a new introduction by Jurgen Herbst. See also, Philip D. Jordan, "Josiah Strong and a Scientific Social Gospel," *The Iliff Review* 42 (Winter 1985), 21–31.

23. Strong, *Our Country*, 218–19.

24. Josiah Strong, "Address," in *Papers Read at the Fifty-eighth Annual Meeting of the American Home Missionary Society* (New York: American Home Missionary Society, 1885), 31–33.

25. *First Report of Bishop Randall of Colorado to the Board of Missions of the Protestant Episcopal Church, October 1866* (New York: Sanford, Harroun and Co., 1866), 16; *The Colorado Transcript,* August 25, 1869.

26. *Thirteenth Annual Report of the Missionary Bishop of Colorado* (1866). Copy, John F. Spalding Papers, Western Heritage Center, Denver, Colorado.

27. E. P. Tenney, *The New West as Related to the Christian College* (Cambridge: Riverside Press, 1878).

28. Alice Cowan Cochran, *Miners, Merchants, and Missionaries: The Roles of Missionaries and Pioneer Churches in the Colorado Gold Rush and Its Aftermath, 1858–1870* (Metuchen, N.J.: Scarecrow Press, 1980), 25.

29. W. A. Seward Sharp, "History of Kansas Baptists" (1939), Manuscript, Kansas Historical Society, Topeka, 56.

30. Hussen, as cited in Daniel S. Tuttle, *Reminiscences of a Missionary Bishop,* 59; *Daily Oklahoman,* April 23, 1939.

31. Ward Platt, *The Frontier* (Cincinnati: Jennings and Graham, 1908).

32. Cf. *Cheyenne Daily Leader,* July 16, 1862, in Church History Vertical File, Wyoming Historical Society, Cheyenne.

33. Frank Milton Bristol, *The Life of Chaplain McCabe* (Cincinnati: Jennings and Graham, 1908), 259.

34. John B. Hill, "Timothy Hill and Western Presbyterianism;" *Denver Republican,* March 10, 1902, in Frank Spalding Scrapbook, Colorado Heritage Center, Denver; Darley Manuscripts, Western Historical Collection, University of Colorado, Boulder; J. D. Stewart, *A Brief Autobiography* (n. p., 1913).

35. Robert W. Lind, *From the Ground Up: The Story of 'Brother Van Orsdel,' Montana Pioneer Minister, 1848–1919* (Polson, Mont.: privately published, 1961), 47.

36. Harrison A. Brann, "Bibliography of Sheldon Jackson Collection in the Presbyterian Historical Society," *Journal of the Presbyterian Historical Society* 30 (September 1952), 145. See also the three articles by Alvin K. Bailey, "Sheldon Jackson, Planter of Churches," *Journal of the Presbyterian Historical Society,* 26 (September 1948), 129–148; (December 1948), 193–215; 27 (March 1949), 21–40.

37. Robert L. Stewart, *Sheldon Jackson* (New York: Revell, 1908), 118–122.

38. Minutes of the Presbytery of Montana, vol. A. Copy, Montana Historical Society, Missoula.

39. See Ted C. Hinckley, "Sheldon Jackson: Gilded Age Apostle," *Journal of the West* 23 (January 1984), 16–25; Norman Bender, "Sheldon Jackson's Crusade to Win the West for Christ, 1869–1880," *The Midwest Review* 4 (Spring 1982), 1–12; and Jackson's own summary in "Sheldon Jackson Invades the Rocky Mountains, 1869–76,"*Journal of Presbyterian History* 37 (1959), 122–128.

40. John B. Hill, "Timothy Hill and Western Presbyterianism," 197.

41. Cited in Fanny H. McDougal, *A History of Trinity Presbyterian Church,* 12. Pamphlet, Arizona Historical Society, Tucson.

42. Cf. the examples in Robert Hickman Adams, *White Churches of the Plains: Examples from Colorado* (Boulder: Colorado Associated University Press, 1970).

43. Cited in Eliott West, *The Saloon on the Rocky Mountain Mining Frontier* (Lincoln: University of Nebraska Press, 1979), 134.

42. "Bells of the Empire," *Rocky Mountain Empire Magazine,* Sunday, April 6, 1947; J. B. Schooland, "A Pioneer Church, First Presbyterian Church of Boulder Colorado Territory" (unpublished manuscript, 1972); Al Look, comp., *Sidelights on Colorado* (Denver: Golden Bell Press, 1967), 91.

45. *Diary and Letters of the Reverend Joseph W. Cook, Missionary to Cheyenne* (Laramie, Wyo.: The Laramie Republican, 1919), 91.

46. Cited in the *North Dakota Evangel,* October 6, 1881; cited in Merle W. Wells, "Presbyterians in the Mountain West: Response to a Regional Challenge,"*Journal of Presbyterian History* 62 (Summer 1984), 139–151.

47. Albuquerque *Morning Democrat,* May 14, 1893, as cited in Betty

Danielson, "Our Homeless Congregation Erects House of Faith." Leaflet, First Baptist Church, Albuquerque.

48. Frederick C. Luebke, *Immigrants and Politics: The Germans of Nebraska, 1880–1900* (Lincoln: University of Nebraska, 1967), 45.

49. *Commemoration, Seventy-fifth Anniversary, 1877–1952,* Mennonite Brethren Church, Henderson, Nebraska. Pamphlet, Nebraska Historical Society.

50. Benjamin Kelson, "The Jews of Montana," *Western States Jewish Historical Quarterly* 3 (January 1971), 176.

51. Mrs. Harold W. Preiss, comp., "The First Methodist Church [of Tucson]," typescript, Arizona Historical Society.

52. Cheyenne *Daily Leader,* September 20, 1878; December 3, 1882, in Vertical Files, Church History, Wyoming Historical Society, Cheyenne.

53. Cf. Ming-Ogu Li, "An Introduction to the Study of the History of the Methodist Churches in El Paso, Texas" (Master's thesis, Texas Western College, 1949), 56–58.

54. Stella to Sister, January 28, 1866, Stella File, Nebraska Historical Society.

55. The [Cheyenne] *Daily Sun Leader,* November 28, 1895.

56. Autobiography of Jacob Adriance (1903), typescript, Western Historical Collections, Denver Public Library.

57. Jacob Adriance to R. M. Hussey, August 29, 1892, Adriance Collection, Western Historical Collections, Denver Public Library.

58. James Wilkinson to Lewis Bodwell, April 28, 1867, Congregational File, Kansas Historical Society, Topeka.

59. Diary of Joseph W. Cook (transcript of letters, slightly different from the published version), Beinecke Library, Yale University, 18.

60. Thomas H. Thompson and Albert A. West, *History of Nevada* (Oakland, Calif.: Thompson and West, 1881), 200.

61. Rollin L. Hartt to Mother, January 19, 1897, Hartt Manuscripts, Montana Historical Society, Helena.

62. James H. White, comp., *The First Hundred Years of Central Presbyterian Church, Denver, Colorado, 1860–1960* (Denver, 1960), 9; "Methodism Begins in Arizona Territory," pamphlet, Arizona Historical Society, 3.

63. *Laramie Daily Boomerang,* May 11, 1944.

64. Pamphlet in Gray Manuscripts, box 1, Western Heritage Collection, Laramie.

65. C. H. McLenathan to J. Mills Kendrick, August 22, 1895, Kendrick Manuscripts, Diocese of the Rio Grande, Albuquerque; *Boulder County News,* October 15.

Chapter Two

1. Ann Douglas, *The Feminization of American Culture* (New York: Knopf, 1977). See also Alice Cowan Cochran, *Miners, Merchants, and Missionaries: The Roles of Missionaries and Pioneer Churches in the Colorado Gold Rush and Its Aftermath, 1858–1870* (Metuchen, N.J.: Scarecrow Press, 1980). v.

2. Lawrence Larsen, *The Urban West at the End of the Frontier* (Lawrence: The Regents Press of Kansas, 1978); Robert Dykstra, *The Cattle Towns* (New York: Knopf, 1968).

3. Verdon R. Adams, *Methodism Comes to the Pass: A History of Trinity United Methodist Church of El Paso* (El Paso: Guynes Printing Co., 1975), 5.

4. Nolie Mumey, ed., *Alexander Taylor Rankin (1803–1885): His Diary and Letters* (Boulder: Johnson, 1966), 90.

5. A. M. Hough, "Establishment of Our Mission in Montana: Notes from My Diary," Montana Historical Society, Helena.

6. Spencer Wilson, ed., "Montana Memories," *Montana* 29 (January 1979), 16–28.

7. *Photography and the Old West* (New York: Harry N. Abrams, in association with the Amon Carter Museum, 1978), 147–51.

8. Look, *Sidelights on Colorado,* 9; William M. Breckenridge, *Helldorado: Bringing the Law to the Mesquite* (Glorieta, N.M.: Rio Grande Press, [1928]; rpt., 1980), xviii; Autobiography of William Bladen Jett (1858–1941), 55, University of Arizona, Special Collections; Dyer, *Snow-Shoe Itinerant,* 262; Diary of Joseph Witherspoon Cook, January 14, 1868, to May 9, 1869, Bienecke Library, Yale University.

9. Robert W. Lind, *From the Ground Up: The Story of 'Brother Van' Orsdel, Pioneer Montana Minister, 1848–1919* (Polson, Mont.: privately published, 1961), 14.

10. Joshua C. Taylor, *America as Art* (New York: Harper and Row, 1976), 176–77; cf. the comments in Samuel E. West, *Cross on the Range: Missionary in Wyoming* (Philadelphia: The Church Historical Society, 1947), 23. H. Craig Miner, *Wichita: The Early Years, 1865–80* (Lincoln: University of Nebraska Press, 1982), 127.

11. Al Hobbs, "The Cowboy Spirit" (sermon 1890), copy, Western Heritage Center, Denver. Francis P. Weisenburger, "God and Man in a Secular City: The Church in Virginia City, Nevada," *Nevada Historical Quarterly* 14 (Summer 1971), 3–5.

12. *Diary and Letters of the Reverend Joseph W. Cook, Missionary to Cheyenne* (Laramie, Wyo.: The Laramie Republican Company, 1919), 11–13; Mary Ann Norman Smallwood, "Childhood on the Southern Plains Frontier, 1870–1910" (Ph.D. diss., Texas Tech, 1975), quoted on 104.

13. Jonathan Blanchard to Milton Badger, August 9, 1864, Blanchard File, Montana Historical Society, Helena; Diary of Joseph W. Cook; C. W. Towne, *Her Majesty Montana: High Lights in the History of a State Fifty Years Old in 1939* (Helena: Montana Power Co., 1939), 37.

14. Everett Dick, *The Sod-House Frontier, 1854–1890* (Lincoln: University of Nebraska Press, 1935; rpt., 1979), 334; Hiram Stone, "Memoirs of a Pioneer Missionary and Chaplain in the United States Army," in *Collections of the Kansas State Historical Society, 1913–1914,* 13 (1915), 344; Diary of Joseph W. Cook.

15. Robert K. De Arment, *Knights of the Green Cloth: The Saga of the Frontier Gamblers* (Norman: University of Oklahoma Press, 1982), 22–23. See also Gary L. Cunningham, "Gambling in Kansas Cattle Towns: A Prominent and Somewhat Honorable Profession," *Kansas History* (Spring 1982), 1–22.

16. Motier A. Bullock, *Congregational Nebraska* (Lincoln: Western Publishing and Engraving Company, 1905), 183–188.

17. Alex M. Darley, "The Faro Dealer's Funeral," clipping, box 1, folder 58, Darley Manuscripts, Western Historical Collections, University of Colorado, Boulder.

18. See Marion S. Goldman, *Gold Diggers and Silver Mines: Prostitution and Social Life on the Comstock Lode* (Ann Arbor: University of Michigan Press, 1981); Carol Leonard and Isidor Wallimann, "Prostitution and Changing Morality in the Frontier Cattle Towns of Kansas," *Kansas History* 2 (Spring 1979), 34–53; Elliott West, "Scarlet West: The Oldest Profession in the Trans-Mississippi West," *Montana* 31 (April 1981), 16–26; Paula Petrik, "Prostitution in Helena, Montana, 1865–1900," *Montana* 31 (April 1981), 28–42; and Marion Goldman, "Sexual Commerce on the Comstock Lode," *Nevada Historical Society Quarterly* 21 (Summer 1978), 99–123. Ruth Rosen's *The Lost Sisterhood: Prostitution in America, 1900–1918* (Baltimore: The Johns Hopkins University Press, 1982), ignores the West.

19. Dorothea R. Muller, "Church Building and Community Making on the Frontier, a Case Study: Josiah Strong, Home Missionary in Cheyenne, 1871–1873," *Western Historical Quarterly* 10 (April 1979), 191–216; Arps, ed., *Faith on the Frontier,* 14.

20. New York *World,* January 1, 1888, in Dawson Scrapbooks, Colorado Heritage Center.

21. Byron A. Johnson and Sharon P. Johnson, *Gilded Palaces of Shame: Albuquerque's Redlight Districts, 1880–1914* (Albuquerque: Gilded Age Press, 1983), 47–48.

22. Helen O. Belknap, *The Church on the Changing Frontier: A Study of the Homesteader and His Church* (New York: George H. Doran, 1922).

23. Idaho Tri-Weekly *Statesman,* February 11, 1873; Avis R. Anderson, ed., "Pastor on the Prairie," *Montana* 24 (January 1974), 36–54; "History

of the First Baptist Church, Hinton, Oklahoma, 1902–1952," typescript, Oklahoma Historical Society, Oklahoma City.

24. El Paso *Herald Post,* May 28, 1936.

25. Elliott West, *The Saloon on the Rocky Mountain Mining Frontier*; Richard Erdoes, *Saloons of the Old West* (New York: Alfred A. Knopf, 1979). Thomas J. Noel, *The City and the Saloon: Denver, 1858–1916* (Lincoln: University of Nebraska Press, 1982).

26. C. L. Sonnichsen, *Pass of the North: Four Centuries on the Rio Grande* (El Paso: Texas Western Press, 1968), 277.

27. William W. Sweet, "The Churches as Moral Courts of the Frontier," *Church History* 2 (March 1933), 3–21.

28. J. B. Schooland, "A Pioneer Church, First Presbyterian Church of Boulder, Colorado Territory" (unpublished manuscript, 1972), 90 ff. The two best accounts of Presbyterians in Colorado are Andrew E. Murray, *The Skyline Synod: Presbyterianism in Colorado and Utah* (Denver: Golden Bell Press, 1971); and Norman J. Bender, "Crusade of the Blue Banner in Colorado," *Colorado Magazine* 47 (Spring 1970), 91–118.

29. El Paso *Times,* February 16, 1932.

30. Don Meschter, typescript of speech, "Address for the Centennial of the First Presbyterian Church, Rawlins, Wyoming," Vertical Files, Wyoming Historical Society; Cheyenne *Tribune-Eagle,* May 4, 1969; tape recorded interview with W. Hamilton Wright, June 11, 1975, Texas Tech Library, Lubbock, Texas.

31. Jane T. Poore, "A Baptist Pioneer in Montana," typescript, Montana Historical Society, Helena.

32. Undated clipping, Frank Spalding Scrapbooks, Colorado Heritage Center, Denver, 3; John L. Dyer, *Snow-Shoe Itinerant*; W. S. Rainsford, *A Preacher's Story of His Work* (New York: Outlook Co., 1904), 212–13; Hiram Stone, "Memoirs of a Pioneer Missionary and Chaplain in the United States Army," *Collections of the Kansas State Historical Society, 1913–1914* 13 (1915), 334; Ralph Hall, *The Main Trail* (San Antonio: The Naylor Company, 1971); John Howard Melish, *Franklin Spencer Spalding: Man and Bishop* (New York: Macmillan, 1917), 214.

33. Earl F. Stover, *Up from Handyman: The United States Army Chaplaincy, 1865–1920,* vol. 3 (Washington, D.C.: Department of the Army, 1977), 69; Lind, *From the Ground Up,* 99; Cyrus Townsend Brady, *Recollections of a Missionary in the Great West* (New York: Scribner's, 1900), 51.

34. Robert P. Wilkins and Wynona H. Wilkins, *God Giveth the Increase: The History of the Episcopal Church in North Dakota* (Fargo: North Dakota Institute for Regional Studies, 1959), 109.

35. John Howard Melish, *Franklin Spencer Spalding: Man and Bishop,* 124.

36. James F. Walker, pamphlet, author's collection.

37. John Mills Kendrick Manuscripts, Diocese of the Rio Grande Archives, Albuquerque.

38. *Annual Report on Domestic Missions* (1890–91), 61–62.

39. C. W. Boynton to John Mills Kendrick, January 19, 1902, box 1; William M. Jeffers to John M. Kendrick, March 26, 1895, box 1; C. W. Boynton to John Mills Kendrick, n.d, Kendrick Collection, box 1.

40. Cyrus Brady, *Recollections,* 38, 113.

41. Ethelbert Talbot, *My People of the Plains* (New York: Harper and Brothers, 1906), 55.

42. Al Look, comp., *Sidelights on Colorado,* 72.

43. Myron J. Fodge, "Brother Van's Call to Frontier Montana," *Montana* 22 (October 1972); Myron J. Fodge, "The Protestant Minister Faces Frontier Montana," *Montana* 15 (January 1965), 34.

44. Esther Derbyshire MacCallum, *The History of St. Clement's Church, El Paso, Texas, 1870–1925* (El Paso: The McGrath Co., 1925). "The First Church in El Paso, 1870–1935," pamphlet, El Paso Public Library.

45. Samuel A. Riggs, "Address at Service in Memory of Rev. Richard Cordley, D.D., Nov. 20, 1904," Riggs Manuscripts, Kansas Historical Society, Topeka.

46. Statement by Reverend Somerville in Cordley Manuscripts, Kansas Historical Society, Topeka.

47. Denver *News,* March 25, 1920.

48. Romulus A. Windes, "Pioneer Baptist Missionary of Arizona," typescript, Arizona Historical Society, Tucson, 64.

49. Chandler W. Sterling, "Leigh Richmond Brewer: Frontier Bishop on the Loose," *Montana* 11 (July 1961), 39–54; Carrie M. Townley, "Bishop Whittaker's School for Girls," *Nevada Historical Society Quarterly* 19 (Fall 1970), 171–81; John Linton Struble, "The People's Bishop," *Montana* 6 (Winter 1956), 20–28; Betty Derig, "Pioneer Portraits," *Idaho Yesterdays* 12 (Winter 1968), 13–22; Daniel S. Tuttle, *Reminiscences of a Missionary Bishop* (New York: Thomas Whittaker, 1906; rpt., Helena Letter Shop, 1977).

50. Undated clipping, Dawson Scrapbooks, Colorado Heritage Center, Denver.

51. Undated clipping, Dawson Scrapbooks, 36.

52. Tuttle to Wife, September 15, 1867, Tuttle letters on microfilm, Montana Historical Society.

53. Henry Pickering Walker, "Preacher in Helldorado," *Journal of Arizona History* 15 (Autumn 1974), 223–47.

54. Brady, *Recollections,* 18–24.

55. Typescript, Church History, Wyoming Historical Society, Cheyenne.

56. Lind, *From the Ground Up,* 133.

57. John Hoskins, "Sky Pilot Tales," *The Frontier* (November 1930), 70. Copy, Western Historical Collections, University of Colorado.

58. Tuttle, *Reminiscences,* 215.

59. Robert William Monday, *Pioneers and Preachers: Stories of the Old Frontier* (Chicago: Nelson Hall, 1980), 189; Theodore C. Blegen, ed., "John B. Blegen: A Missionary Journey on the Dakota Prairies in 1888," *North Dakota Historical Quarterly* 1 (1927), 16–29. The quotation is on p. 23.

60. Tuttle to Wife, August 27, 1867; Windes, as quoted in Hester Cattel, "A Pioneer Minister," *The Rail* 2 (August 1909), 15.

61. Claton Rice, *Ambassador to the Saints* (Boston: Christopher Publishing House, 1965), 138.

62. *Diary and Letters of the Reverend Joseph W. Cook, Missionary to Cheyenne,* 45–46.

63. Tuttle to Wife, April 12, 1868. Tuttle Microfilm.

64. Cornelia B. Kennedy, "Organized Religion in South Dakota before 1900" (Master's thesis, University of South Dakota, 1932), 2; Virgil Couvsey, *Indian-Pioneer Papers,* vol. 51, Oklahoma Historical Society, 249; Motier A. Bullock, *Congregational Nebraska* (Lincoln: Western Publishing and Engraving Company, 1905), 188, 195. For a much more critical view of clerical social work, see Peter H. Argersinger, "The Divines and the Destitute," *Nebraska History* 51 (Fall 1970), 303–18.

65. Jacob Adriance Diary (1859), Colorado Heritage Center.

66. Letters, reports, and articles by Albert Stewart, typescript from *Sunday School Missionary* (February 1919), Arizona Historical Society.

67. Stover, *Up from Handyman,* 45.

68. Fanny A. Adriance, "Reminiscences" (1905), Western Heritage Collection, Denver Public Library.

69. Cheyenne *Daily Leader,* September 20, 1876.

70. Leadville *Daily Democrat,* January 18, 1880.

71. Interview with Beth Hoddel, Albuquerque, New Mexico.

72. Tuttle to Wife, March 19, 1868. Tuttle Microfilm.

73. Cook to Bishop Randall, March 16, 1868. Letter of Rev. Joseph W. Cook to Rt. Rev. R. H. Clarkson and Rt. Rev. George M. Randall, typescript, Bienecke Library.

74. Rollin L. Hartt to Mother, January 19, 1897; October 5, 1896, Hartt Manuscripts, Montana Historical Society.

75. Leaflet on Grace Episcopal Church, 1917, Arizona Historical Society.

Chapter Three

1. Dodge City *Times,* May 11, 1882. This copy was lent to me by Hana Samek.

2. Joseph B. Clark, *The Closing Decade* (New York: American Home

Missionary Society, 1891), 8; William N. Sloan, *Spiritual Conquest along the Rockies* (New York: George H. Doran Company, 1913), 11.

3. Lyle Dorsett, *The Queen City: A History of Denver* (Boulder: Pruett, 1977), 88–89.

4. Carole Rifkind, *A Field Guide to American Architecture* (New York: New American Library, 1980), 146–49; Roger G. Kennedy, *American Churches* (New York: Stewart, Tabori and Chang, 1982), is the best pictorial survey of American church architecture.

5. Denver *Post,* October 20, 1912.

6. William H. Haupt, "History of the American Church Known in Law as the Protestant Episcopal Church in the State of Kansas," *Collections of the Kansas State Historical Society* 16 (1923–1925), 395; Louis L. Perkins, "Samuel Gautier French: 1838–1882," *Historical Magazine of the Protestant Episcopal Church* 62 (March 1973), 37–45.

7. Cook to Randall, February 13, 1868. Letters of Rev. Joseph W. Cook to Rt. Rev. R. H. Clarkson and Rt. Rev. George M. Randall, typescript, Bienecke Library, Yale University.

8. Cornelia B. Kennedy, "Organized Religion in South Dakota" (Master's thesis, University of South Dakota, 1932), 6.

9. Will V. McGee manuscripts, private collection, Cottage Grove, Oregon.

10. Rudolf Glanz, "Notes on the Early Jews in Arizona," *Western States Jewish Historical Quarterly* 5 (July 1973), 248. Thomas H. Thompson and Albert A. West, *History of Nevada* (Oakland, Calif.: Thompson and West, 1881), 227–28. Marjorie Hornbein, "Denver's Rabbi William S. Friedman: His Ideas and Influence," *Western States Jewish Historical Quarterly* 13 (January 1981), 149.

11. Ward, quoted in Don O. Shelton, *Heroes of the Cross in America* (New York: The Young People's Missionary Movement, 1904), 237; Dana in North Dakota *Evangel,* September 18, 1888.

12. *Baptist Home Missions in North America* (New York: Baptist Home Mission Rooms, 1883), 178; James H. Hitchman, *Liberal Arts Colleges in Oregon and Washington: 1842–1980* (Bellingham, Wash.: Center for Pacific Northwest Studies, 1981), discusses this crusade in the Pacific Northwest. His story stresses the important role these church-related schools played in the region.

13. Cited in Betty Derig, "Pioneer Portraits," *Idaho Yesterdays* 12 (Winter 1968), 13–22.

14. *Twenty-first Anniversary of the First Congregational Church of Crete, Nebraska* (1891), 4. Pamphlet, Arley B. Shaw Collection, Nebraska Historical Society.

15. Quoted in "Welcome to Historic Del Norte" (pamphlet, 1975),

copy in Del Norte Clippings, Menaul Historical Library of the Southwest, Albuquerque.

16. Arthur B. Kinsolving, *Texas George: The Life of George Herbert Kinsolving, Bishop of Texas, 1892–1928* (Milwaukee: Morehouse, 1932), 53.

17. Edward Murphy, "Diary," Idaho Historical Society, Boise.

18. William D. Walker, "Report of the Missionary Bishop of North Dakota," in *Annual Report upon Domestic Missions by the Board of Managers of the Domestic and Foreign Missionary Society of the Protestant Episcopal Church in the USA* (New York, 1890), 49.

19. William Robert Dubois III, "A Social History of Cheyenne Wyoming, 1875–1885" (Master's thesis, University of Wyoming, 1963).

20. J. B. Schooland, "A Pioneer Church, First Presbyterian Church of Boulder, Colorado Territory" (unpublished manuscript, 1972). Cheyenne *Daily Leader,* February 10, 1876; September 10, 1876.

21. Clippings, Methodist File, Sharlott Hall Library, Prescott, Ariz.; unidentified clipping, February 15, 1878, Sharlott Hall Scrapbook 4, p. 5, Prescott, Ariz.

22. Cited in Vernon R. Adams, *A History of Trinity United Methodist Church El Paso* (El Paso: Guyne Printing Co., 1975), 39.

23. Central City paper, as cited in Olaf S. Olsen, "A History of the Baptists of the Rocky Mountain Region, 1849–1890" (Ph.D. diss., University of Colorado, 1952), 210.

24. Abbie E. (Noyes) Raymond, "The Ladies Social Circle," in Richard Cordley Manuscripts, Kansas Historical Society.

25. *Cheyenne Daily Leader,* September 10, 1876.

26. Cf. the account in Lucy Crane, "Silverton: Social Life in the Early Days" (unpublished paper, University of New Mexico).

27. The quotation is from E. Franklin Frazier, *The Negro Church in America* (New York: Schocken, 1963; 1974), 35; W. Sherman Savage, *Blacks in the West* (Westport, Conn.: Greenwood Press, 1976), 185.

28. Bruce David Forbes, "Presbyterian Beginnings in South Dakota, 1840–1900," *South Dakota History* 7 (Spring 1977), 140.

29. Colin B. Goodykoontz, *Home Missions on the American Frontier* (Caldwell, Ida.: Caxton Printers, 1939), especially chapter 13.

30. F. L. Bennett to W. J. Johnson, October 1895; W. J. Jerome to J. Mills Kendrick, November 29, 1899; see also C. M. Randall to J. Mills Kendrick, February 23, 1893, Kendrick Papers, box 3.

31. "The Life and Ministry of William Vance Shook, Pioneer Oklahoma Minister of the Gospel," Western History Collections, University of Oklahoma, Norman.

32. Jacob Adriance, "My First Ten Years," manuscript, Western History Collections, Denver Public Library; J. D. Stewart, *A Brief Autobiography* (n.p., 1913), Western History Collections, University of Colorado, Boulder;

Romulus A. Windes, Pioneer Baptist Missionary of Arizona (Autobiography), typescript, Arizona Historical Society; Ralph Hall, *The Main Trail* (San Antonio: The Naylor Company, 1971), 16.

33. M. F. Platt, "Reminiscences of Early Days in Nebraska," in *Transactions and Reports of the Nebraska State Historical Society* 10 (1892), 90.

34. Olive Price Holder, "Circuit Riding Experiences of William Perryman Garvin on the Texas Frontier, 1891–1898" (Master's thesis, Texas Technological College, 1935), 30.

35. "1923 Reminiscences of Mrs. Anna Moore Simpson, Wife of Rev. Wm. G. Simpson, Methodist Pastor," Idaho Historical Society; Ennen Reaves Hall, *One Saint and Seven Sinners: The Life of a Baptist Circuit-Riding Pastor and His Family at the Turn of the Century* (New York: Thomas Y. Crowell, 1959), 27; interview with John W. Miller, typescript, Idaho Historical Society.

36. Mary M. Gaylord, *Life and Labors of Reuben Gaylord: Home Missionary for Iowa and Nebraska* (Omaha: Rees Printing Co., 1889), 253; Franklin Moore, "Autobiography of a Pioneer Missionary," typescript, Fort Collins Public Library, 21, p. 2.

37. Hall, *One Saint and Seven Sinners,* 47.

38. Cited in Robert Moats Miller, *Harry Emerson Fosdick: Preacher, Pastor, Prophet* (New York: Oxford University Press, 1985), 312.

Chapter Four

1. E. Lyman Hood, "Why Plant Mission Schools in New Mexico" (pamphlet, ca. 1890).

2. E. P. Tenney, *The New West as Related to the Christian College* (Cambridge: Riverside Press, 1878), 3–4.

3. "Wyoming," pamphlet, Gray Collection, box 2, Western Heritage Center, University of Wyoming.

4. W. Barrows, "Eight Weeks on the Frontier" (Boston, 1876), sermon, Bienecke Library, Yale University; R. L. Bachman, "Home Missions in the New West," sermon given at the First Presbyterian Church, Utica, N.Y., February 17, 1875, Bienecke Library, Yale University.

5. Tuttle to wife, July 19, 1867, Bishop Tuttle Letters, Montana Historical Society (microfilm).

6. E. P. Tenney, *Looking Forward into the Past* (Nahant, Mass.: Romford Press, 1910), 101.

7. William Kincaid, "Practical Measures in the Present Stage" (New York, 1870), pamphlet, Congregational Historical Society, Boston.

8. Hunter Farish, *The Circuit Rider Dismounts* (Richmond: Dietz Press, 1938).

9. Cited in Hamilton W. Pierson, *In the Brush; Or, Old-time Social and Religious Life in the Southwest* (New York: B. Appleton and Co., 1881), 4.

10. Ward Platt, *The Frontier* (Cincinnati: Jennings and Graham, 1908), xi.

11. Edward Laird Mills, *Plains, Peaks and Pioneers: Eighty Years of Methodism in Montana* (Portland: Binfords and Mort, 1947), 62.

12. Seth K. Humphrey, *Following the Prairie Frontier* (Minneapolis: University of Minnesota Press, 1931), 78; Robert P. Wilkins and Wynona H. Wilkins, *God Giveth the Increase: The History of the Episcopal Church in North Dakota* (Fargo: North Dakota Institute for Regional Studies, 1959) 14n; Faye C. Lewis, *Nothing to Make a Shadow* (Ames: Iowa State University Press, 1971), ix.

13. *Western Story: The Recollections of Charley O'Kieffe, 1884–1898* (Lincoln: University of Nebraska Press, 1960).

14. Interview with Mrs. Mae Embery (daughter of Baptist minister S. Y. Jackson), Spring 1980, Albuquerque, New Mexico.

15. Lewis, *Nothing to Make a Shadow*, esp. chap. 10; Ross G. Barnes, *The Sod House* (Lincoln: University of Nebraska Press, 1930; 1970), chap. 16; Everett Dick, *The Sod House Frontier, 1854–1890* (Lincoln: University of Nebraska Press, 1935), esp. chap. 24; Joanna L. Stratton, *Pioneer Women: Voices from the Kansas Frontier* (New York: Simon and Schuster, 1981), 171–83. Margaret Wasson, "Texas Methodism's Other Half," *Methodist History* 19 (July 1981), 209.

16. Wilferd T. Knight, *Pioneer's Heritage* (Franklin, Wisc.: privately published, 1979), 25. Interview with Liff Sanders, July 5, 1958, Texas Tech (tape recording); interview with Mae Embery; Wasson, "Texas Methodism's Other Half," 206–10.

17. Ralph Hall, *The Main Trail* (San Antonio: The Naylor Company, 1971), 69.

18. "John Mallory Bates," typescript, in George Allen Beecher Manuscripts, Nebraska Historical Society, Lincoln, box 2; Virginia Driving Hawk Sneve, *That They May Have Life: The Episcopal Church in South Dakota, 1859–1976* (New York: Seabury Press, 1976), 90–91.

19. George Allen Beecher, "Journal of Events, 1891–1894," Nebraska Historical Society, Lincoln.

20. Cited in Wilkins and Wilkins, *God Giveth the Increase,* 49–50.

21. *Annual Report upon Domestic Missions by the Board of Managers of the Domestic and Foreign Missionary Society of the Protestant Episcopal Church in the USA* (New York, 1890–91); Walker, *Annual Report,* 1895, 87–88.

22. Lawrence T. Slaght, *Multiplying the Witness: 150 Years of Ameri-*

can Baptist Educational Ministry (Valley Forge: Judson Press, 1974), 47–50.

23. Daniel G. Stevens, *The First Hundred Years of the American Baptist Publication Society* (Philadelphia: American Baptist Publication Society, n.d.), 41.

24. Martin L. Massaglia, "Colporter Ministry," *Foundations* 24 (October–December 1981), 328–339.

25. Antoine Loving Brady, *Thornton Kelly Tyson: Pioneer Home Missionary* (Kansas City, Mo.: Western Baptist Publishing Co., 1915), 93–117. Cf. Nina Ellis Dosker, "Edwin M. Ellis, Montana's Bicycling Minister," *Montana* 30 (Winter 1980), 42–50.

26. O'Kieffe, *Western Story: The Recollections of Charley O'Kieffe*, 5, 58.

27. Eve Ball, *Riodoso* (San Antonio: Naylor, 1963), 14.

28. J. M. Somerndike, *By-Products of the Rural Sunday School* (Philadelphia: Westminster Press, 1914), 12, 138.

29. W. H. Schureman, *Pioneer Sabbath School Missions in Colorado and Wyoming, 1898 to 1923,* 2.

30. Joanna L. Stratton, *Pioneer Women: Voices from the Kansas Frontier* (New York: Simon and Schuster, 1981), chap. 10.

31. Mary Blake Salmans, "Mrs. Blake's Sunday Schools," *New Mexico Historical Review* 38 (October 1963), 312–322; *Pioneer Sabbath School Missions,* 2.

32. O'Kieffe, *Western Story: The Recollections of Charley O'Kieffe,* 69.

33. J. D. Stewart, *A Brief Autobiography* (n.p., 1913), 89ff.

34. Eugene Parsons, "History of Colorado Baptists" [1923], manuscript, Colorado Heritage Center, Denver.

35. Schureman, *Pioneer Sabbath School Missions,* passim; Louise Barry, ed., "Circuit-Riding in Southwest Kansas in 1885 and 1886: The Letters of Jeremiah Evarts Platt," *Kansas Historical Quarterly* 12 (November 1943), 378–89.

36. Pamphlet in Albert L. Johnson Manuscripts, Nebraska Historical Society.

37. Letters, reports, and articles by Albert Stewart, typescript, copied from Sunday School Missionary (February 1918), in Arizona Historical Society, Tucson.

38. W. H. Schureman, *Pioneer Sabbath School Missions,* 24.

39. George Allen Beecher, "My Dear Fellow Workers," address (ca. 1934), in George Allen Beecher Manuscripts, Nebraska Historical Society, box 1. There is an old Plains saying that advises: Either you love Nature or you hate it. Bates fell in the former category.

40. New Mexico Baptist College Catalogue (Alamogordo, 1909), 7.

41. Embery interview.

42. Merton L. Dillon, "Religion in Lubbock," in Lawrence L. Graves,

ed., *A History of Lubbock* (Lubbock: West Texas Museum Association, 1962), 449–516.

43. Cited in Vernon R. Adams, *A History of Trinity United Methodist Church of El Paso* (El Paso: Guynes Printing Co., 1975), 43.

44. Fred P. Force, "The Life Story of L. R. Millican" (Master's thesis, Texas Western College of the University of Texas, 1956), 25–27.

45. W. D. Smithers, *Circuit Riders of the Big Bend* (El Paso: Texas Western Press, 1981), 18–20.

46. El Paso *Times,* February 13, 1933. Indeed, as one minister observed in 1986, Great Plains religious conditions were still similar to those of the 1880s. *Albuquerque Journal,* September 14, 1986.

47. El Paso *Herald Post,* April 19, 1938.

48. Margaret Hook Olsen, *Patriarch of the Rockies: The Life Story of Joshua Gravett* (Denver: Golden Bell, 1960), 104; Leroy L. Lane, "Frontier Methodism," in William M. Kramer, ed., *The American West and the Religious Experience* (Los Angeles: Will Kramer, 1975), 29; Lauretta I. Randall, *The Odyssey of a Great Grandmother* (Spokane: Spokane Lithographing Co., n.d.), 49, 78.

49. The standard account is, Charles A. Johnson, *The Frontier Camp Meeting: Religion's Harvest Time* (Dallas: Southern Methodist University Press, 1955; rpt., 1985, with new introduction by Ferenc M. Szasz).

50. Charles A. Parker, "The Camp Meeting on the Frontier and the Methodist Religious Resort in the East—Before 1900," *Methodist History* 18 (April 1980), 179–92.

51. Quoted in Betty Danielson, "Albuquerque, 1888—America's Hardest Mission Field," leaflet, First Baptist Church, Albuquerque.

52. Joe M. Evans, *The Cowboys' Hitchin' Post* (El Paso: n.p., 1938; ca. 1941), 17.

53. Austin and Alta Fife, *Heaven on Horseback: Revivalist Song and Verse in the Cowboy Idiom* (Logan: Utah State University Press, 1970), 24.

54. Neil M. Clark, "God's Round Up," *Saturday Evening Post* (March 6, 1943); cf. also Clifford Westermeier, "The Cowboy and Religion," *The Historical Bulletin* (January 1950).

55. C. Kenneth Smith of Marfa, Texas, Texas Tech, July 29, 1972 (tape recording).

56. Pamphlet, "Wyoming Mission Motors," Vertical File, Wyoming Historical Society.

Chapter Five

1. Alice Felt Tyler, *Freedoms Ferment* (Minneapolis: University of Minnesota Press, 1941), still offers the best account. See also, Winthrop S.

Hudson, *Religion in America* (New York: Charles Scribner's Sons, 1981); John Augustus Williams, *Life of Elder John Smith* (Cincinnati: Standard Publishing Company, n.d.); *The Evidences of Christianity: A Debate between Robert Owen, of New Lanark Scotland, and Alexander Campbell...* (St. Louis: Christian Board of Publication, n.d.); *A Debate on the Roman Catholic Religion* (Cincinnati: J. A. James, 1837).

2. Stephen D. Eckstein, "The History of Churches of Christ in Texas, 1824–1950" (Ph.D. diss., Texas Technological College, 1959), 211–24; the quotation is on p. 224.

3. A good collection of these pamphlets may be found in the Arthur B. Duncan Papers, Southwest Collection, Texas Technological University, Lubbock. Warlick's quotation is from the "Introduction," 25. Eckstein, "History of Churches of Christ," 185.

4. William Warren Sweet, *The Story of Religion in America* (New York: Harper and Brothers, 1950), 223–242.

5. Edward Cross, "Good and Bad Foundations in Time of Flood" (1895), sermon pamphlet, in J. Mills Kendrick Manuscripts, Miscellaneous Documents, 1892–1900, Archdiocese of the Rio Grande, Albuquerque.

6. John L. Peters, *Christian Perfectionism and American Methodism* (New York: Abington, 1956), 150; Anne C. Loveland, "Domesticity and Religion in the Ante-bellum Period: The Career of Phoebe Palmer," *The Historian* 39 (May 1977), 455–471. See also Timothy L. Smith, *Called unto Holiness: The Story of the Nazarenes, The Formative Years* (Kansas City: Nazarene Publishing House, 1962); David Edwin Harrell, Jr., *Oral Roberts: An American Life* (Bloomington: Indiana University Press, 1985), esp. 1–35, and Charles E. Jones, *Perfectionist Persuasion: The Holiness Movement and American Methodism, 1867–1936* (Metuchen, N.J.: Scarecrow, 1974).

7. Clark C. Spence, *The Salvation Army Farm Colonies* (Tucson: University of Arizona Press, 1985), is the best study.

8. Mary Lucille Hathaway, *An Album of Memories* Tucson: n. p., 1972), 16–17; *Los Angeles Times,* as quoted in the *Tucson Citizen,* January 6, 1908; *Denver Post,* June 7, 1904; March 22, 1905.

9. "Reminiscences of Mrs. Nye," Nye File, Arizona Historical Society; C. B. Forsberg, "John McIntyre: Life on the Sunnyside," *Que Pasa* (October 1976). Copy in Arizona Historical Society; *Tucson Citizen,* December 24, 1970.

10. Eckstein, "History of Churches of Christ," passim. See David E. Harrell, Jr., "The Sectional Origins of the Churches of Christ," *Journal of Southern History* 30 (August 1964), 261–277.

11. Hartt to Mother, Hartt Manuscripts, Montana Historical Society.

12. Isaac Gardner, "Quarterly Report," May 2, 1893, American Home Missionary Society, microfilm, reel 162; E. Lyman Hood to Brother Choate,

April 24, 1893, AHMS, reel 168; Geo. Wicks to Brethren, April 17, 1893, AHMS, reel 162.

13. Cited in Thomas S. Goslin II, "Henry Kendall, Missionary Statesman," *Journal of the Presbyterian Historical Society* 27 (June 1949), 74.

14. Figures from Vander Velde Manuscripts, Kansas Historical Society, and Moitier Bullock, *Congregational Nebraska* (Lincoln: Western Publishing and Engraving Company, 1905), 286–87.

15. Robert P. Wilkins and Wynona H. Wilkins, *God Giveth the Increase: The History of the Episcopal Church in North Dakota* (Fargo: North Dakota Institute for Regional Studies, 1959), 106–7; 117.

16. Cheyenne *Leader,* September 25, 1877.

17. H. M. Burr letter, April 17, 1893, AHMS, reel 15, Wyoming.

18. Tuttle to wife, microfilm, Montana Historical Society.

19. *La Plata Miner,* Silverton, Colorado, March 28, 1885.

20. Samuel E. West, *Cross on the Range: Missionary in Wyoming* (Philadelphia: The Church Historical Society, 1947), 32–35; Melish, *Franklin Spencer Spalding.*

21. Clifford S. Higby, "Reminiscences of a Wyoming Preacher," Manuscript, p. 40, Western Heritage Collection, Laramie, Wyoming.

22. Samuel S. West, *Cross on the Range,* 32; Franklin Moore, "Autobiography of a Pioneer Missionary," typescript, Fort Collins Public Library, chap. 19, p. 3. This even extended to the Catholics. As an 1867 Denver journalist admitted (upon looking at Catholic Central City Hospital), "Much as opposing denominations may denounce the Roman Catholic Church, all must admit that in the work for general good our Catholic church of this city has by no means become laggard, but on the contrary [has] led the advance." Quoted in Alice Cowan Cochran, *Miners, Merchants, and Missionaries: The Roles of Missionaries and Pioneer Churches in the Colorado Gold Rush and Its Aftermath, 1858–1970* (Metuchen, N.J.: Scarecrow Press, 1980), 127.

23. Zachary Eddy, *The Evangelization of Our Country* (New York: American Home Missionary Society, 1877), 18. Cf. Charles A. Johnson, *The Frontier Camp Meeting: Religion's Harvest Time* (Dallas: Southern Methodist University Press, 1955; rpt., 1985).

24. James D. Moffat, "The Attitude of Ministers toward Current Discussions in Theology" (Pittsburgh, 1889). Pamphlet, Presbyterian Historical Society, Philadelphia.

25. Cited in Szasz, *Divided Mind,* 16.

26. Mrs. James B. Collison, *Indian-Pioneer Papers,* vol. 2, p. 364. Oklahoma Historical Society.

27. W. W. Van Dusen, *Blazing the Way; Or, Pioneer Experiences in Idaho, Washington, and Oregon* (Cincinnati: Jennings and Graham, 1905), 84.

28. Claton Rice, *Ambassador to the Saints* (Boston: Christopher Publishing House, 1965), 138; Samuel E. West, *Cross on the Range,* 41.

29. Mrs. Earle Ragsdale, "Skull Valley Church History," typescript, Sharlott Hall, Prescott, Arizona; Frank Schweissing, *The History of Wyoming Baptists,* 26. Pamphlet, vertical files, Wyoming Historical Society, Cheyenne; Putnam Burton Peabody, "Coming Back: A Missionary Experience," unpublished manuscript, Bienecke Library, Yale University; "Data Relating Experiences of James F. Walker," typescript, author's collection.

30. Francis P. Weisenburger, "God and Man in a Secular City: The Church in Virginia City, Nevada," *Nevada Historical Society* 14 (Summer 1971), 8. "The Hold Up in Jerico Canyon," W. D. B. Gray Manuscripts, Western Heritage Center, Laramie, Wyoming.

31. Cited in Myron T. Fogde, "Brother Van's Call to Frontier Montana," *Montana* 22 (October 1972), 4.

32. Watson Parker, *Deadwood: The Golden Years* (Lincoln: University of Nebraska Press, 1981), 162–63.

33. Conrad Vander Velde, "The Cumberland Presbyterian Church, Wichita Presbytery 1878–1903," Vander Velde Manuscripts, Kansas Historical Society; Denver *News,* June 17, 1901.

34. Canadian minister, as quoted in B. G. Smillie and N. T. Threinen, "Protestants: Prairie Visionaries of the New Jerusalem, The United and Lutheran Churches in Western Canada," in Smillie, ed., *Visions of the New Jerusalem: Religious Settlement on the Prairies* (Edmonton: NeWest Press, 1983), 80.

35. James F. Walker pamphlet, author's possession.

36. "Early Religious Activity in Tonkawa," in Mrs. Edna Hatfield Collection, University of Oklahoma Western Collection.

37. Chalmers Martin, "A Journal, May–September, 1981," South Dakota Historical Society; Cyrus R. Rice, "Experience of a Pioneer Missionary," *Collections of the Kansas State Historical Society* 13 (1913–1914), 229; Ralph Hall, *The Main Trail* (San Antonio: Naylor, 1971); Romulus A. Windes, "Pioneer Baptist Missionary of Arizona," manuscript, Arizona Historical Society, 70; Jacob Adriance, "Dear Brethren," Western Historical Collections, Denver Public Library.

38. Austin and Alta Fife, *Heaven on Horseback: Revivalist Songs and Verse in the Cowboy Idiom* (Logan: Utah State University Press, 1970), 85–91.

39. M. A. DeWolfe Howe, *The Life and Labors of Bishop Hare: Apostle to the Sioux* (New York: Sturgis and Walton, 1911), 302.

40. Spencer Wilson, ed., "Montana Memories," *Montana* 29 (January 1979), 25.

41. Unidentified clipping, May 29, 1899, Sharlott Hall; ibid., August 18, 1898; Colorado Springs *Gazette-Telegram,* May 5, 1946.

42. William B. Goode, *Outposts of Zion, with Limnings of Mission Life* (Cincinnati: Poe and Hitchcock, 1864), 425.

43. *Courier,* January 18, 1870, copy in Sharlott Hall; undated clipping, March 31, 1897, ibid.

44. *Leadville Daily Democrat,* February 8, 1880; Rollin L. Hartt to Mother, October 16, 1896, Hartt Manuscripts, Montana Historical Society.

45. John Howard Melish, *Franklin Spencer Spalding: Man and Bishop* (New York: Macmillan, 1917), 139.

46. Cf. the analysis in Lowell B. Harlan, "Theology of Eighteenth Century English Hymns," *Historical Magazine of the Protestant Episcopal Church* 48 (June 1979), 167–93. Charles W. Hughes, et al., *American Hymns, Old and New* (New York: Columbia University Press, 1980) is the standard work. See also the thematic analysis and discussion in Sandra S. Sizer, *Gospel Hymns and Social Religion* (Philadelphia: Temple University Press, 1978).

47. Angie Debo, *Tulsa: From Creek Town to Oil Capital* (Norman: University of Oklahoma Press, 1943), 72; Fife and Fife, *Heaven on Horseback,* vii–2.

48. Edward A. Geary, "For the Strength of the Hills: Imagining Mormon Country," in Thomas Alexander and Jessie L. Embry, eds., *After 150 Years: The Latter-day Saints in Sesquicentennial Perspective* (Provo: Charles Redd Center for Western Studies, 1983), 78–79; Wilfred C. Bailey, "Folklore Aspects in Mormon Culture," *Western Folklore* 10 (1951), 217–25.

49. Isadore Papermaster, "A History of North Dakota Jewry and Their Pioneer Rabbi," Part 2, *Western Jewish Historical Quarterly* 10 (January 1978), 172.

50. Cited in Don O. Shedton, *Heroes of the Cross in America* (New York: The Young People's Missionary Movement, 1904), 200.

51. Edward D. Terry, "Methodism in Arizona: The First Seventy Years," *Arizona and the West* 3 (Summer 1961), 248; "A Reminiscent Chapter by a Wyoming Pioneer, 1889–1915," 7. Manuscript, Western Heritage Center, Laramie, Wyoming.

52. Betty Derig, "Pioneer Portraits," *Idaho Yesterdays* 12 (Winter 1968), 20.

53. Cheyenne *Leader,* February 23, 1873. E. A. Babcock to Bro. Kincaid, March 23, 1893, American Home Missionary Society, microfilm, reel 15.

54. Joyce S. Kendall to Mrs. Frank Goodwin, May 12, 1974, Manuscript 456, box 12, Southwest folder, Idaho Historical Society.

55. Fife and Fife, *Heaven on Horseback,* 3–4.

56. H. Craig Miner, *West of Wichita: Settling the High Plains of Kansas, 1865–1900* (Lawrence: University Press of Kansas, 1986), 52 ff.

Chapter Six

1. Diary of Sister Monica, Special Collections, University of Arizona, Tucson.

2. El Paso *Times,* February 8, 1895. In Carl Hayden File, Arizona Historical Society; cf. H. W. Read File, New Mexico Baptist Convention, Albuquerque.

3. Transcriptions of letter from Read from *Baptist Home Monthly,* December 1948; New Mexico Baptist Convention, Albuquerque.

4. Ibid.

5. James M. Stoney, *Lighting the Candle: The Episcopal Church on the Upper Rio Grande* (Santa Fe: The Rydal Press, 1961), 1–6; Olaf S. Olsen, "A History of the Baptists of the Rocky Mountain Region, 1849–1890" (Ph.D. diss., University of Colorado, 1952), 99. Cf. Ernest Stapleton, Jr., "The History of Baptist Missions in New Mexico, 1849–1866" (Master's thesis, University of New Mexico, 1954).

6. *Original Record,* vol. 1, vol. 2, in folders, "New Mexico Baptist Convention," Albuquerque; P. W. Longfellow, "Baptist Beginnings and Progress in New Mexico" (Roswell 1909); pamphlet, ibid.

7. Thomas Harwood, *History of New Mexico Spanish and English Missions of the Methodist Episcopal Church from 1820 to 1910,* 2 vols. (Albuquerque: El Abogado Press, 1908–1910), tells their story.

8. *El Abogado Cristiano* (October 1907).

9. Carolyn Atkins, "Menaul School, 1881–1930 . . . Not Leaders, Merely, but Christian Leaders," *Journal of Presbyterian History* 58 (Winter 1980), 279–98.

10. Earl S. Bell, "Evangelical Beginnings in the Arizona Territory, 1804–1912," typescript, Southern Baptist Convention, quoted on 13–16. Cf. James W. Byrkit, "The Word on the Frontier: Anglo Protestant Churches in Arizona, 1854–1899," *Journal of Arizona History* 21 (Winter 1980), 63–86.

11. Diary of William Bladen Jett, Arizona Historical Society. Figures from typescript, Sharlott Hall Library, Prescott, Arizona.

12. Wallace, as cited in Roland F. Dickey, "Lew Wallace: One of 'Them Literary Fellers,' " *New Mexico Magazine* 63 (January 1985), 15–17. Ruth Ealy, *Water in a Thirsty Land* (n. p., 1955), 36–39; Norman J. Bender, ed., *Missionaries, Outlaws and Indians: Taylor F. Ealy at Lincoln and Zuni, 1878–1881* (Albuquerque: University of New Mexico Press, 1984).

13. Mario T. Garcia, *Desert Immigrants: The Mexicans of El Paso, 1880–1920* (New Haven: Yale University Press, 1981), 219; Robert West, "Missouri, Arkansas, Indian Territory and Texas as a Mission Field" (1881), 5, pamphlet, Congregational Library, Boston.

14. *The Southwest Baptist* (Texico, N.M.) July 25, 1907.

15. Fred P. Force, "The Spanish Baptist Publishing House," Manuscripts, Special Collections, University of Texas at El Paso.

16. Marta Weigle, *Brothers of Light, Brothers of Blood: The Penitentes of the Southwest* (Albuquerque: University of New Mexico Press, 1976), 72–75.

17. Alice Corbin Henderson, *Brothers of Light: The Penitentes of the Southwest* (New York: Harcourt, Brace and Company, 1937), presents the first favorable view of the order.

18. *Fifth Annual Report of the New West Commission; First Annual Report of Colorado, Wyoming, and New Mexico* (1874) 16; Bruce Kinney, *Frontier Missionary Problems,* 102–3.

19. Alexander M. Darley, *The Passionists of the Southwest, or The Holy Brotherhood* (Pueblo: n.p., 1893); rprt. Glorieta, N.M.: Rio Grande Press, 1968), 58.

20. Cited in Ray John de Aragon, *Padre Martinez and Bishop Lamy* (Las Vegas, N.M.: Pan-American, 1978), 58.

21. Santa Fe *New Mexican,* May 18, 1912.

22. In spite of this criticism, Paul Horgan, *Lamy of Santa Fe* (New York: Farrar, Straus and Giroux, 1975), is the definitive biography of the archbishop. See also John Charles Scott, "Between Fiction and History: An Exploration into Willa Cather's *Death Comes for the Archbishop*" (Ph.D. diss., University of New Mexico, 1980); Thomas J. Steele, S.J., "Peasant Religions: Retablos and Penitentes," in Jose de Onis, ed., *The Hispanic Contribution to the State of Colorado* (Boulder: Westview Press, 1976), 124–136; Aragon, *Padre Martinez and Bishop Lamy,* 115.

23. Alice Blake, "History of Presbyterian Missions in Colorado and New Mexico," Manuscripts, Menaul Historical Society, 71–78.

24. Olsen, "History of the Baptists of the Rocky Mountain Region," 113–15.

25. Ernest Stapleton, Jr., "The History of Baptist Missions in New Mexico, 1849–1866" (Master's thesis, University of New Mexico, 1954), 203, 216–218; *El Abogado Cristiano* (December 1903); Jay S. Stowell, *Home Mission Trails* (New York: Abingdon Press, 1920), 47–48.

26. Melba H. Swartout, "Missionaries to Their Own People," *Menaul Historical Review* 13 (Fall 1986), 1–7; Gabino Rendon's autobiography is *Hand on My Shoulder.* As Alfredo Nañez shows in "The Transition from Anglo to Mexican-American Leadership in the Rio Grande Conference," *Methodist History* 16 (January 1978), 67–74, the Methodists in Texas usually assigned the Hispanic evangelists to a secondary role until after World War I. See also R. Douglas Brackenridge and Francisco O. García-Treto, "Presbyterians and Mexican Americans: From Paternalism to Partnership," *Journal of Presbyterian History* 55 (Summer 1977), 161–78.

27. Sister M. Lilliana Owens, "Most Reverend Anthony J. Schuler, S.J.,"

Jesuit Studies—Southwest (El Paso, 1953), 183–193; the quotation is on p. 190. See also Garcia, *Desert Immigrants,* 219–22.

28. *Revista Católica,* June 27, 1897; March 29, 1896; March 20, 1881; June 4, 1899. Cf. the account in Dianna Everett, "The Public School Debate in New Mexico, 1850–1891," *Arizona and the West* 26 (Summer 1984), 107–35.

29. Quoted in Everett, "Public School Debate"; Thomas Harwood, *History of New Mexico Spanish and English Missions,* vol. 2, 171–81.

30. Sheldon, cited in chap. 1 of William B. Hale, "Charles Elkanah Hodgin: Educator" (Ph.D. diss., University of New Mexico, 1983); *New Mexico: A Guide to the Colorful State* (New York: Hastings House, 1953 [1940]), 127.

31. Sister Richard Marie Barbour, L.L., *Light in Yucca Land* (Santa Fe: Shifani Brothers, 1952), tells their story; Rev. J. B. Salpointe, *Soldiers of the Cross: Notes on the Ecclesiastical History of New Mexico, Arizona, and Colorado* (Albuquerque: Calvin Horn, 1967 [1898]), 234–41.

32. Louis Avanti, "The History of Catholic Education in New Mexico since the American Occupation" (Master's thesis, University of New Mexico, 1940), 20, 24. Jane C. Atkins, "Who Shall Educate: The Schooling Question in Territorial New Mexico, 1846–1911" (Ph.D. diss., University of New Mexico, 1982) is a superb story of the conflict over education.

33. Harwood, *History of New Mexico Spanish and English Missions,* vol. 1, 205; Thomas J. Steele, S.J., *Works and Days: A History of San Felipe Neri Church, 1867–1895* (Albuquerque: The Albuquerque Museum, 1983), 38.

34. Frederick G. Bohme, "The Italians in New Mexico," *New Mexico Historical Review* 34 (April 1959), 103.

35. *El Abogado Cristiano* (October 1907).

36. Clipping in Sheldon Jackson Scrapbook, 1–55. Microfilm from the Presbyterian Historical Society. George G. Smith to Sheldon Jackson, August 24, 1875, Jackson Correspondence, 386 (microfilm).

37. Thomas Harwood, *History of New Mexico Spanish and English Missions,* 2 vols.; Carolyn Atkins, comp., "Presbyterian Schools in New Mexico and Southern Colorado," Menaul Historical Library, Archives, Albuquerque; Ruth Barber, "History of the Allison James School," typescript, "Allison James" folder, Menaul School Archives, Albuquerque. See also Frank D. Reeve, "The Church in Territorial New Mexico," unpublished manuscript, 1964, Coronado Room, University of New Mexico, 7–8.

38. Frank D. Reeve, "The Old University of New Mexico in Santa Fe," *New Mexico Historical Review* 8 (July 1933), 201–9.

39. E. Lyman Hood, *The New West Education Commission, 1880–1893,* 79. Pamphlet.

40. Clipping File, Del Norte, Menaul Historical Library of the Southwest.

41. Quoted in Edith J. Agnew and Ruth K. Barber, "The Unique Presbyterian School System of New Mexico," *Journal of Presbyterian History* 49 (Fall 1921), 205.

42. Ruth Barber, typescript, "History of the Presbyterian Medical Work in New Mexico," "Bible in the South West" folder, Menaul School Archives, Albuquerque.

43. J. M. Bernal, "Our Teacher—Alice Hyson" [1960], Alice Hyson folder, Menaul School; cf. Alice Hyson, "Experiences with Little Mexicans," *Home Mission Monthly* (November 1917); Cheryl J. Foote, "Alice Blake of Trementina: Mission Teacher of the Southwest," *Journal of Presbyterian History* 60 (Fall 1982), 228–42.

44. D. E. F., "Why? Where? How? When?," *Home Mission Monthly* 4 (April 1890), 7.

45. *Home Mission Monthly* 3 (1889), 5, 131.

46. *Home Mission Monthly* 2 (November 1887), 9.

47. *Christian Education and New West Gleaner* 8 (August and September 1891), 26.

48. The *Home Mission Monthly* has many stories of such incidents.

49. Benjamin M. Read, *Illustrated History of New Mexico* (Santa Fe: New Mexican Printing Co., 1912), 525.

50. *The Old Faith and Old Glory, 1846–1946; Story of the Church in New Mexico since the American Occupation* (n.p., 1946), 12–13.

51. Santa Fe *New Mexican,* May 18, 1912.

52. *El Abogado Cristiano,* March 1903.

53. Ralph E. Twitchell, ed., *The Leading Facts of New Mexican History,* vol. 2 (Cedar Rapids: Torch Press, 1911–1917), 205–6.

54. For overviews of the situation, see R. Douglas Brackenridge and Francisco O. García-Treto, *Iglesia Presbiteriana: A History of Presbyterians and Mexican Americans in the Southwest* (San Antonio: Trinity University Press, 1974); and Randi Jones Walker, "Protestantism in the Sangre de Cristos: Factors in the Growth and Decline of the Hispanic Protestant Churches in Northern New Mexico and Southern Colorado, 1850–1920" (Ph.D. diss., Claremont Graduate School, 1983).

Chapter Seven

1. Jan Shipps, *Mormonism: The Story of a New Religious Tradition* (Urbana: University of Illinois Press, 1985). See also Jan Shipps, "Brigham Young and His Times: A Continuing Force in Mormonism," in Ferenc M. Szasz, ed., *Religion in the West* (Manhattan, Kan.: Sunflower University Press, 1984).

2. Burton, as cited in Davis Bitton, "The Ritualization of Mormon History," *Utah Historical Quarterly* 43 (Winter 1975), 71.

3. Rodman W. Paul, "The Mormons of Yesterday and Today," *Idaho Yesterdays* 19 (Fall 1975), 2–7.

4. The best overall study is Robert Joseph Dwyer, *The Gentile Comes to Utah: A Study in Religious and Social Conflict, 1862–1890* (Salt Lake City: Western Epics, 1971); for a more specific focus, see A. J. Simmons, *The Gentile Comes to Cache Valley* (Logan: Utah State University Press, 1976).

5. Thomas W. Haskins to Mrs. Hamilton, December 10, 1891, Utah Historical Society.

6. Illegible to McLeod, February 3, 1865; American Home Missionary Society Papers, microfilm, reel 4, 243.

7. McLeod to Dr. B. Coe, January 16, 1873, reel 4, 243.

8. *World's Fair Ecclesiastical History of Utah* (Salt Lake City, 1893), 166.

9. Undated clipping, AHMS, microfilm, reel 243; "Mr. McLeod's Work Among the Mormons," undated flyer, ibid.

10. Haskins to Hamilton, December 10, 1891, Utah Historical Society.

11. Quoted in James T. Addison, *The Episcopal Church in the United States, 1789–1931* (New York: Charles Scribner's Sons, 1951), 233. T. Edgar Lyon, "Religious Activities and Development in Utah, 1847–1910," *Utah Historical Quarterly* 35 (February 1967), 292–306. Sara Napper, "The History of the Episcopal Church in Utah," typescript, Utah Historical Society.

12. John D. Thornley, "Religion in Utah," typescript, Utah Historical Society, 34.

13. McLeod to D. B. Coe, October 28, 1872, AHMS, reel 243.

14. Rob W. Stafford to W. W. Storrs, ibid., November 4, 1876; Walter M. Barrows to A. H. Clapp, April 2, 1877, ibid., reel 244.

15. James B. Funsten, "The Making of an American on the West Side of the Rockies," *Outlook* 71 (June 14, 1902), 452. E. Lyman Hood, *The New West Education Commission, 1880–1893* (Jacksonville: H. and W. R. Drew Co., 1905), 125.

16. Hood, *The New West Education Commission,* 103–22.

17. Bruce Kinney, *Mormonism: The Islam of America* (New York: Fleming H. Revell, 1912), 9, 164.

18. Bruce Kinney, *Frontier Missionary Problems* (New York: Fleming H. Revell, 1918), 96.

19. R. Maud Ditmars, "A History of Baptist Missions in Utah, 1871–1931" (Master's thesis, University of Colorado, 1931), 48.

20. It is reprinted in James D. Gillilan, *Thomas Corwin Iliff: Apostle of Home Missions in the Rocky Mountains* (New York: Methodist Book Concern, 1919).

21. Henry M. Merkel, *History of Methodism in Utah* (Colorado Springs: Denton Printing Co., 1938), 71–78.

22. Store Notes from Logan Block Teachers Minute book, 1860–1875, J. Duncan Bright Collection (hereafter cited as JDB), Utah State University, Logan.

23. *Minutes of the Synod of Utah,* 1914, 15; 1896. Newton E. Clemenson, "Important Work in Utah," pamphlet, 1896, JDB Collection, box 4, folder 2.

24. Paul Jesse Baird, *The Mystery of Ministry in the Great Basin* (Globe, Ariz.: Pabsco Printers, 1976), 1–3; 37. S. M. Padden, *Is Mormonism Changing?* (New York: Home Missions Council, 1919).

25. *Ten Reasons: Being a Statement Why Christians Cannot Fellowship with Mormons* (1921), pamphlet, Utah Historical Society. Ditmars, "A History of Baptist Missions in Utah," 13–14.

26. John D. Thornley, "Religion in Utah," 36.

27. Leonard J. Arrington and Jon Haupt, "Intolerable Zion: The Image of Mormonism in Nineteenth Century American Literature," *Western Humanities Review* 22 (1968), 244n.

28. Cited in Frederick E. Maser, "The Way We Were in 1884," *Methodist History* 22 (January 1984), 125–26.

29. Davis Bitton, "Early Mormon Lifestyles; or the Saints as Human Beings," in F. Mark McKiernan, et al., eds. *The Restoration Movement: Essays in Mormon History* (Lawrence, Kan.: Coronado Press, 1973), 286.

30. Cited in John Howard Melish, *Franklin Spencer Spalding: Man and Bishop* (New York: Macmillan, 1917), 169.

31. Ditmars, "A History of Baptist Missions in Utah," 78.

32. *Home Mission Monthly* 11 (1887–1888), 6.

33. William Wise, *Massacre at Mountain Meadows: An American Legend and a Monumental Crime* (New York: Thomas Y. Crowell, 1976).

34. On this controversial subject, see: Leonard J. Arrington and Davis Bitton, *The Mormon Experience: A History of the Latter-day Saints* (New York: Alfred A. Knopf, 1979), 167–68. Leonard J. Arrington, *Brigham Young: American Moses* (New York: Alfred A. Knopf, 1985), 257–60, 278–80, 385–86, 479–80; and Juanita Brooks, *The Mountain Meadows Massacre* (Stanford, 1950; reprt., Norman: University of Oklahoma Press, 1962, 1970).

35. Henry M. Merkel, *History of Methodism in Utah* (Colorado Springs: Denton Printing Co., 1938), quoted on 54.

36. Merkel, *History of Methodism in Utah,* quoted on 67.

37. Young as quoted in Hood, *The New West Education Commission,* 41. John D. Thornley, "Religion in Utah," Utah Historical Society, 36–37.

38. *Public Discussion of the Doctrines of the Gospel of Jesus Christ*

(Salt Lake City: George Q. Cannon and Sons, 1897), 2d ed., pamphlet, Utah Historical Society.

39. F. S. Spalding, *Joseph Smith, Jr., as a Translator,* pamphlet, Utah Historical Society; Sara Napper, "The History of the Episcopal Church in Utah," typescript, Utah Historical Society, 15–17; Melish, *Franklin Spencer Spalding,* 171–75. John Sillito and Martha Bradley, "Franklin Spencer Spalding: An Episcopal Observer of Mormonism," *Historical Magazine of the Protestant Episcopal Church* 54 (December 1985), 339–49.

40. Cf. Walter Martin, *The Maze of Mormonism* (Ventura, Calif.: Vision House, 1962; 1984), and the contemporary efforts of Jerald and Sandra Tanner's Modern Microfilm company.

41. T. Edgar Lyon, "Evangelical Protestant Missionary Activity in Mormon Dominated Areas: 1865–1900" (Ph.D. diss., University of Utah, 1962), 67–69.

42. Young, as quoted in Brigham D. Madsen, "Frolics and Free Schools for the Youthful Gentiles of Corinne," *Utah Historical Quarterly* 48 (Summer 1980), 220–31.

43. N. Hamlet-Sanchez to J. Winkless, October 18, 1869, private collection, copy lent by Chantall Winkless.

44. William Henry Jackson, *Time Exposure* (New York: G. P. Putnam's Sons, 1940; rprt. University of New Mexico Press, 1986), 145.

45. S. S. Ivins, "Free Schools Come to Utah," *Utah Historical Quarterly* 22 (July 1954), 329. Charles S. Peterson, "A New Community: Mormon Teachers and the Separation of Church and State in Utah's Territorial Schools," *Utah Historical Quarterly* 48 (Summer 1980), 293–312.

46. Herbert W. Reherd, "An Outline History of the Protestant Churches of Utah," in W. Wain Sutton, ed., *Utah: A Centennial History* (New York: n. p., 1949); L. Lyman Hood, *The New West Education Commission,* preface.

47. W. M. Bonais to A. H. Clapp, April 2, 1877, AHMS papers, reel 244.

48. J. Duncan Brite, "History of the Presbyterian Churches and Schools in Cache Valley," manuscript, Utah State University, 8. A good, overall study is Carl Winkler, "History of Presbyterian Schools in Utah" (Master's thesis, University of Utah, 1968).

49. W. M. Barrows to A. H. Clapp, April 2, 1877, American Home Missionary Society Papers, reel 244. *Annual Report upon Domestic Missions of the Protestant Episcopal Church, 1891,* 5.

50. Theodore D. and Marian E. Martin, et al., comp., "Presbyterian Work in Utah, 1869–1969," Manuscript, Utah Historical Society, 572.

51. Olaf B. Olsen, "A History of the Baptists of the Rocky Mountain Region, 1849–1890" (Ph.D. diss., University of Colorado, 1952), 335.

52. E. Lyman Hood, *The New West Education Commission,* 137–147.

The figures include missionaries for both New Mexico and Utah. For the experiences of one woman missionary, see Gary Topping, "The Ogden Academy: Gentile Assault on Mormon Country," in Szasz, ed., *Religion in the West,* 37–47.

53. Interview with Nellie Wood Simpson, JDB Collection, box 3, folder 6.

54. Joseph A. Vinatieri, "The Growing Years: Westminster College from Birth to Adolescence," *Utah Historical Quarterly* 43 (Fall 1975), 344–61.

55. H. D. Fisher, *The Gun and the Gospel,* 268.

56. Paul Jesse Baird, *The Shepherd's Dog: The Story of Peacock Country* (Mexico: Casa de Publicaciones, 1974), 56.

57. Paul Jesse Baird, *The Shepherd's Dog,* 11.

58. Stanley B. Kimball, "The Utah Gospel Mission, 1900–1950," *Utah Historical Quarterly* 44 (Spring 1976), 149–55.

59. Rice, *Ambassador to the Saints.*

60. Ibid., 65.

61. Cited in Bright, "Non-Mormon Schools and Churches," 315–18.

62. Gentile School. Logan Block Minute Book, 1860–1875.

63. *Home Mission Monthly* 11 (1886–87), 60.

64. Edward Murphy, "Diary," Idaho Historical Society, 46.

65. Hans P. Freece, "Are You That Damned Presbyterian Devil?," *Presbyterian Magazine* (October 1931), offprint, Utah Historical Society.

66. Duncan J. McMillan, "Early Education Days in Utah," 10.

67. C. Merrill Hough, "Two School Systems in Conflict: 1867–1890," *Utah Historical Quarterly* 28 (April 1960), 113–128.

68. Merkel, *A History of Methodism in Utah,* 120.

69. John D. Thornley, "Religion in Utah," 62n, 69–71; appendix.

70. Duncan J. McMillan, "Early Education Days in Utah," 8; Lee A. Butler, "The Benjamin Presbyterian Church 1886–1916," *Utah Historical Quarterly* 51 (Summer 1983), 259–271.

71. Rice, *Ambassador to the Saints,* 182–84.

72. *Annual Report* (1897), 91. Kinney, *Mormonism: The Islam of America,* 161.

73. *Home Missionary Monthly* 3 (1888–1889), 228, 91; Henry M. Merkel, *History of Methodism in Utah,* quoted on 90.

74. D. Michael Quinn, "Utah's Educational Innovation: LDS Religion Classes, 1890–1929," *Utah Historical Quarterly* 43 (Fall 1975), 379–95.

75. *Doctrine and Covenants,* 160; 238–39.

76. For example, Rev. J. H. Worcester of Vermont once observed that beyond a "wholesome and needed recreation, mere play is not the business of a man and a Christian;" J. J. Worcester, *The House of Mirth* (Burlington: Tuttle and Stacy, 1850), 19. Sermon pamphlet, Stowe–Day Library, Hartford, Connecticut.

77. *Doctrine and Covenants,* 255.

78. Quoted in Eugene E. Campbell, "Social, Cultural, and Recreational Life," in Joel E. Ricks, ed., *The History of a Valley* (Logan: Cache Valley Centennial Commission, 1956), 414–16.

79. Daniel S. Tuttle, *Reminiscences of a Missionary Bishop* (New York: Thomas Whittaker, 1906), 309.

80. Herbert W. Reherd, "An Outline History of the Protestant Churches of Utah," in W. Wain Sutton, ed., *Utah: A Centennial History* (1949), vol. 2, 650.

81. Tuttle, *Reminiscences,* 314.

82. Henry Ward Beecher, *A Circuit of the Continent* (New York: Fords, Howard, and Hulbert, 1884), 12–13.

83. Merkel, *History of Methodism in Utah,* 93.

84. The best story of Utah during this era, although it does not concentrate on Gentile influences, is Thomas G. Alexander, *Mormonism in Transition: A History of the Latter-day Saints, 1890–1930* (Urbana: University of Illinois Press, 1986).

Chapter Eight

1. All studies of missions to the Indians should begin with James P. Ronda and James Axtell, eds., *Indian Missions, A Critical Bibliography* (Bloomington: Indiana University Press, published for the Newberry Library, 1978). The best surveys are Robert F. Berkhofer, Jr., *Salvation and the Savage* (New York: Atheneum, 1972), and Henry Warner Bowden, *American Indians and Christian Missions* (Chicago: University of Chicago Press, 1981). For the individual denominations, see Clifford M. Drury, *Presbyterian Panorama: One Hundred and Fifty Years of National Missions History* (Philadelphia: Board of Christian Education, 1952). Natalie Morrison Denison, "Missions and Missionaries of the Presbyterian Church, U.S., Among the Choctaws—1866–1907," *Chronicles of Oklahoma* 24 (Winter 1946–47), 426–47; *Baptist Home Missions in North America* (New York: Baptist Home Mission Rooms, 1883). S. C. Bartlett, *Historical Sketch of the Missions of the American Board among the North American Indians* (Boston: American Board, 1880). Clyde A. Milner II, *With Good Intentions: Quaker Work among the Pawnees, Otos, and Omahas: The 1870s* (Lincoln: University of Nebraska Press, 1982). See also Clyde A. Milner II and Floyd A. O'Neal, eds., *Churchmen and Western Indians, 1820–1920* (Norman: University of Oklahoma Press, 1985).

2. The classic account is R. Pierce Beaver, *Church, State, and the American Indian* (St. Louis: Concordia, 1966).

3. Cited in George F. McAfee, *Missions Among the North American*

Indian (New York: Women's Board of Home Missions of the Presbyterian Church, ca. 1920), 39, pamphlet, Oklahoma Historical Society, Oklahoma City.

4. R. Pierce Beaver, "The Churches and the Indians: Consequences of 350 Years of Missions," in Beaver, ed., *American Missions in Bicentennial Perspective* (South Pasadena, Calif.: William Carey Library, 1977), 275–331.

5. The best account is Francis Paul Prucha, *American Indian Policy in Crisis: Christian Reformers and the Indian, 1865–1900* (Norman: University of Oklahoma Press, 1976).

6. Prucha, *American Indian Policy in Crisis,* 30. See also Robert M. Utley, "The Celebrated Peace Policy of General Grant," *North Dakota History* 20 (July 1953), 121–42.

7. Henry E. Fritz, *The Movement for Indian Assimilation, 1860–1890* (Philadelphia: University of Pennsylvania Press, 1963), 80.

8. Fritz, *Movement for Indian Assimilation,* 76–79.

9. Francis Paul Prucha, *The Churches and the Indian Schools, 1888–1912* (Lincoln: University of Nebraska Press, 1979), is the most thorough account.

10. Fritz, *Movement for Indian Assimilation,* 92.

11. The best study is Robert H. Keller, Jr., *American Protestantism and United States Indian Policy, 1869–82* (Lincoln: University of Nebraska Press, 1983). Figures are from 233–35.

12. Loring Benson Priest, *Uncle Sam's Stepchildren: The Reformation of United States Indian Policy, 1865–1887* (New York: Octagon Books, 1969), 28.

13. Pond, as quoted in Mark Banker, "Presbyterians and Pueblos: A Protestant Response to the Indian Question, 1872–1892," *Journal of Presbyterian History* 60 (Spring 1982), 74. Albert Keiser, *Among the American Indians* (Minneapolis: Augsburg Publishing House, 1922), 128. Norman J. Bender, ed., *Missionaries, Outlaws, and Indians: Taylor F. Ealy at Lincoln and Zuni, 1878–1881* (Albuquerque: University of New Mexico Press, 1984).

14. Warren Harding Onken, Jr., "Pioneer Missionary: The Life of John Roberts, 1853–1949" (Master's thesis, University of Wyoming, 1977), 52.

15. Alice B. Nash, " 'The Hidden Hero' of Wyoming Brought to Light," undated clipping from *The Spirit of Missions,* vertical files, Wyoming Historical Society, Cheyenne.

16. Kate McBeth, "Miss S. L. McBeth," typescript, Oklahoma Historical Society. Typescript, box 10, Crawford Manuscript Collection, Idaho Historical Society, Boise.

17. The best discussion of her position may be found in Michael C.

Coleman, *Presbyterian Missionary Attitudes toward American Indians, 1837–1893* (Jackson: University Press of Mississippi, 1985).

18. Kate C. McBeth, "Monthly Letter for February 1883," Idaho Historical Society.

19. Kate C. McBeth, "Monthly Letter for February, 1883," Camp Meeting Program, ibid. See also Kate C. McBeth, *The Nez Perce Indians since Lewis and Clark* (New York: Fleming H. Revell, 1908), 163–83.

20. F. F. Ellinwood, "Three Heroines of the Nez Perce's Mission" (March 1894), unidentified article, McBeth Manuscripts, Idaho Historical Society.

21. Michael C. Coleman, "Christianizing and Americanizing the Nez Perce: Sue L. McBeth and Her Attitudes to the Indians," *Journal of Presbyterian History* 53 (1985), 339–61. The most complete biography is Allen Conrad Morrill and Eleanor Dunlap Morrill, *Out of the Blanket: The Story of Sue and Kate McBeth, Missionaries to the Nez Perces* (Moscow, Ida.: University of Idaho Press, 1978).

22. Mary Louise Fulweiler, "The Right Reverend William Hobart Hare," typescript of 1939 radio broadcast, South Dakota Historical Society.

23. M. A. DeWolfe Howe, *The Life and Labors of Bishop Hare: Apostle to the Sioux* (New York: Sturgis and Walton, 1911).

24. Virginia Driving Hawk Sneve, *That They May Have Life: The Episcopal Church in South Dakota, 1859–1976* (New York: Seabury Press, 1976).

25. Quoted in DeWolfe, *The Life and Labors of Bishop Hare,* 90.

26. Cornelia B. Kennedy, "Organized Religion in South Dakota before 1900" (Master's thesis, University of South Dakota, 1932), 36–40.

27. *Annual Report Upon Domestic Missions* (New York: 1889–1890), 11; cf. *Annual Report* (1895), 50; *Annual Report* (1898), 111.

28. The only biography is by his daughter: Minnie Cook, *Apostle to the Pima Indians: The Story of Charles H. Cook, the First Missionary to the Pimas* (Tiburon, Calif.: Omega Books, 1979).

29. Edward H. Spicer, *Cycles of Conquest: The Impact of Spain, Mexico, and the United States on the Indians of the Southwest, 1533–1960* (Tucson: University of Arizona Press, 1962), 149–50; 512–21. *American Indian Missions,* Presbyterian pamphlet, Arizona Historical Society, Tucson.

30. Spicer, *Cycles of Conquest,* 520. Beaver, "The Churches and the Indians. " 309–10.

31. Cited in Hugh D. Corwin, "Protestant Missionary Work among the Comanches and Kiowas," *Chronicles of Oklahoma* 46 (Spring 1968), 40–57.

32. J. J. Methvin, "Reminiscences of Life among the Indians," *Chronicles of Oklahoma* 5 (June 1927), 166–79.

33. A. E. Butterfield, "Comanche Kiawa [*sic*] and Apache Missions," typescript, Oklahoma Historical Society.

34. "Necrology: Rev. Dr. Joseph Samuel Morrow," *Chronicles of Oklahoma* 7 (December 1929), 487–89.

35. Frank A. Balyeat, "Joseph Samuel Murrow, Apostle to the Indians," *Chronicles of Oklahoma* 35 (Autumn 1957), 297–313.

36. Charles E. Creager, *Father Murrow and His Ninety Busy Years* (Muskogee: Times-Democrat, n.d.). Copy, Western History Collections, University of Oklahoma; W. H. Underwood, "Joseph Samuel Morrow, DD," typescript, Oklahoma Historical Society. A good study of the impact of education on the Seminoles is Michael E. Welsh, "The Road to Assimilation: The Seminoles in Oklahoma, 1839–1936," Ph.D. diss., University of New Mexico, 1983.

37. C. C. Wilson, *Indian Pioneer Papers,* vol. 2, Oklahoma Historical Society, 454–55).

38. *Home Mission Monthly* 14 (January 1892) typescript, Oklahoma Historical Society.

39. Kinney, *Frontier Missionary Problems,* 35.

40. Samuel Czarina, *Indian Pioneer Papers,* Oklahoma Historical Society, 434; Mrs. Sam Sanders, *Indian Pioneer Papers,* vol. 9, Oklahoma Historical Society, 165; Charles F. Haymaker, *Indian Pioneer Papers,* vol. 63, 479; Stephen A. Wood, ibid., vol. 11, 584; Ted Byron Hall, *Oklahoma Indian Territory* (Fort Worth: American Reference Publishers, 1971), 205–6.

41. *Annual Report* (1895), 96–97.

42. Julia C. Emery to JMK, August 9, 1906; Emery to JMK, June 6, 1900, and miscellaneous letters, file 4, box 1. John Mills Kendrick manuscripts, Archdiocese of the Rio Grande, Albuquerque, N.M.; Appeal for Cornelia Jay Memorial (ca. 1904); Mary W. Bockee to JMK, December 28, 1898. Ibid.

43. Cornelia Jay to JMK, August 8, August 15, 1900; Julia C. Emery to JMK, August 9, 1900. Ibid.

44. The best study is Margaret Connell Szasz, *Education and the American Indian: The Road to Self-Determination since 1928* (Albuquerque: University of New Mexico Press, 1977).

45. Quoted in W. H. Underwood, "Joseph Samuel Murrow," typescript, Oklahoma Historical Society.

46. Priest, *Uncle Sam's Stepchildren,* 143.

47. Prucha, *American Indian Policy in Crisis,* 265.

48. Warren Harding Onken, Jr., *Pioneer Missionary: The Life of John Roberts, 1853–1949,* quoted on 17.

49. Francis Paul Prucha, *The Churches and the Indian Schools, 1888–1912,* 205.

50. Prucha, *American Indian Policy in Crisis,* 288.

51. Figures from H. L. Morehouse, *The North American Indians and*

Our Home Mission Work among Them (New York: American Baptist Home Mission Society, 1900).

52. *Nutshell Items,* leaflet, Arizona Historical Society.

53. Historical Circular of Indian Training School, Tucson Indian Training School, box 2, Arizona Historical Society; cf. H. G. B. to Mrs. L. S. Borgers, November 30, 1908, Letter book, Tucson Indian Training School, Arizona Historical Society.

54. Robert T. Handy, *We Witness Together: A History of Cooperative Home Missions* (New York: Friendship Press, 1956), 54–55.

55. Kinney, *Frontier Missionary Problems,* 77.

56. Cornelia B. Kennedy, *Organized Religion in South Dakota before 1900,* 27.

57. Cook, *Apostle to the Pima Indians;* Howe, *The Life and Labors of Bishop Hare;* 281.

58. Stephen R. Riggs, *Mary and I: Forty Years with the Sioux* (Williamstown, Mass.: Corner House, 1971 [1880]); Arne Hassing, "Father Benard Haile, O.F.M., and the Navajos," in Ferenc M. Szasz, ed., *Religion in the West* (Manhattan, Kan.: Sunflower University Press, 1984), 91–96.

59. Carolyn Thomas Foreman, "The Cherokee Gospel Tidings of Dwight Mission," Grant Foreman Collection, box 9, Oklahoma Historical Society.

60. "Among the Blanket Indians" (*Baptist Home Mission Monthly [1894]*), typescript, Oklahoma Historical Society.

61. Beaver, *"The Churches and the Indians: Consequences of 350 Years of Missions,"* 310–15. See also L. G. Moses and Margaret Connell Szasz, *"'My Father, Have Pity on Me!': Indian Revitalization Movements of the Late-Nineteenth Century," Journal of the West* 23 (January 1984), 5–15.

62. Angie Debo, *Tulsa: From Creek Town to Oil Capital* (Norman: University of Oklahoma Press, 1943), 45.

63. McAfee, *Missions among the North American Indians,* 31.

Chapter Nine

1. Thomas B. McLeod, "Save the City for the Nation's Sake," sermon at the annual meeting of the Congregational Home Mission Society, 1898. Copy, Congregational Library, Boston; William Kinaid, *Practical Measures in the Present Stress* (New York, 1890), pamphlet, ibid.; Josiah Strong, *Our Country* (New York: Home Missionary Society, 1885), 128.

2. Walter Rauschenbusch, *Christianity and the Social Crisis* (New York, 1907); Walter Rauschenbusch, *A Theology for the Social Gospel* (New York: Macmillan, 1917).

3. C. Howard Hopkins, *The Rise of the Social Gospel in American Protestantism, 1865–1915* (New Haven: Yale University Press, 1940), 319.

See also the classic accounts by Henry F. May, *Protestant Churches and Industrial America* (New York: Harper and Row, 1949; 1967); Robert T. Handy, ed., *The Social Gospel in America* (New York: Oxford University Press, 1966); and Ronald C. White, Jr., and C. Howard Hopkins, eds., *The Social Gospel: Religion and Reform in Changing America* (Philadelphia: Temple University Press, 1976).

4. On the South, see: Kenneth K. Bailey, "Southern White Protestantism at the Turn of the Century," *American Historical Review* 68 (1963); Hugh C. Bailey, *Liberalism in the New South: Southern Social Reformers and the Progressive Movement* (Coral Gables: University of Miami Press, 1969); Jane C. Zimmerman, "The Penal Reform Movement in the South during the Progressive Era, 1890–1917," *Journal of Southern History* 17 (1951); and Wayne Flynt, "Dissent in Zion: Alabama Baptists and Social Issues, 1900–1914," *Journal of Southern History* 25 (1969).

5. Charles V. LaFontaine, S.A., "Apostle to the Meatpackers: The Associate Mission of Omaha, Nebraska, 1891–1902," *Historial Magazine of the Protestant Episcopal Church* 47 (September 1978), 233–53.

6. D. G. Paz, "The Anglican Response to Urban Social Dislocation in Omaha, 1875–1920," *Historical Magazine of the Protestant Episcopal Church* 51 (June 1978), 131–146. D. G. Paz, "For Zion's Sake Will I Not Hold My Peace: John Williams, Radical Omaha Priest, 1877–1914," *Nebraska History* 63 (Spring 1982), 87–107.

7. Facts from Uzzell vertical file, Western Historical Collections, Denver Public Library. See, especially, Denver *Times,* October 26, 1901; ibid., February 17, 1901; "He did his level best," *Greeley Sunday Journal,* October 16, 1966.

8. *The Colorado Graphic* 3 (October 1, 1887), 1.

9. Facts from the Reed file of Denver Public Library. See, especially, *Daily News,* March 5, 1899; Denver *Times,* January 30, 1899; Denver *Daily News,* May 7, 1897; Denver *Republican,* February 2, 1899.

10. The *American* (January 1917), copy, Dawson Scrap Books, Colorado Heritage Center.

11. *Annual Report of the Holy Trinity Italian Evangelical Institutional Church* (Denver, 1912); *Rocky Mountain News,* December 16, 1929.

12. George N. Rainsford, "Dean Henry Martyn Hart and Public Issues," *Colorado Magazine* 48 (1971), 204–20.

13. Their stories may be found in Erie *Herald,* October 17, 1914, Spalding Scrapbooks; John Howard Melish, *Franklin Spencer Spalding: Man and Bishop* (New York: Macmillan, 1917), 237–56; and Salt Lake *Herald Republican,* September 25, 1914, Spalding Scrapbooks, Colorado Heritage Center. Copies of the rare *Woodrow's Monthly* may be found in the University of Oklahoma.

14. The best study of this is Lawrence H. Larsen, *The Urban West at*

the End of the Frontier (Lawrence: The Regents Press of Kansas, 1976); Hugh Latimer Burleson, *Our Church and Our Country* (New York: Domestic and Foreign Missionary Society, 1918), 48.

15. See J. Alton Templin, Allen D. Breck, and Martin Rist, eds., *The Methodist, Evangelical, and United Brethren Churches in the Rockies, 1850–1926* (Denver: The Rocky Mountain Conference of the United Methodist Church, 1977).

16. Leroy A. Halbert, *Across the Way: A History of the Work of Central Church, Topeka Kansas in Tennessee Town* (1900). Pamphlet, Kansas Historical Society, Topeka.

17. "Churches and Schools of Rock Springs," typescript, Wyoming Historical Society, Cheyenne; vertical files.

18. Quoted in Szasz, *Divided Mind,* 48–49.

19. Jon C. Teaford, *The Twentieth-Century American City: Problem, Promise, and Reality* (Baltimore: Johns Hopkins University Press, 1986), 30–43.

20. Nancy Farrar, *The Chinese in El Paso* (El Paso: Texas Western Press, 1972), 4–5, 7.

21. *Phoenix Gazette,* 1886, in "Chinese" folder, Sharlott Hall Museum, Prescott, Arizona.

22. Stuart Creighton Miller, *The Unwelcome Immigrant: The American Image of the Chinese, 1785–1882* (Berkeley: University of California, 1969).

23. John Wunder, "The Courts and the Chinese in Frontier Idaho," *Idaho Yesterdays* 25 (1981), 23–32; John Wunder, "Law and Chinese in Montana," *Montana* 30 (July 1980), 18–30.

24. Flagstaff *Champion,* October 5, 1889.

25. Rev. John Hoskins, "Sky Pilot Tales," *The Frontier* (November 1930), 71. Copy, Western Heritage Center, Denver.

26. *As a Chinaman Saw Us: Passages from His Letters to a Friend at Home* (New York: Appleton and Co., 1910), 281–82.

27. Helen Webster, "The Chinese School of the Central Presbyterian Church of Denver," *Colorado Magazine,* 40 (January 1963), 57–62; and (April 1963), 132–37; "Two Years—The First Baptist Church of Denver, 1890–1892," manuscript, Colorado Heritage Center; Grant K. Anderson, "Deadwood's Chinatown," *South Dakota History* 5 (Summer 1975), 266–85. Elizabeth Lee and Kenneth A. Abbott, "Chinese Pilgrims and Presbyterians in the United States, 1851–1977," *Journal of Presbyterian History* 55 (Summer 1977), 125–44.

28. Cited in Jack Benham, *Silverton and Neighboring Ghost Towns* (Ouray, Colo.: Bear Creek Publishers, n.d.).

29. Webster, "Chinese School of the Central Presbyterian Church of Denver," 57–62; 132–37.

30. Karen Shane, "New Mexico: Salubrious El Dorado," *New Mexico Historical Review* 56 (1981), 387–99.

31. Bradford Luckingham, *The Urban Southwest: A Profile History of Albuquerque–El Paso–Phoenix–Tucson* (El Paso: Texas Western Press, 1982), quoted on 43; *La Aurora,* May 15, 1908.

32. Jake W. Spidle, Jr., "An Army of Tubercular Invalids: New Mexico and the Birth of a Tuberculosis Industry," *New Mexico Historical Review* 61 (July 1986), 179–201. *La Aurora,* November 15, 1914.

34. Cf. the account in John E. Baur, *Health Seekers of Southern California* (San Marino: The Huntington Library, 1959).

35. *La Aurora,* December 15, 1913; Marion Woodham, *A History of Presbyterian Hospital, 1908–1976* (Albuquerque, 1976), 1–13.

36. Lillian D. Ashe to J. Mills Kendrick, box 1, John Mills Kendrick Manuscripts, Albuquerque.

37. Daniel S. Tuttle, *Reminiscences of a Missionary Bishop* (New York: Thomas Whittaker, 1906), 403.

38. James B. Funsten, "The Making of an American on the West Side of the Rockies, *Outlook* 21 (June 14, 1902), 452.

39. Charles M. Sheldon, *In His Steps: The Seventieth Anniversary 1897–1967,* commemorative ed. (Topeka, 1967).

40. A new biography is Timothy Miller, *Following In His Steps* (Knoxville: University of Tennessee Press, 1986).

Conclusion

1. Edwin Scott Gaustad, *Historical Atlas of Religion in America* (New York: Harper and Row, 1962; 1976), 46.

2. W. D. B. Gray, *Strength and Outlook of Congregationalism in the Rocky Mountain District of the United States* (ca. 1915). Pamphlet, Gray Manuscripts, Western Heritage Center, Laramie, Wyoming.

3. Sarah Griswold Spalding, ed., "John Franklin Spalding, Bishop of Colorado, 1874–1902," *Colorado Magazine* 22 (March 1945); (May 1945); (July 1934). The citation is from May 1945, p. 133.

4. Quoted in Edward Ring, "The Episcopal Diocese of Colorado," *The Colorado Magazine* 13 (July 1936), 124.

5. Gaustad, *Historical Atlas of Religion in America,* 46.

6. For some figures on the high rate of collapse in the Plains, see Conrad Vander Velde, "History of the First Presbyterian Church of Emporia," typescript, box 1, Vander Velde Manuscripts, Kansas Historical Society; and Motier Bullock, *Congregational Nebraska* (Lincoln: Western Publishing and Engraving Company, 1905), 286–87.

7. Margaret Hook Olsen, *Patriarch of the Rockies: The Life Story of Joshua Gravett* (Denver: Golden Bell, 1960), 50.

8. Thomas H. Thompson and Albert A. West, *History of Nevada* (Oakland, Calif., 1881), 191.

9. William Henry Jackson, *Time Exposure* (New York: G. P. Putnam's Sons, 1940; rprt. University of New Mexico Press, 1986), 102.

10. This is the thesis of Mark Banker, "Making Haste Slowly: A History of Presbyterian Mission Work in the Southwest" (Ph.D. diss., University of New Mexico, 1987).

11. I have borrowed these ideas from the work of Sidney E. Mead, especially his *The Old Religion in the Brave New World* (Berkeley: University of California Press, 1977), and *The Nation with the Soul of a Church* (New York: Harper and Row, 1975).

12. For representative statements, see the letters by Maggie Brown in Elizabeth Byrd Gibbens, "Impact of the Western Frontier on Family Configuration: The Charles Albert Brown Collection of Letters (1874–1930), a Study in Literary Analysis of Correspondence" (Ph.D. diss., University of New Mexico, 1983).

13. M. A. DeWolfe Howe, *The Life and Labors of Bishop Hare: Apostle to the Sioux* (New York: Sturgis and Walton, 1911), 404–5.

14. Thomas S. Goslin II, "Henry Kendall, Missionary Statesman," *Journal of the Presbyterian Historical Society* 27 (June 1949), 69–87.

15. Thompson and West, *History of Nevada,* 192.

16. *World's Work* 18 (October 1909), 12090–91.

17. Roosevelt, from *Addresses and Papers* (New York: Sun Dial Classics, 1909), as quoted in R. Maud Ditmars, "A History of Baptist Missions in Utah, 1871–1931" (Master's thesis, University of Colorado, 1931), 2–3.

18. Ray A. Billington, *America's Frontier Culture* (College Station: Texas A and M University Press, 1977), 77.

19. Judge Louis H. Blackledge, "In Memory of Rev. John Mallory Bates," typescript, in G. A. Beecher Papers, box 12, Nebraska Historical Society, Lincoln.

20. Martindale, quoted in Ted Byron Hall, *Oklahoma: Indian Territory* (Fort Worth: American Reference Publishers, 1971), 242.

Bibliography

Books

Adams, Robert Hickman. *White Churches of the Plains: Examples from Colorado.* Boulder: Colorado Associated University Press, 1970.

Adams, Verdon R. *Methodism Comes to the Pass: A History of Trinity United Methodist Church of El Paso.* El Paso: Guynes Printing Co., 1975.

Addison, James T. *The Episcopal Church in the United States, 1789–1931.* New York: Charles Scribner's Sons, 1951.

Alexander, Thomas G. *Mormonism in Transition: A History of the Latter-day Saints, 1890–1930.* Urbana: University of Illinois Press, 1986.

Allen, T. D. *Not Ordered by Men.* Santa Fe: The Rydal Press, 1967.

Arps, Louise Ward, ed., *Faith on the Frontier: Religion in Colorado before August, 1876.* Denver: Colorado Council of Churches, 1976.

Arrington, Leonard J. *Brigham Young: American Moses.* New York: Alfred A. Knopf, 1985.

Arrington, Leonard J., and Davis Bitton. *The Mormon Experience: A History of the Latter-day Saints.* New York: Alfred A. Knopf, 1979.

As a Chinaman Saw Us: Passages from His Letters to a Friend at Home. New York: Appleton and Company, 1910.

Bailey, Hugh C. *Liberalism in the New South: Southern Social Reformers and the Progressive Movement.* Coral Gables, Fla.: University of Miami Press, 1969.

Baird, Paul Jesse. *The Mystery of Ministry in the Great Basin.* Globe, Ariz.: Pabsco Printers, 1976.

257

————. *The Shepherd's Dog: The Story of Peacock Country.* Mexico: Casa de Publicaciones, 1974.

Ball, Eve. *Riodoso.* San Antonio: Naylor, 1963.

Baptist Home Missions in North America. New York: Baptist Home Mission Rooms, 1883.

Barbour, Sister Richard Marie. *Light in Yucca Land.* Santa Fe: Schifani Brothers, 1952.

Barnes, Ross G. *The Sod House.* Lincoln: University of Nebraska Press, 1930; 1970.

Baur, John E. *Health Seekers of Southern California.* San Marino, Calif.: The Huntington Library, 1959.

Beaver, R. Pierce. *Church, State, and the American Indian.* St. Louis: Concordia, 1966.

————, ed. *American Missions in Bicentennial Perspective.* South Pasadena, Calif.: William Carey Library, 1977.

Beecher, George Allen. *A Bishop of the Great Plains.* Philadelphia: Church Historical Society, 1950.

Beecher, Henry Ward. *A Circuit of the Continent.* New York: Fords, Howard, and Hulbert, 1884.

Beecher, Lyman. *A Plea for the West.* Cincinnati: Truman, 1835.

Belknap, Helen O. *The Church on the Changing Frontier: A Study of the Homesteader and His Church.* New York: George H. Doran, 1922.

Bender, Norman J., ed. *Missionaries, Outlaws and Indians: Taylor F. Ealy at Lincoln and Zuni, 1878–1881.* Albuquerque: University of New Mexico Press, 1984.

Benham, Jack. *Silverton and Neighboring Ghost Towns.* Ouray, Colo.: Bear Creek Publishers, n.d.

Bergon, Frank, and Zeese Papanikolas, eds. *Looking Far West: The Search for the American West in History, Myth, and Literature.* New York: Mentor, 1978.

Berkhofer, Robert F. *Salvation and the Savage.* New York: Atheneum, 1972.

Billington, Ray A. *America's Frontier Culture.* College Station: Texas A and M University Press, 1977.

Bodo, Charles R. *The Protestant Clergy and Public Issues, 1812–1848.* Princeton: Princeton University Press, 1954.

Bowden, Henry Warner. *American Indians and Christian Missions.* Chicago: University of Chicago Press, 1981.

Boyer, Paul. *Urban Masses and Moral Order in America, 1870–1920.* Cambridge: Harvard University Press, 1978.

Brackenridge, R. Douglas, and Francisco O. García–Treto. *Iglesia Presbiteriana: A History of Presbyterians and Mexican Americans in the Southwest.* San Antonio: Trinity University Press, 1974.

Brady, Antoine Loving. *Thornton Kelly Tyson: Pioneer Home Missionary.* Kansas City, Mo.: Western Baptist Publishing Co., 1915.

Breck, Allen duPont. *The Episcopal Church in Colorado, 1860–1963.* Denver: Big Mountain Press, 1963.

Bristol, Frank Milton. *The Life of Chaplain McCabe.* Cincinnati: Jennings and Graham, 1908.

Brooks, Juanita. *The Mountain Meadows Massacre.* Stanford, Calif.: Stanford University Press, 1950; rprt., Norman: University of Oklahoma Press, 1962, 1970.

Bullock, Motier A. *Congregational Nebraska.* Lincoln: Western Publishing and Engraving Company, 1905.

Bushnell, Horace. *Barbarism the First Danger: A Discourse for Home Missions.* New York: American Home Missionary Society, 1847.

Caspar, Henry W. *History of the Catholic Church in Nebraska.* 3 vols. Milwaukee: Bruce/Catholic Life, 1960–69.

Castaneda, Carlos. *Our Catholic Heritage in Texas, 1519–1936.* 7 vols. Austin, Tex.: Von Boeckmann-Jones, 1936.

Chesham, Sallie. *Born to Battle: The Salvation Army in America.* Chicago: Rand McNally, 1965.

Clark, Joseph B. *The Closing Decade.* New York: American Home Missionary Society, 1891.

Clarke, Joseph B. *Leavening the Nation: The Story of American [Protestant] Home Missions.* New York: Revell, 1908; 1913.

Cochran, Alice Cowan. *Miners, Merchants, and Missionaries: The Roles of Missionaries and Pioneer Churches in the Colorado Gold Rush and Its Aftermath, 1858–1870.* Metuchen, N.J.: Scarecrow Press, 1980.

Coleman, Michael. *Presbyterian Missionary Attitudes toward American Indians, 1837–1893.* Jackson: University Press of Mississippi, 1985.

Connor, Ralph (Charles Williams Gordon). *The Sky Pilot: A Tale of the Foothills.* London: Hodder and Stoughton, 1899; 1903.

Cook, Minnie. *Apostle to the Pima Indians: The Story of Charles H. Cook, the First Missionary to the Pimas.* Tiburon, Calif.: Omega Books, 1979.

Darley, Alexander M. *The Passionists of the Southwest, or the Holy Brotherhood.* Pueblo: n.p. 1893; rprt., Glorieta, N.M.: Rio Grande Press, 1968.

De Aragon, Ray John. *Padre Martinez and Bishop Lamy.* Las Vegas, N.M.: Pan American, 1978.

De Arment, Robert K. *Knights of the Green Cloth: The Saga of the Frontier Gamblers.* Norman: University of Oklahoma Press, 1982.

Debo, Angie. *Tulsa: From Creek Town to Oil Capital.* Norman: University of Oklahoma Press, 1943.

Diary and Letters of the Reverend Joseph W. Cook, Missionary to Cheyenne. Laramie, Wyo.: The Laramie Republican, 1919.

Dick, Everett. *The Sod-House Frontier, 1854–1890.* Lincoln: University of Nebraska Press, 1935; rprt., 1979.

Dorsett, Lyle. *The Queen City: A History of Denver.* Boulder: Pruett, 1977.

Douglas, Ann. *The Feminization of American Culture.* New York: Knopf, 1977.

Drury, Clifford M. *Marcus and Narcissa Whitman and the Opening of Old Oregon.* Seattle, Wash.: Pacific Northwest National Parks and Forests Association, 1986.

———. *Presbyterian Panorama: One Hundred and Fifty Years of National Missions History.* Philadelphia: Board of Christian Education, 1952.

Durand, George H. *Joseph Ward of Dakota.* Boston: The Pilgrim Press, 1913.

Dwyer, Robert Joseph. *The Gentile Comes to Utah: A Study in Religious and Social Conflict, 1862–1890.* Salt Lake City: Western Epics, 1971.

Dyer, John L. *The Snow-Shoe Itinerant: An Autobiography of the Rev. John L. Dyer.* Cincinnati: Methodist Book Concern, 1890.

Dykstra, Robert. *The Cattle Towns.* New York: Alfred A. Knopf, 1968.

Eddy, Zachary. *The Evangelization of Our Country.* New York: American Home Missionary Society, 1877.

Erdoes, Richard. *Saloons of the Old West.* New York: Alfred A. Knopf, 1979.

Evans, Joe M. *The Cowboys' Hitchin' Post.* El Paso: n.p., 1938; ca. 1941.

Farish, Hunter. *The Circuit Rider Dismounts.* Richmond: Dietz Press, 1938.

Farrar, Nancy. *The Chinese in El Paso.* El Paso: Texas Western Press, 1972.

Fife, Austin, and Alta Fife. *Heaven on Horseback: Revivalist Songs and Verse in the Cowboy Idiom.* Logan: Utah State University Press, 1970.

Foster, Charles I. *An Errand of Mercy: The Evangelical United Front, 1790–1837.* Chapel Hill: University of North Carolina Press, 1960.

Frazier, E. Franklin. *The Negro Church in America.* New York: Schocken, 1963; 1974.

Fritz, Henry E. *The Movement for Indian Assimilation, 1860–1890.* Philadelphia: University of Pennsylvania Press, 1963.

García, Mario T. *Desert Immigrants: The Mexicans of El Paso, 1880–1920.* New Haven: Yale University Press, 1981.

Gaylord, Mary M. *Life and Labors of Reuben Gaylord: Home Missionary for Iowa and Nebraska.* Omaha: Rees Printing Co., 1889.

Gillilan, James D. *Thomas Corwin Iliff: Apostle of Home Missions in the Rocky Mountains.* New York: Methodist Book Concern, 1919.

Goode, William B. *Outposts of Zion, with Limnings of Mission Life.* Cincinnati: Poe and Hitchcock, 1864.

Goodykoontz, Colin B. *First Congregational Church of Boulder: An Historical Sketch, 1864–1939.* Boulder: First Congregational Church, 1939.

———. *Home Missions on the American Frontier.* Caldwell, Idaho: Caxton Printers, 1939; rprt., 1971.

Griffin, Clifford S. *Their Brothers' Keepers: Moral Stewardship in the United States, 1820–1865.* New Brunswick, N.J.: Rutgers University Press, 1960.

Guarneri, Carl and David Alvarez, eds. *Religion and Society in The American West: Historical Essays.* New York: University Press of America, 1987.

Hall, Ennen Reaves. *One Saint and Seven Sinners: The Life of a Baptist Circuit-Riding Pastor and His Family at the Turn of the Century.* New York: Thomas Y. Crowell, 1959.

Hall, Ralph. *The Main Trail.* San Antonio: The Naylor Company, 1971.

Hall, Ted Byron. *Oklahoma: Indian Territory.* Fort Worth: American Reference Publishers, 1971.

Handy, Robert T. *We Witness Together: A History of Cooperative Home Missions.* New York: Friendship Press, 1956.

————, ed. *The Social Gospel in America.* New York: Oxford University Press, 1966.

Harrell, David Edwin, Jr. *Oral Roberts: An American Life.* Bloomington: Indiana University Press, 1985.

Harwood, Thomas. *History of New Mexico Spanish and English Missions of the Methodist Episcopal Church from 1820 to 1910.* 2 vols. Albuquerque: El Abogado Press, 1908–1910.

Henderson, Alice Corbin. *Brothers of Light: The Penitentes of the Southwest.* New York: Harcourt, Brace and Company, 1937.

Hitchman, James H. *Liberal Arts Colleges in Oregon and Washington: 1842–1980.* Bellingham, Wash.: Center for Pacific Northwest Studies, 1981.

Hood, E. Lyman. *The New West Education Commission, 1880–1893.* Jacksonville, Fla.: H. and W. B. Drew Co., 1905.

Hopkins, C. Howard. *The Rise of the Social Gospel in American Protestantism, 1865–1915.* New Haven: Yale University Press, 1940.

Horgan, Paul. *Lamy of Santa Fe.* New York: Farrar, Straus and Giroux, 1975.

Howe, M. A. DeWolfe. *The Life and Labors of Bishop Hare: Apostle to the Sioux.* New York: Sturgis and Walton, 1911.

Hudson, Winthrop S. *Religion in America.* New York: Charles Scribner's Sons, 1981.

Humphrey, Seth K. *Following the Prairie Frontier.* Minneapolis: University of Minnesota Press, 1931.

Jackson, William Henry. *Time Exposure.* New York: G. P. Putnam's Sons, 1940; rprt. University of New Mexico Press, 1986.

Johnson, Byron A., and Sharon P. Johnson. *Gilded Palaces of Shame: Albuquerque's Red Light Districts, 1880–1914.* Albuquerque: Gilded Age Press, 1983.

Johnson, Charles A. *The Frontier Camp Meeting: Religion's Harvest Time.* Dallas: Southern Methodist University Press, 1955; rprt., 1985.

Jones, Charles E. *Perfectionist Persuasion: The Holiness Movement and American Methodism, 1867–1936.* Metuchen, N.J.: Scarecrow Press, 1974.

Keller, Robert H. *American Protestantism and United States Indian Policy, 1869–82.* Lincoln: University of Nebraska Press, 1983.

Kennedy, Roger G. *American Churches.* New York: Stewart, Tabori and Chang, 1982.

Kinney, Bruce. *Frontier Missionary Problems.* New York: Fleming H. Revell, 1918.

———. *Mormonism: The Islam of America.* New York: Fleming H. Revell, 1912.

Kinsolving, Arthur B. *Texas George: The Life of George Herbert Kinsolving, Bishop of Texas, 1892–1928.* Milwaukee: Morehouse, 1932.

Knight, Wilferd T. *Pioneer's Heritage.* Franklin, Wisc.: privately published, 1979.

Kramer, William M., ed. *The American West and the Religious Experience.* Los Angeles: Will Kramer, 1970.

Larsen, Lawrence. *The Urban West at the End of the Frontier.* Lawrence: The Regents Press of Kansas, 1978.

Lewis, Faye C. *Nothing to Make a Shadow.* Ames: Iowa State University Press, 1971.

Lind, Robert W. *From the Ground Up: The Story of 'Brother Van' Orsdel, Montana Pioneer Minister, 1848–1919.* Polson, Mont.: privately published, 1961.

Look, Al, comp. *Sidelights on Colorado.* Denver: Golden Bell Press, 1967.

Luebke, Frederick C. *Immigrants and Politics: The Germans of Nebraska, 1880–1900.* Lincoln: University of Nebraska, 1967.

The Lutherans in North America. Philadelphia: Fortress Press, 1975.

McBeth, Kate C. *The Nez Perce Indians Since Lewis and Clark.* New York: Fleming H. Revell, 1908.

McGrath, Roger D. *Gunfighters, Highwaymen and Vigilantes: Violence on the Frontier.* Berkeley: University of California Press, 1984.

Martin, Walter. *The Maze of Mormonism.* Ventura, Calif.: Vision House, 1962; 1984.

Marty, Martin E. *Righteous Empire: The Protestant Experience in America.* New York: Dial, 1970.

May, Henry F. *Protestant Churches and Industrial America.* New York: Harper and Row, 1949; 1967.

Mead, Sidney E. *The Lively Experiment: The Shaping of Christianity in America.* New York: Harper and Row, 1963.

———. *The Old Religion in the Brave New World: Reflections on the*

Relation between Christendom and the Republic. Berkeley: University of California, 1977.

———. *The Nation with the Soul of a Church.* New York: Harper and Row, 1975.

Melish, John Howard. *Franklin Spencer Spalding: Man and Bishop.* New York: Macmillan, 1917.

Merkel, Henry M. *History of Methodism in Utah.* Colorado Springs: Denton Printing Co., 1938.

Miller, Robert Moats. *Harry Emerson Fosdick: Preacher, Pastor, Prophet.* New York: Oxford University Press, 1985.

Miller, Stuart Creighton. *The Unwelcome Immigrant: The American Image of the Chinese, 1785–1882.* Berkeley: University of California Press, 1969.

Mills, Edward Laird. *Plains, Peaks and Pioneers: Eighty Years of Methodism in Montana.* Portland, Ore.: Binfords and Mort, 1947.

Mills, Samuel J., and Daniel Smith. *Report of a Missionary Tour through that Part of the United States which Lies West of the Allegheny Mountains: Performed under the Direction of the Massachusetts Missionary Society.* Andover, Mass.: Flagg and Gould, 1815.

Milner, Clyde A. II. *With Good Intentions: Quaker Work among the Pawnees, Otos, and Omahas in the 1870s.* Lincoln: University of Nebraska Press, 1982.

———, and Floyd A. O'Neal, eds. *Churchmen and Western Indians, 1820–1920.* Norman: University of Oklahoma Press, 1985.

Miner, H. Craig. *West of Wichita: Settling the High Plains of Kansas, 1865–1900.* Lawrence: University Press of Kansas, 1986.

Mondy, Robert William. *Pioneers and Preachers: Stories of the Old Frontier.* Chicago: Nelson Hall, 1980.

Moorhead, James H. *American Apocalypse: Yankee Protestants and the Civil War.* New Haven: Yale University Press, 1978.

Murray, Andrew E. *The Skyline Synod: Presbyterianism in Colorado and Utah.* Denver: Golden Bell Press, 1971.

Myers, Lewis A. *A History of New Mexico Baptists.* Albuquerque: Baptist Convention of New Mexico, 1965.

Olsen, Margaret Hook. *Patriarch of the Rockies: The Life Story of Joshua Gravett.* Denver: Golden Bell, 1960.

Parker, Watson. *Deadwood: The Golden Years.* Lincoln: University of Nebraska Press, 1981.

Peters, John L. *Christian Perfectionism and American Methodism.* New York: Abington, 1956.

Phares, Ross. *Bible in Pocket, Gun in Hand: The Story of Frontier Religion.* Lincoln: University of Nebraska Press, 1962; 1964.

Pierson, Hamilton W. *In the Brush; or, Old-time Social and Religious Life in the Southwest.* New York: B. Appleton and Co., 1881.

Platt, Ward. *The Frontier.* Cincinnati: Jennings and Graham, 1908.

Plumb, Beatrice. *The Goodwill Man: Edgar James Helms.* Minneapolis: S. Denison and Company, 1965.

Priest, Loring Benson. *Uncle Sam's Stepchildren: The Reformation of United States Indian Policy, 1865–1887.* New York: Octagon Books, 1969.

Prucha, Francis Paul. *American Indian Policy in Crisis: Christian Reformers and the Indian, 1865–1900.* Norman: University of Oklahoma Press, 1976.

———. *The Churches and the Indian Schools, 1888–1912.* Lincoln: University of Nebraska Press, 1979.

Puddefoot, W. G. *The Minute Man on the Frontier.* Chicago: Thomas Y. Crowell, 1895.

Rainsford, W. S. *A Preacher's Story of His Work.* New York: Outlook Co., 1904.

Randall, Lauretta I. *The Odyssey of a Great Grandmother.* Spokane, Wash.: Spokane Lithographing Co., n.d.).

Read, Benjamin. *Illustrated History of New Mexico.* Santa Fe: New Mexican Printing Co., 1912.

Rice, Claton. *Ambassador to the Saints.* Boston: Christopher Publishing House, 1965.

Riegel, Robert E. *Young America, 1830–1840.* Norman: University of Oklahoma Press, 1949.

Rifkind, Carole. *A Field Guide to American Architecture.* New York: New American Library, 1980.

Riggs, Stephen R. *Mary and I: Forty Years with the Sioux.* Minneapolis: Ross and Haines, 1969 [1880].

Rochlin, Harriet, and Fred Rochlin. *Pioneer Jews: A New Life in the Far West.* Boston: Houghton Mifflin Company, 1984.

Ronda, James P., and James Axtell, eds. *Indian Missions, A Critical Bibliography.* Bloomington: Indiana University Press; published for the Newberry Library, 1978.

Rosen, Ruth. *The Lost Sisterhood: Prostitution in America, 1900–1918.* Baltimore: The John Hopkins University Press, 1982.

Rothenberg, Gunther, and Israel C. Carmel. *Congregation Albert, 1897–1972.* Albuquerque, n.p., 1972.

Salpointe, J. B. *Soldiers of the Cross: Notes on the Ecclesiastical History of New Mexico, Arizona, and Colorado.* Albuquerque: Calvin Horn [1898], 1967.

Savage, W. Sherman. *Blacks in the West.* Westport, Conn.: Greenwood Press, 1976.

Shelton, Don O. *Heroes of the Cross in America.* New York: The Young People's Missionary Movement, 1904.

Shipps, Jan. *Mormonism: The Story of a New Religious Tradition.* Urbana: University of Illinois Press, 1985.

Simmons, A. J. *The Gentile Comes to Cache Valley.* Logan: Utah State University Press, 1976.

Sizer, Sandra S. *Gospel Hymns and Social Religion.* Philadelphia: Temple University Press, 1978.

Slaght, Lawrence T. *Multiplying the Witness: 150 Years of American Baptist Educational Ministry.* Valley Forge, Pa.: Judson Press, 1974.

Sloan, William N. *Spiritual Conquest along the Rockies.* New York: George H. Doran Company, 1913.

Smillie, B. G., ed. *Visions of the New Jerusalem: Religious Settlement on the Prairies.* Edmonton: NeWest Press, 1983.

Smith, Timothy L. *Called unto Holiness: The Story of the Nazarenes, The Formative Years.* Kansas City: Nazarene Publishing House, 1962.

Smithers, W. D. *Circuit Riders of the Big Bend.* El Paso: Texas Western Press, 1981.

Sneve, Virginia Driving Hawk. *That They May Have Life: The Episcopal Church in South Dakota, 1859–1976.* New York: Seabury Press, 1976.

Somerndike, J. M. *By-Products of the Rural Sunday School.* Philadelphia: Westminster Press, 1914.

Sonnichsen, C. L. *Pass of the North: Four Centuries on the Rio Grande.* El Paso: Texas Western Press, 1968.

Spence, Clark C. *The Salvation Army Farm Colonies.* Tucson: University of Arizona Press, 1985.

Starkey, Marion L. *The Congregational Way: The Role of the Pilgrims and Their Heirs in Shaping America.* Garden City, N.Y.: Doubleday and Company, 1966.

Stevens, Daniel G. *The First Hundred Years of the American Baptist Publication Society.* Philadelphia: American Baptist Publication Society, n.d.

Stewart, J. D. *A Brief Autobiography.* n.p., 1913.

Stewart, Robert L. *Sheldon Jackson.* New York: Revell, 1908.

Stoney, James M. *Lighting the Candle: The Episcopal Church on the Upper Rio Grande.* Santa Fe: The Rydal Press, 1961.

Stover, Earl F. *Up from Handyman: The United States Army Chaplaincy, 1865–1920.* Vol. 3. Washington, D.C.: Office of the Chief of Chaplains, Department of the Army, 1977.

Stowell, Jay S. *Home Mission Trails.* New York: Abingdon Press, 1920.

Stratton, David H. *The First Century of Baptists in New Mexico, 1849–1950.* Albuquerque: Women's Missionary Union of New Mexico, 1954.

Stratton, Joanna L. *Pioneer Women: Voices from the Kansas Frontier.* New York: Simon and Schuster, 1981.

Sweet, William Warren. *The Story of Religion in America.* New York: Harper and Brothers, 1950.

———. *Religion on the American Frontier.* 4 vols. Chicago and New York: Henry Holt, 1931–46.

Szasz, Ferenc Morton. *The Divided Mind of Protestant America, 1880–1930.* University: University of Alabama Press, 1982.

———, ed. *Religion in the West.* Manhattan, Kan.: Sunflower University Press, 1984.

Szasz, Margaret Connell. *Education and the American Indian: The Road to Self-Determinaton since 1928.* Albuquerque: University of New Mexico Press, 1977.

———. *First Congregational Church of Albuquerque, New Mexico, A Centennial History: 1880–1980.* Albuquerque: AVC Printers, Inc., 1980.

Talbot, Ethelbert. *My People of the Plains.* New York: Harper and Brothers, 1906.

Taylor, Joshua C. *America as Art.* New York: Harper and Row, 1976.

Templin, J. Alton, Allen D. Breck, and Martin Rist, eds. *The Methodist, Evangelical, and United Brethren Churches in the Rockies, 1850–1926.* Denver: The Rocky Mountain Conference of the United Methodist Church, 1977.

Tenney, E. P. *Looking Forward into the Past.* Nahant, Mass.: Romford Press, 1910.

Tenney, E. P. *The New West as Related to the Christian College.* Cambridge, Mass.: Riverside Press, 1878.

Thompson, Thomas H., and Albert A. West. *History of Nevada.* Oakland, Calif.: Thompson and West, 1881.

Towne, C. W. *Her Majesty Montana: High Lights in the History of a State Fifty Years Old in 1939.* Helena: Montana Power Co., 1939.

Tuttle, Daniel S. *Reminiscences of a Missionary Bishop.* New York: Thomas Whittaker, 1906; rprt., Helena Letter Shop, 1977.

Twitchell, Ralph E., ed. *The Leading Facts of New Mexico History.* 5 vols. Cedar Rapids, Iowa: Torch Press, 1911–17.

Tyler, Alice Felt. *Freedom's Ferment.* Minneapolis: University of Minnesota Press, 1941.

Van Dusen, W. W. *Blazing the Way; or, Pioneer Experiences in Idaho, Washington, and Oregon.* Cincinnati: Jennings and Graham, 1905.

Webb, Walter Prescott. *The Great Plains.* Boston: Ginn and Co., 1931.

Weigle, Marta. *Brothers of Light, Brothers of Blood: The Penitentes of the Southwest.* Albuquerque: University of New Mexico Press, 1976.

West, Elliott. *The Saloon on the Rocky Mountain Mining Frontier.* Lincoln: University of Nebraska Press, 1979.

West, Samuel E. *Cross on the Range: Missionary in Wyoming.* Philadelphia: The Church Historical Society, 1947.

Western Story: The Recollections of Charley O'Kieffe, 1884–1898. Lincoln: University of Nebraska Press, 1960.

White, Ronald C., Jr., and C. Howard Hopkins, eds. *The Social Gospel: Religion and Reform in Changing America.* Philadelphia: Temple University Press, 1976.

Wilkins, Robert P., and Wynona H. Wilkins. *God Giveth the Increase: The History of the Episcopal Church in North Dakota.* Fargo: North Dakota Institute for Regional Studies, 1959.

Wise, William. *Massacre at Mountain Meadows: An American Legend and a Monumental Crime.* New York: Thomas Y. Crowell, 1976.

Articles

Anderson, Avis R., ed. "Pastor on the Prairie." *Montana* 24 (January 1974), 36–54.

Anderson, Grant K. "Deadwood's Chinatown." *South Dakota History* 5 (Summer 1975), 266–85.

Argersinger, Peter H. "The Divines and the Destitute." *Nebraska History* 51 (Fall 1970), 303–18.

Arrington, Leonard J. , and Jon Haupt. "Intolerable Zion: The Image of Mormonism in Nineteenth Century American Literature." *Western Humanities Review* 22 (1968), 243–60.

Atkins, Carolyn. "Menaul School, 1881–1930 . . . Not Leaders, Merely, but Christian Leaders." *Journal of Presbyterian History* 58 (Winter 1980), 279–98.

Bailey, Alvin K. "Sheldon Jackson, Planter of Churches." *Journal of the Presbyterian Historical Society* 26 (September 1948), 129–48; (December 1948), 193–215; 27 (March 1949), 21–40.

Bailey, Kenneth K. "Southern White Protestantism at the Turn of the Century." *American Historical Review* 68 (1963), 618–35.

Bailey, Wilfrid C. "Folklore Aspects in Mormon Culture." *Western Folklore* 10 (1951), 217–25.

Banner, Lois. "Religious Benevolence as Social Control: A Critique of an Interpretation." *Journal of American History* 60 (1973), 23–41.

Baun, Louise, ed. "Circuit-riding in Southwest Kansas in 1885 and 1886: The Letters of Jeremiah Evarts Blatt." *Kansas Historical Quarterly* 12 (November 1943), 378–89.

Bender, Norman J. "Crusade of the Blue Banner in Colorado." *Colorado Magazine* 47 (Spring 1970), 91–118.

Bender, Norman. "Sheldon Jackson's Crusade to Win the West for Christ, 1869–1880." *The Midwest Review* 4 (Spring 1982), 1–12.

Blegen, Theodore C., ed. "John B. Blegen: A Missionary Journey on the Dakota Prairies in 1888." *North Dakota Historical Quarterly* 1 (1927), 16–29.

Bohme, Frederick G. "The Italians in New Mexico." *New Mexico Historical Review* 34 (April 1959), 98–116.

Brackenridge, R. Douglas, and Francisco O. García-Treto. "Presbyterians and Mexican Americans: From Paternalism to Partnership." *Journal of Presbyterian History* 55 (Summer 1977), 161–78.

Bitton, Davis. "Early Mormon Lifestyles: or, The Saints as Human Beings," 273–305. In Mark McKiernan et al, eds., *The Restoration Movement: Essays in Mormon History.* Lawrence, Kan.: Coronado Press, 1973.

————. "The Ritualization of Mormon History." *Utah Historical Quarterly* 43 (Winter 1975), 67–85.

Butler, Lee A. "The Benjamin Presbyterian Church, 1886–1916." *Utah Historical Quarterly* 51 (Summer 1983), 259–71.

Byrkit, James W. "The Word on the Frontier: Anglo Protestant Churches in Arizona, 1854–1899." *Journal of Arizona History* 21 (Winter 1980), 63–68.

Campbell, Eugene E. "Social, Cultural, and Recreational Life." In Joel E. Ricks, ed., *The History of a Valley.* Logan, Utah: Cashe Valley Centennial Commission, 1956.

Derig, Betty. "Pioneer Portraits." *Idaho Yesterdays* 12 (Winter 1968), 13–22.

Dickey, Roland F. "Lew Wallace: One of 'Them Literary Fellers.'" *New Mexico Magazine* 63 (January 1985), 15–17.

Dillon, Merton L. "Religion in Lubbock." In Lawrence L. Graves. ed., *A History of Lubbock.* Lubbock: West Texas Museum Association, 1962.

Dosker, Nina Ellis. "Edwin M. Ellis, Montana's Bicycling Minister." *Montana* 30 (Winter 1980), 42–50.

Everett, Dianna. "The Public School Debate in New Mexico, 1850–1891." *Arizona and the West* 26 (Summer 1984), 107–35.

Finnie, Gordon E. "Some Aspects of Religion on the American Frontier." In Stuart Henry, ed., *A Miscellany of American Christianity: Essays in Honor of H. Sheldon Smith.* Durham, N.C.: Duke University Press, 1965.

Flynt, Wayne. "Dissent in Zion: Alabama Baptists and Social Issues, 1900–1914." *Journal of Southern History* 25 (1969), 523–42.

Foote, Cheryl J. "Alice Blake of Trementina: Mission Teacher of the Southwest." *Journal of Presbyterian History* 60 (Fall 1982), 228–42.

Forbes, Bruce David. "Presbyterian Beginnings in South Dakota, 1840–1900." *South Dakota History* 7 (Spring 1977), 115–53.

Funsten, James B. "The Making of an American on the West Side of the Rockies." *Outlook* 71 (June 14, 1902).

Geary, Edward A. "For the Strength of the Hills: Imagining Mormon Country," 74–93. In Thomas A. Alexander and Jessie L. Embry, eds., *After 150 Years: The Latter-day Saints in Sesquicentennial Perspective.* Provo, Utah: Charles Redd Center for Western Studies, 1983.

Glanz, Rudolf. "Notes on the Early Jews in Arizona." *Western States Jewish Historical Quarterly* 5 (July 1973), 243–56.

Goldman, Marion. "Sexual Commerce in the Comstock Lode." *Nevada Historical Society Quarterly* 21 (Summer 1978), 99–127.

Griffin, Clifford S. "Religious Benevolence as Social Control, 1815–1860." *Mississippi Valley Historical Review* 44 (1957), 423–44.

Harlan, Lowell B. "Theology of Eighteenth Century English Hymns." *Historical Magazine of the Protestant Episcopal Church* 48 (June 1979), 167–93.

Haupt, William H. "History of the American Church Known in Law as the Protestant Episcopal Church in the State of Kansas." *Collections of the Kansas State Historical Society* 16 (1923–1925), 353–402.

Harrell, David E., Jr. "The Sectional Origins of the Churches of Christ." *Journal of Southern History* 30 (August 1964), 261–77.

Helmreich, Ernest C., ed. "Letters of Pastor Christian Helmreich: Establishing a Lutheran Congregation in Weyerts, Nebraska, 1887–1888." *Nebraska History* 58 (Summer 1977), 175–92.

Hinckley, Ted C. "Sheldon Jackson: Gilded Age Apostle." *Journal of the West* 23 (January 1984), 16–25.

Hornbein, Marjorie. "Denver's Rabbi William S. Friedman: His Ideas and Influence." *Western States Jewish Historical Quarterly* 13 (January 1981), 142–54.

Hough, C. Merrill. "Two School Systems in Conflict: 1867–1890." *Utah Historical Quarterly* 28 (April 1960), 113–28.

Ivins, S. S. "Free Schools Come to Utah." *Utah Historical Quarterly* 22 (July 1954), 321–42.

Jackson, Sheldon. "Sheldon Jackson Invades the Rocky Mountains, 1869–76." *Journal of Presbyterian History* 37 (1959), 122–28.

Jordan, Philip D. "Josiah Strong and a Scientific Social Gospel." *The Iliff Review* 42 (Winter 1985), 21–31.

Kelson, Benjamin. "The Jews of Montana." *Western States Jewish Historical Quarterly* 3 (January 1971), 170–89.

Kimball, Stanley B. "The Utah Gospel Mission, 1900–1950." *Utah Historical Quarterly* 44 (Spring 1976), 149–55.

LaFontaine, Charles V. "Apostle to the Meatpackers: The Associate Mission of Omaha, Nebraska, 1891–1902." *Historical Magazine of the Protestant Episcopal Church* 47 (September 1978), 233–53.

Lee, Elizabeth, and Kenneth A. Abbott. "Chinese Pilgrims and Presbyterians in the United States, 1851–1977." *Journal of Presbyterian History* 55 (Summer 1977), 125–44.

Leonard, Carol, and Isidor Wallimann. "Prostitution and Changing Morality in the Frontier Cattle Towns of Kansas." *Kansas History* 2 (Spring 1979), 34–53.

Loveland, Anne C. "Domesticity and Religion in the Ante-bellum Period: The Career of Phoebe Palmer." *The Historian* 39 (May 1977), 455–71.

Lyon, T. Edgar. "Religious Activities and Development in Utah, 1847–1910." *Utah Historical Quarterly* 35 (February 1963), 292–306.

Madsen, Brigham D. "Frolics and Free Schools for the Youthful Gentiles of Corinne." *Utah Historical Quarterly* 48 (Summer 1980), 220–31.

Maser, Frederick E. "The Way We Were in 1884." *Methodist History* 22 (January 1984), 115–26.

Massaglia, Martin L. "Colporter Ministry." *Foundations* 24 (October–December 1981), 328–39.

Nañez, Alfredo. "The Transition from Anglo to Mexican-American Leadership in the Rio Grande Conference." *Methodist History* 15 (January 1978), 67–74.

Papermaster, Isadore. "A History of North Dakota Jewry and Their Pioneer Rabbi." Part 2. *Western Jewish Historical Quarterly* 10 (January 1978), 170–84.

Parker, Charles A. "The Camp Meeting on the Frontier and the Methodist Religious Resort in the East—Before 1900." *Methodist History* 18 (April 1980), 179–92.

Paul, Rodman W. "The Mormons of Yesterday and Today." *Idaho Yesterdays* 19 (Fall 1975), 2–7.

Paz, D. G. "The Anglican Response to Urban Social Dislocation in Omaha, 1875–1920." *Historical Magazine of the Protestant Episcopal Church* 51 (June 1978), 131–46.

———. " 'For Zion's Sake Will I Not Hold My Peace': John Williams, Radical Omaha Priest, 1877–1914." *Nebraska History* 63 (Spring 1982), 87–107.

Perkins, Louis L. "Samuel Gautier French: 1838–1882." *Historical Magazine of the Protestant Episcopal Church* 62 (March 1973), 37–45.

Peterson, Charles S. "A New Community: Mormon Teachers and the Separation of Church and State in Utah's Territorial Schools." *Utah Historical Quarterly* 48 (Summer 1980), 293–312.

Petrik, Paula. "Prostitution in Helena, Montana, 1865–1900." *Montana* 31 (April 1981), 28–42.

Platt, M. J. "Reminiscences of Early Days in Nebraska." *Transactions and Reports of the Nebraska State Historical Society* 10 (1892).

Priestley, Lee. "Shalam, Land of Children." *La Cronica de Nuevo México* (November 1978), 2–3.

Quinn, D. Michael. "Utah's Educational Innovation: LDS Religion Classes, 1890–1929." *Utah Historical Quarterly* 43 (Fall 1975), 379–95.

Rainsford, George N. "Dean Henry Martyn Hart and Public Issues." *Colorado Magazine* 48 (1971), 204–20.

Reeve, Frank D. "The Old University of New Mexico in Santa Fe." *New Mexico Historical Review* 8 (July 1933), 201–9.

Reherd, Herbert W. "An Outline History of the Protestant Churches of Utah." W. Wain Sutton, ed., *Utah: A Centennial History.* New York: n. p., 1949.

Shane, Karen. "New Mexico: Salubrious El Dorado." *New Mexico Historical Review* 56 (1981), 387–99.

Shinn, Charles H. "Glimpses of Frontier Ministers." *Outlook* (September 20, 1902), 167–70.

Sillito, John and Martha Bradley. "Franklin Spencer Spaulding: An Episcopal Observer of Mormonism." *Historical Magazine of the Protestant Episcopal Church* 54 (December 1985), 339–49.

Singleton, Gregory H. " 'Mere Middle-Class Institutions': Urban Protestantism in Nineteenth-Century America." *Journal of Social History* 6 (Summer 1973), 489–504.

Spidle, Jake W. " 'An Army of Tubercular Invalids': New Mexico and the Birth of a Tuberculosis Industry." *New Mexico Historical Review* 61 (July 1986), 179–201.

Steele, Thomas J. "Peasant Religions: Retablos and Penitentes," 124–36. In José de Onis, ed., *The Hispanic Contribution to the State of Colorado.* Boulder, Colo.: Westview Press, 1976.

Stone, Hiram. "Memoirs of a Pioneer Missionary and Chaplain in the United States Army." *Collections of the Kansas State Historical Society, 1913–1914* 13 (1915), 298–344.

Stratton, David H. "The Army and the Gospel in the West." *Western Humanities Review* 8 (Summer 1954), 247–67.

Swartout, Melba H. "Missionaries to Their Own People." *Menaul Historical Review* 13 (Fall 1986), 1–7.

Sweet, William W. "The Churches as Moral Courts of the Frontier." *Church History* 2 (March 1933), 3–21.

Terry, Edward D. "Methodism in Arizona: The First Seventy Years." *Arizona and the West* 3 (Summer 1961).

Topping, Gary. "Religion in the West." *Journal of American Culture* 3 (Summer 1980), 330–50.

Twaddell, Elizabeth. "The American Tract Society, 1814–1860." *Church History* 15 (1946), 116–32.

Utley, Robert M. "The Celebrated Peace Policy of General Grant." *North Dakota History* 20 (July 1953), 121–42.

Vinatieri, Joseph A. "The Growing Years: Westminister College from Birth to Adolescence." *Utah Historical Quarterly* 43 (Fall 1975), 344–61.

Walker, Henry Pickering. "Preacher in Helldorado." *Journal of Arizona History* 15 (Autumn 1974), 223–67.

Wasson, Margaret. "Texas Methodism's Other Half." *Methodist History* 19 (July 1981), 206–23.

Webster, Helen. "The Chinese School of the Central Presbyterian Church of Denver." *Colorado Magazine* 40 (January 1963), 57–62; (April 1963), 132–37.

Weisenburger, Francis P. "God and Man in a Secular City: The Church in Virginia City, Nevada." *Nevada Historical Quarterly* 14 (Summer 1971), 3–23.

Wells, Merle W. "Presbyterians in the Mountain West: Response to a Regional Challenge." *Journal of Presbyterian History* 62 (Summer 1984), 139–51.

West, Elliott. "Scarlet West: The Oldest Profession in the Trans-Mississippi West." *Montana* 31 (April 1981), 16–26.

Wilson, Spencer, ed. "Montana Memories." *Montana* 29 (January 1979), 16–28.

Wunder, John. "The Courts and the Chinese in Frontier Idaho." *Idaho Yesterdays* 25 (1981), 23–32.

———. "Law and Chinese in Montana." *Montana* 30 (July 1980), 18–30.

Zimmerman, Jane C. "The Penal Reform Movement in the South during the Progressive Era, 1890–1917." *Journal of Southern History* 17 (1951), 462–92.

Unpublished Materials

Carroll, Horace Bailey. "Social Life in West Texas from 1875 to 1890." Master's thesis, Texas Technological College, 1928.

Ditmars, R. Maud. "A History of Baptist Missions in Utah, 1871–1931." Master's thesis, University of Colorado, 1931.

Dubois, William Robert III. "A Social History of Cheyenne, Wyoming, 1875–1885." Master's thesis, University of Wyoming, 1963.

Eckstein, Stephen D. "The History of Churches of Christ in Texas, 1824–1950." Ph.D. dissertation, Texas Technological College, 1959.

Hale, William B. "Charles Elkanah Hodgin: Educator." Ph.D. dissertation, University of New Mexico, 1983.

Hill, John B. "Timothy Hill and Western Presbyterianism: A Review of the

Life and Letters of a Superintendent of Missions." Typescript, Kansas Historical Society, Topeka.

Holder, Olive Price. "Circuit Riding Experiences of William Perryman Garvin on the Texas Frontier, 1891–1898." Master's thesis, Texas Technological College, 1935.

Kennedy, Cornelia B. "Organized Religion in South Dakota Before 1900." Master's thesis, University of South Dakota, 1932.

Li, Ming-Ogu. "An Introduction to the Study of the History of the Methodist Churches in El Paso, Texas." Master's thesis, Texas Western College, 1949.

Lyon, T. Edgar. "Evangelical Protestant Missionary Activity in Mormon Dominated Areas: 1865–1900." Ph.D. dissertation, University of Utah, 1962.

Moore, Franklin. "Autobiography of a Pioneer Missionary." Typescript, Fort Collins Public Library.

Onken, Warren Harding, Jr. "Pioneer Missionary: The Life of John Roberts, 1853–1949." Master's thesis, University of Wyoming, 1977.

Scott, John Charles. "Between Fiction and History: An Exploration into Willa Cather's *Death Comes for the Archbishop*." Ph.D. dissertation, University of New Mexico, 1980.

Smallwood, Mary Ann Norman. "Childhood on the Southern Plains Frontier, 1870–1910." Ph.D. dissertation, Texas Tech, 1975.

Stapleton, Ernest, Jr. "The History of Baptist Missions in New Mexico, 1849–1866." Master's thesis, University of New Mexico, 1954.

Walker, Randi Jones. "Protestantism in the Sangre de Cristos: Factors in the Growth and Decline of the Hispanic Protestant Churches in Northern New Mexico and Southern Colorado, 1850–1920." Ph.D. dissertation, Claremont Graduate School, 1983.

Welsh, Michael E. "The Road to Assimilation: The Seminoles in Oklahoma, 1839–1936." Ph.D. dissertation, University of New Mexico, 1983.

Winkler, Earl. "History of Presbyterian Schools in Utah." Master's thesis, University of Utah, 1968.

Index